The Public Affairs Guide to

Wales

The Handbook of Effective and Ethical Lobbying

The Public Affairs Guide to
Wales

The Handbook of Effective
and Ethical Lobbying

Daran Hill

welsh academic press

Cardiff

Published in Wales by Welsh Academic Press, an imprint of
Ashley Drake Publishing Ltd
PO Box 733
Cardiff
CF14 7ZY

www.welsh-academic-press.wales
First Edition - 2020

ISBN
Paperback - 978 1 86057 1428

British Library Cataloguing-in-Publication Data.
A CIP catalogue for this book is available from the British Library.

Cover designed by Welsh Books Council, Aberystwyth, Wales
Typeset by Prepress Plus, India (www.prepressplus.in)

Contents

Acknowledgements		vii
Foreword		ix
Preface		xi
Introduction		xiii

1.	Stripping Away the Mysteries: Timing	1
2.	Stripping Away the Mysteries: Who to target	7
3.	Stripping Away the Mysteries: How to target	12
4.	Political Monitoring	20
5.	Working with Welsh Government	27
6.	Working with Members of the Senedd	46
7.	Working with Political Parties	54
8.	Responding to Consultations	60
9.	Influencing Senedd Committees	71
10.	Engaging with the Legislative Process	78
11.	Non-Government Legislation	98
12.	The Financial Process	103
13.	Oral and Written Questions	119
14.	Other Senedd Business in Plenary Session	126
15.	Statements of Opinion	135
16.	Petitions	141
17.	Cross-Party Groups	152
18.	Events at the Senedd	161
19.	Party Conferences	167
20.	Manifesto Compilation	178
21.	Working at a Local or Regional Level	186
22.	Partnership Working	195
23.	Working with the Media	203
24.	Online Communications	214
25.	Operating Bilingually	226
26.	Any Other Business	235

Index		239

In memory of my wonderful friend Carl Sargeant,
the best lobbyist I ever met

Acknowledgements

No book of this nature can be written with any confidence and accuracy without the support, input and insight of others, especially my friends and co-workers Dafydd Huw, Naomi Williams, Rhodri ab Owen and Susan Bowen. They gave me not only case studies and critical review, but also the time and patience to compile this book. I will always be grateful and they share in the achievement of this publication. It was a long endeavour and would never have been completed without the support and belief of Ashley Drake from Welsh Academic Press, who has enabled me to compile a guide for an area of policy development which is little understood and usually misunderstood. Although I am yet to meet them, Robert McGeachy and Mark Ballard, who jointly-authored *The Public Affairs Guide to Scotland*, with Mr McGeachy having since also written *The Public Affairs Guide to Westminster* (both published by Welsh Academic Press), also offered me inspiration as well as a clear narrative structure so that I could maintain the integrity of the this series of important books.

After over 20 years of devolution, the shape and depth of public affairs has evolved mostly for the better. I have learnt not just from my co-workers like Beryl Wichard, Kate Evans, Steve Jones and Tom Griffin, but from my clients and friends like David Taylor, Claire Lawson, Pip Ford, Iestyn Davies and Joe Ferris, and from alumni of the public affairs scene like Lia Murphy, John Pockett, Fay Jones and Leigh Jeffes. Especially powerful has been my experience at the centre of two referendum campaigns, and I am grateful one of my sternest yet kindest tutors, Leighton Andrews, has been good enough to contribute to and commend this book.

There are hundreds of others that should be referenced too. Many of these are politicians, who of course have shaped two decades of devolution and the shape of public affairs in Wales. I have been privileged to know so many of them, and to call so many friends and confidantes. I hope I will offend none of them by either inclusion or omission if I single out particularly Alun Davies, Nick Ramsay, Bethan Sayed, Ann Jones, Anna McMorrin, Jonathan Davies, Lesley Griffiths, Ken Skates, Jonathan Morgan, William Powell, Dafydd Elis-Thomas,

Paul Davies, Darren Millar, Rhodri Glyn Thomas, Nick Bourne, Hefin David, Ali Thomas, Russell Goodway, Eluned Morgan, Byron Davies, Craig Williams, Guto Davies and Jack Sargeant for having stimulated, tolerated, nudged and indulged me at different points.

I hold Jack in particular love and esteem. If I had had his talent at his age, I would probably have achieved more in the first decade of devolution, and certainly written a book like this ten years earlier. What, perhaps, most unites us both is that we have both been shaped by Carl Sargeant more than any other person. Carl would never have recognised what a profound effect he has had on us, both in life and in death, and it is to the 'Captain' that this book is dedicated. Not that he would ever have bothered reading it or needed to.

Daran Hill
Cardiff
November 2019

Foreword

When I was elected to the National Assembly for Wales in 2003, I had a very simple response to letters from pressure groups, lobbyists and others seeking my involvement in events that they were holding or demands that they were making: I wrote back, saying: please set out for me, on no more than two sides of paper, precisely what your organisation has to offer my constituents. That soon dealt with the time-wasters.

Time is precious for politicians. It's one of the few resources that they have. Time matters. They have fixed terms and only a limited political time-span in which to get things done and to make a difference: to stand up for their constituency or region; to learn about an issue; to be an advocate for a cause that matters to them; to pass legislation or amend it; to scrutinise government.

It's no surprise then that those who can convey a complex case in a clear and direct way will get a better hearing than those who can't. Those who understand the pressures on politicians' time, who direct their communications at the right stage of a piece of legislation, or to the right committee or the appropriate official, adviser or Minister, will make more impact than those who don't.

Daran Hill has written a book which is designed to help people get their message across. It's more than a book about public affairs in Wales. It's a summary of the peculiar twists and turns in the story of Welsh devolution since 1997, and the growth of powers of the National Assembly for Wales and the development of what is now known as the Welsh Government. It explains the development of Welsh devolution from the first Government of Wales Act to the latest legislation. Daran understands how the Assembly works and how the Government operates. He understands the responsibilities of the National Assembly and the Welsh Government, what is devolved and what is reserved to UK or England and Wales level. It's a book that I would be happy for my postgraduate students to use to get a general understanding of devolution in Wales.

Devolution in Wales is under-reported at UK level. It's no wonder that public affairs staff at the centre of major corporations, UK public sector bodies or third sector organisations often get things wrong. Even UK media organisations still, in late 2019, make simple mistakes. Even Ministers and Government departments at a UK level, whose responsibilities may sometimes operate across the England and Wales boundary, still make the elementary mistake of designing services on an English template, with all the cost and disruption that can cause.

Daran Hill has played a central role in Welsh devolution since the outset. I have worked with him on two referendums, in 1997 and 2011, as we sought to persuade the people of Wales first to vote for devolution, then to give Wales the law-making process that it deserved. The National Assembly for Wales remains the only political institution that the people of Wales have voted to create.

It's essential, of course, that those who seek to influence politicians, whether on behalf of corporate interests, public bodies, trades unions or the third sector, understand the rules and are transparent and open in their dealings. Welsh democracy bedded down in the early 2000s with a commitment from the late Rhodri Morgan to open government. Cabinet minutes are published, and so are Cabinet papers which don't contain policy still in development or commercially confidential material. Modern Welsh democracy grew up in the Nolan era, and has avoided most of the scandals that beset Westminster. The new era of Welsh democracy abolished the quango culture based on cronyism and insider contacts. Long may that be the case.

Daran's book is a valuable handbook on effective – and ethical – lobbying, written by someone who has been there and who enjoys good relationships across the Assembly. It also provides distinctive insights into a democracy that is still developing. I am sure it will get put to good use.

Leighton Andrews
Professor of Practice in Public Service Leadership and
Innovation, Cardiff Business School
former Assembly Member and Welsh Government Minister
November 2019

Preface

Lobbying must rank amongst the oldest professions in the world. From time immemorial, people have sought to have their voice heard, to try to make those in positions of influence to see their point of view, or to accept their way of doing things.

Here in Wales, public affairs, lobbying, government relations, whatever you may wish to call it, is a relatively recent addition to Welsh political life. When I first became involved in this work in the mid-1980s, the focus of attention was, of course, at Westminster. For us in Wales, it was a somewhat remote activity, perhaps carried out in the shadows of the corridors of power, miles away at the other end of the M4. Much of this activity would often be carried out by London-based agencies or consultants on behalf of clients in Wales; there were few indigenous lobbying companies or consultants here. All of this changed greatly when the National Assembly for Wales was set up in 1999, and businesses and organisations quickly realised that they needed their voice heard in Cardiff Bay as much as, if not more than, at Westminster.

With the gradual flow of greater powers to the National Assembly, the work of ethical, effective political lobbying is increasingly important for the political life of Wales, and for the continued development of our National Assembly as it gains ever more responsibilities. For those of us seeking to help our AMs to understand and, dare I say, take on the views and legitimate aspirations of Welsh businesses and organisations, knowing how to do this without fear of crossing the red lines is essential if we are to be effective. *The Public Affairs Guide to Wales* does precisely that, which is why it is a significant and very useful tool to us all, even those of us who have been working in this profession for many years.

I can think of no one better positioned or experienced to write this definitive handbook of political lobbying in Wales than Daran. He was at the heart of the *Ie dros Gymru / Yes for Wales* campaign in 1997 and has become one of our leading public affairs professionals, as well as a highly respected political commentator.

Daran has succeeded, concisely, to explain the complex minefield of ethical, but effective, political lobbying to the whole spectrum of those of us involved in political activity, whether as professional or would be politicians, public affairs practitioners or, indeed, interested onlookers who want to become better informed. *The Public Affairs Guide to Wales*, with its detailed technical know-how and reliable political insight, is the go-to point of reference for all those working to improve Wales, for the better.

John Pockett
Pontypridd
November 2019

Introduction

A common misconception is that you need to be 'in politics' in some way to have a political impact. You do not.

Context is the key to successful public affairs activity. It is about talking to the right person, or an influencer of the right person, in the right way, about the right things, at the right time. Perhaps this book could end here with this fundamental truism, but it would not have been a very substantial read. To make true sense of the opening statement, you need context. This guide attempts to offer that context in order to enable you to make better informed and better targeted public affairs interventions.

The first context is that it is particularly and peculiarly Welsh, just like the devolution system which it seeks to describe. The system we have in Wales is unique. It may not – like the British constitution more generally – have been designed in the way that it exists and operates. The point is that it is distinctive, both operationally and culturally, and needs to be understood on that basis. To superimpose systems and public affairs practices from other nations, even other nations within the United Kingdom (UK) would not provide an accurate context.

Yes, the principles of a parliamentary democracy remain the same in Wales as they are in Scotland and in Westminster. There are patterns of accountability through scrutiny processes found in any democratic political system. There are checks and balances which offer a degree of separation of powers between government and legislature, such as the budget process which has been developed over two decades – based on the fundamental principle enshrined since the English Civil War – that the parliament or legislature makes the financial award to government to spend.

Fundamentally, however, the processes and applications of those principles are different in Wales – the Welsh parliamentary system is unique – and explaining how they operate here is the overarching intention of this guide: to assist the reader in making better informed and better planned strategic political interventions within the Welsh context.

Let me qualify that for the moment. I am not writing from some introverted or even overtly patriotic standpoint when I make a claim to uniqueness. The distinctive pattern of politics, administration and public affairs has grown over time in response to challenges, opportunities and influences at work within the Welsh body politic. Some of that development has been stunted and led into cul de sacs. There were fundamental flaws in the first devolution settlement when the Assembly was established in 1999, perhaps the most profound of which was the hybrid nature of the institution. The executive arm, what was termed early on as the Cabinet of the National Assembly for Wales was indistinct in law or practice from the parliamentary arm, the Assembly itself. Cabinet Ministers sat on committees and policy was often developed at a committee level rather than a governmental level.

No wonder Rhodri Morgan, in one of his first big actions on becoming First Secretary (not First Minister) in 2000, decided to name the executive arm the Welsh Assembly Government. It was an appropriate reflection of the confusion from which it was born and, I would argue, continued to contribute to the confusion in the minds of the electorate throughout the following decade. I am reminded of a story a former opposition party leader told me about one of his Assembly Members who put up a sign in their constituency office window proclaiming they were a member of the Welsh Assembly Government. Only one of those words were correct and, if the AMs themselves did not all understand the fundamental overarching structures, what hope for the public? The sign went pretty speedily; the confusion continued for some years and, some would argue, still continues.

Other cul de sacs have also been part of the road map to the devolved Wales we have today. Between 1999 and 2003 an integral part of the National Assembly's functioning was regional committees, which met every month on Fridays in different towns in the five electoral regions of Wales. They were local talking shops for local people and didn't last long. Between 2007 and 2011 we had the Legislative Competence Order (LCO) system, where the National Assembly was conferred primary legislative power over very specified areas of competence by a process of Order making powers at Westminster. If you find that sentence to be a sudden introduction of overly legalese jargon, don't worry: LCOs are a thing of the past and won't be coming back. You are in the fortunate position of just having read a reference to them rather than living through their convoluted reality.

Some changes and modernisations have just crept along either incrementally, such as the evolution of the Assembly's budgetary process, or the development of its petition system since 2007. Others have been internal choices for the institution such as the introduction of free votes for committee chairs in 2016, or the agreement of a four-stage legislative process from 2011. Yet, as I wrote in a pamphlet for the Bevan Foundation in 2008, there is a clear direction of travel, and it is one I stand by over a decade later:

'When it comes to devolution, 'the arrow of history' is clearly pointing in the direction of more powers exercised for Wales in Wales. The story of the last 50 years has been one of increasing capability for policy divergence between Wales and England. When Ron Davies said famously that devolution was "a process not an event", he was of course right. But it is not true to say that that process began with the Government of Wales Act 1998 or the referendum of 1997. In reality, power through executive responsibilities had been devolved to Wales decades earlier. The story of the last decade is more one of the development of a democratic and stronger civic context for those powers. It is a process, and a dynamic one at that.'[1]

There are, however, seminal points of change that have shaped the political structure in which we now exist. Some of these have required significant legislative change to the powers and functioning of the National Assembly and Welsh Government, which Carwyn Jones unilaterally renamed the Welsh Assembly Government once he had taken the mantle of power. In total we have had four different Wales Acts from Westminster dealing with such powers – Labour Governments passed the 1998 and 2006 Acts, while Conservative-led Governments initiated the Acts of 2014 and 2017. Incidentally, each one of these Acts was intended to stabilise the system and make a further piece of legislation unnecessary, at least in the short to medium term. How wrong they were.

---

1   Daran Hill, Huw Edwards and Leigh Jeffes, *The Evolution of Devolution*, Bevan Foundation (2008).

It says it all that some of these Acts repeal parts of their predecessors. The biggest change was perhaps the jump from 1998 to 2006, when a whole new system of operation and legislation was introduced, legally separating the Government from the Assembly for the first time. The most constant squabble has been one of the most reported but least important, namely the Labour Government's decision in 2006 to stop Assembly Member candidates from standing in both the constituencies and on regional lists at the same time. This element was subsequently overturned in the Wales Act 2014, as a point of principle advocated by the Conservatives but never actually used by them in an Assembly election.

A similar change of mind even occurred between the Wales Acts of 2014 and 2017. In 2014 the law prescribed that, before a degree of income tax raising powers were conferred to the Assembly, a referendum should be held to get popular consent, as had happened in Scotland in 1999. By 2017 the same Conservative Party had concluded that such a referendum could never be won but that it was desirable, for the principle of accountability to have meaning, that the Welsh Government should have some tax raising powers. They therefore abolished the requirement for a referendum and Wales acquired its own partially devolved income tax system from March 2019.

There is, of course, no rule by which referenda must be used and popular consent must be sought. The Electoral Commission governs the conduct of referenda and the questions posed, but no body other than a Government in power can decide, with the agreement of the legislature, to hold a referendum. While one was held in 2011 to bring about direct primary law making powers for the National Assembly, no other change, large or small, has been put to the people of Wales since. This includes not only the issue of income tax already referred to, but also the matter of changing the name of the National Assembly for Wales to the Welsh Parliament. This relatively radical shift in terminology can now be achieved through an Act of the Assembly. The relevant legislation has already been laid in the National Assembly and is likely to come into force by the time of the next election in 2021. The only real form of popular engagement around this shift was an online poll and consultation exercise. The National Assembly considered that to be enough and, in October 2018, they agreed by 44 votes to 1, with 3 abstentions, to allow the legislation to be brought forward. Therefore, we already have the seeds of out-datedness sewn in the very first pages of this guide. Although the legislation turning the Assembly into a

Welsh Parliament has not yet passed, it has been laid and is very likely to pass. So, do I continue to use the terminology of the time of writing or the terminology of the future in drafting this book?

To determine this, let me step back. This guide has been written in a variety of contexts which also need to be understood in order for it to be appreciated for what it actually is: a mixture of present, past and a sprinkling of future. The past will, beyond this introduction, be confined to the past while the vast bulk of this guide will utilise the context of the present, yet we cannot ignore the future of the institution and its operations, where we believe developments and innovations are extremely likely to occur. This predictive category is based on as much sure-footed guesswork as possible, but an unavoidable element underpins it. On that basis, beyond this introduction, I will use the term Senedd, the Welsh language name for both the current National Assembly *and* the Welsh Parliament that it will become.

There may be risk, but that risk can be measured and mitigated. To have just settled on National Assembly would have probably dated the volume too soon. To have chosen Welsh Parliament / Senedd Cymru as the Members appear to have done would have necessitated the full use of the term continuously to distinguish it from the UK Parliament; while there is also a small risk the legislation on the name change will not go through. Such an outcome might make this guide as notorious to the Welsh public affairs community as the *Chicago Daily Tribune* issue of November 1948 which heralded 'Dewey Defeats Truman'.

Turning away from the political structures and looking at the public affairs community in Wales, of which I have been a member since its 'creation' in a devolved context in 1999, it is less easy to be sure footed in some respects. The 2017 review of lobbying in Wales – the practice of public affairs – by the Senedd's Standards Committee did not suggest any significant changes to the system but noted it would revisit the matter later in 2019. This could change the operation of some aspects of lobbying as much as relatively recent legislation in Scotland has altered the profession there.

The absence of absoluteness has, however, been a particular feature of Welsh governance since 1999. Devolution in Wales has indeed been the "process not an event" foretold by former Welsh Secretary Ron Davies back in 1997. We, as lobbyists and public affairs professionals have, if we are operating effectively, moved with the times. We have engaged with the changing processes and maybe even impacted on them and improved them. We have noted and responded to the changes of the context which is integral to the success of our profession. We have also grown significantly and this has been generally welcomed across the political spectrum. Speaking at a lobbyist dinner in Cardiff in 2013, Baroness Randerson, a former Member of the Senedd and a former Minister of the Welsh Government, reflected on this while in her role as a Minister in the Wales Office:

> 'The public affairs profession has grown rapidly in Wales in the last 15 years. The outward and visible sign of this is that almost every charity now has at least a branch here in Wales and puts Cymru after its name, and either does its own PR in Wales or employs another company to do it for them. This is strongly to be welcomed. It is a sign that Wales really is being considered in its own right.'[2]

We do this, to return to my opening point, because context is everything. Effective public affairs is indeed about talking to the right person, or an influencer of the right person, in the right way, about the right things, at the right time. This guide to public affairs in Wales is my attempt to enable more people to do that effectively.

To this end, it is always worth networking with other public affairs professionals. Those working in the health or environmental sectors often have their own established networks based around professional expertise and input, but more generic organisations exist too. Perhaps the best one is Public Affairs Cymru, an umbrella body for public affairs professionals in Wales. PAC, which I helped establish in October 2006, aims to raise awareness of the public affairs industry and to promote good practice. It has close to 200 members who benefit from networking, professional development and information sharing opportunities.

This guide is the first of its kind published for Wales and is intended to be as definitive as any handbook to ethical and effective lobbying can be. It can, I hope perhaps at least in part, offer a structured guide to how public affairs works in Wales and offer some truths and examples that will stand the test of time along the winding path of Welsh devolution and political evolution.

---

2   Speech by Baroness Randerson to the Public Affairs Cymru annual dinner, 13 June 2013.

1

Stripping Away the Mysteries: Timing

Political processes are never as complex as they first seem. A major contextual key is provided by the understanding of the political timelines that are intrinsic to the operation of those processes. Four of these are worth unpicking in respect of the operation of the Senedd.

The Senedd electoral timeline

The first is its own electoral cycle. Following the Government of Wales Act 2014, the life of the Senedd was extended from four to five years, with elections always to take place on the first Thursday in May. There is a process for dissolving the Senedd if a government cannot be formed, but this eventuality has never arisen, so you can set it to one side for the purposes of this guide. You should simply work on the basis that the next Senedd election is due in May 2021, the one after that is May 2026, and so forth.

Aligned to this is the mystery of the Senedd's electoral system, which is in fact is no mystery at all. There are 60 Senedd Members elected on a twin stream electoral process. Forty of these are elected on the traditional 'First Past the Post' system, with their constituencies mirroring the same constituencies at Westminster. The other 20 are elected, four from each, from the five regional lists covering parts of Wales and comprised of blocks of constituencies. The table below displays the split between them:

North	Mid & West	South West	South Central	South East
Alyn & Deeside	Dwyfor Meirionnydd	Gower	Cardiff West	Newport West
Delyn	Ceredigion	Swansea West	Cardiff North	Newport East
Wrexham	Montgomeryshire	Swansea East	Cardiff Central	Caerphilly
Clwyd South	Brecon & Radnorshire	Neath	Cardiff South & Penarth	Islwyn
Vale of Clwyd	Carmarthen East & Dinefwr	Aberavon	Vale of Glamorgan	Torfaen
Clwyd West	Carmarthen West & Pembrokeshire South	Bridgend	Pontypridd	Monmouthshire
Aberconwy	Preseli Pembrokeshire	Ogmore	Cynon Valley	Merthyr Tydfil & Rhymney
Arfon	Llanelli		Rhondda	Blaenau Gwent
Ynys Môn				

To calculate the number of regional list seats allocated to a political party you need to first look at the number of constituency seats won, and by which political party. This is done using a formula where X is the number of seats already won by a party and V is the number of votes gained by that party, expressed like this:

$$\frac{V}{X + 1} = Y$$

The best way to show how it works is by using an example. Taking the homogenous South Wales West as an example (where Labour has won every single constituency seat in every single one of the Senedd elections so far held), we can therefore calculate the original X score to be 7 for Labour and 0 for every other party.

In 2016, the results of the regional list vote for each party was as follows:

- **Welsh Labour**: 66,903
- **Plaid Cymru**: 29,050
- **Welsh Conservatives**: 25,414
- **UKIP**: 23,096
- **Welsh Liberal Democrats**: 10,946

You can then apply these figures to the formula and on the first calculation you get the following outcomes for the five parties respectively

$$\frac{66,903}{7+1} = 8,363 \text{ for } \textbf{Welsh Labour}$$

$$\frac{29,050}{0+1} = 29,050 \text{ for } \textbf{Plaid Cymru}$$

$$\frac{25,414}{0+1} = 25,414 \text{ for } \textbf{Welsh Conservatives}$$

$$\frac{23,096}{0+1} = 23,096 \text{ for } \textbf{UKIP}$$

$$\frac{10,946}{0+1} = 10,946 \text{ for } \textbf{Welsh Liberal Democrats}$$

You will therefore see the Labour score drops significantly when divided by the number of seats held plus one. The party with the highest score on the formula for regional seats was therefore Plaid Cymru, who won the first place and Bethan Jenkins was returned to the Senedd.

To calculate the next regional list place, only the Plaid Cymru score has to be recalculated and this is now done as follows:

$$\frac{29,050}{1+1} = 14,525 \text{ for } \textbf{Plaid Cymru}$$

No further calculations need to be done. The Conservative's Suzy Davies was returned for the second list seat with 25,414; UKIP's Caroline Jones took third with 23,096; and Plaid managed to take the fourth and final place, and a second seat, with Dr Dai Lloyd returned to the Senedd.

Proposals have been submitted to change the electoral system of the Senedd to create larger seats returning more Members on a proportional system, thus doing away with the regional lists and the current constituencies. This will not be in place for the 2021 Senedd election.

All of the elected Members of the Senedd enjoy equal standing in the institution, regardless of whether they are constituency or regional list Members (although this principle was challenged in the Second Senedd by Labour benches as they did not return a regional Member). Thus, it is as legitimate for a regional Member to become First Minister as it is for a constituency Member to do so. Indeed, Alun Michael, who served as First Secretary in the 1999-2000 period represented Mid and West Wales on the regional list, and when Eluned Morgan ran for the Labour leadership in autumn 2018 she did so having been elected for the same region.

The Westminster electoral timeline

The UK Parliament is elected under the Fixed-term Parliaments Act to last for five years. It ran its full course between 2010 and 2015, but the 2015 Parliament was dissolved just two years in. The next Westminster election is therefore forecast to occur in 2022.

It is important to mention this for two particular reasons in the context of the Senedd. Firstly, the Senedd and Westminster elections are completely independent of one another. Indeed, the life of the Senedd was specifically extended from 2015 to 2016 by the Government of Wales Act 2014 to stop the two primary elections happening on the same day.

However, it is also important to realise from a public affairs perspective that a Westminster general election does impact on the work of the Senedd and the Welsh Government. Political temperatures rise, tensions are exacerbated, and there is an increased political and media focus on Westminster. It is not a good time to be launching or cranking up any public affairs activity in the Senedd unless such a campaign is deliberately linked to the potential outcome of the Westminster election.

The Welsh Government year

There are two key cycles that determine how the Welsh Government operates, the legislative cycle and the budgetary cycle. Welsh Government planning is also intersected by these two set timelines, both of which are explored more fully in Chapters 10 and 12. Thinking within Welsh Government will be framed logistically by both of these things, and also the drive to deliver the full legislative programme of the Welsh Government, which is always planned across the five year cycle of the Senedd. It is normal for the First Minister to provide an update on the full programme of government either in July or

September every year. This statement, however, is more of a formality than anything else and does not impact on the bigger timelines.

At roughly the same time the First Minister will also provide an update on the legislative programme. The update will look back at the legislative Bills introduced in the previous year, including the ones which have not yet completed their passage, and will announce which pieces of legislation the Welsh Government will bring forward in the following year. There are usually four or five items and the order in which they will be presented is not set out in detail, though phrases like 'in the autumn term' and 'next year' (i.e. beyond Christmas) are often used as markers, indicating an useful rough timeline for introduction. In the final year of a Senedd, however, it is unusual for more than one or two final Bills to be introduced, and they are then sped through the process in order to be completed before the session finishes with a Senedd election.

The financial timeline is perhaps the most critical one of all. Every year the Welsh Government's Finance Minister oversees an annual budget process that begins over the summer and culminates in a draft budget presented in the autumn, with a more detailed version following some weeks later, along with the local government financial settlement. A final debate is then held between December and the early part of the following year which sets the budget for the Welsh Government from the following April, in line with the normal financial year.

The clarity and structure of the budget process is one of the most important things that the Welsh Government does. Because it operates to a strict timeline you can, from a public affairs perspective, seek to input in a meaningful way. This is best done before the initial draft budget is laid. The later in the process you seek to influence, the harder it is for the Welsh Government to compromise. Having said that, there are some good examples of where organised public affairs campaigns have impacted on the budget process, such as the third sector-led campaign in the autumn of 2017 to protect the distinct 'Supporting People' budget line.

From a financial perspective, there are also some political and procedural impacts that a public affairs practitioner should note. The first is the preoccupation of many Ministers with budgetary matters during the intense budget period, especially those, like the Health Minister or the Local Government Minister, with high spending briefs. Additionally, there is significant pressure on some Senedd Committees during this period, most notably the Finance Committee.

The Senedd week

The Senedd tends to sit for approximately 32 weeks per year, which is somewhat shorter than Westminster. It sits following the pattern of school holidays, including half term breaks, so no session ever tends to be longer than seven weeks and some sessions are as short as four weeks, depending when Easter falls.

When the Senedd is in session, each day of the week is a little different although the weeks are similar in layout and tend to follow the pattern set out below between Plenary (full sessions) and Committee meetings. The business of Plenary and Committees are considered in more detail in later chapters but, essentially, the pattern looks like this:

	Morning	Afternoon
Monday		Currently three committees have Monday meetings
Tuesday	Business Committee Petitions Committee Party political group meetings	Plenary Session – Government business including First Minister's Questions, statements, legislation, budgets
Wednesday	Meetings of Subject Committees	Plenary Session – questions to Government Ministers; followed by Senedd, individual Member and opposition business
Thursday	Meetings of Subject Committees	Over-run of meetings of Subject Committees from the morning
Friday	Constituency/Region day and Scrutiny of the First Minister Committee on a quarterly basis	

TOP TIP: You need to understand and think about timing from the perspective of the institution you are trying to influence, not from the perspective of your own organisation or what suits your campaign. Mistiming things can cause a campaign to fail before it has even begun and will portray you as less clued up, less effective and less professional.

2

Stripping Away the Mysteries: Who to target

Having tried to demystify the different legislative and financial cycles impacting on and shaping the political year in Wales, so as to assist public affairs professionals identify 'the right time' for action, further explanation and probing is necessary in relation to determining what 'the right things' might be. This has to be established before you can determine who the right person is, let alone the right influencer, and that's before we begin to examine the right way to talk about them.

What is devolved to Wales?

The first test that needs to be undertaken in determining 'the right person' to lobby is to ascertain who is the responsible person – the one who can make a decision – and, in order to do that, you need to track back and make sure that an issue is actually devolved to Wales. The Wales Act 2017 for the first time created a clearer list of matters which were fully devolved to Wales. Previously, the system had operated on a conferred model of devolution – the Welsh Government could only act where powers had been expressly conferred upon it by Westminster through a number of separate Acts. There is not much rhyme or reason to the list of devolved matters other than the bulk of them were previously responsibilities of the Welsh Office before devolution in 1999, and then transferred over to the Senedd.

The change in the 2017 Act, taking effect in 2018, was that Wales could now legislate and operate freely on all matters which are not reserved to Westminster. Essentially, the process of definition has been reversed and brings Wales into line with the system of devolution operating in Scotland and Northern Ireland. Therefore, the first step that needs to be taken is to consult the list of reserved powers to Westminster to ensure the matter is devolved. The overarching list of reserved matters at the time of writing is as follows:

Westminster's Reserved Powers	
• the Crown • the making of peace or war • defence • treaties or any relations with foreign states or dominions • naturalisation • external trade • quarantine • navigation (including merchant shipping) • submarine cables	• wireless telegraphy • aerial navigation • lighthouses • currency • copyright • treason • the UK Parliament • registration and funding of political parties • international development • the Home Civil Service

There are also specific reservations covering particular areas of social and economic policy which are reserved to Westminster, and these are listed under 13 'heads':

Head A - Financial and Economic Matters	Head B - Home Affairs
• fiscal, economic and monetary policy • currency • financial services • financial markets • money laundering	• drug abuse • data protection and access to information • elections • firearms • film classification • immigration and nationality • scientific procedures on live animals • national security and counter-terrorism • betting, gaming and lotteries • emergency powers • extradition • lieutenancies • charities

Head C – Trade and Industry	Head D – Energy
• business associations • insolvency • competition • intellectual property • import and export control • sea fishing outside the Scottish zone • customer protection • product standards, safety and liability • weights and measures • telecommunications • postal services • research councils	• electricity • oil and gas • coal • nuclear energy • energy efficiency
Head E - Transport • marine transport • air transport	**Head F – Social Security** • social security schemes • child support • pensions
Head G – Regulation of the Professions • architects • health professions • auditors	**Head H – Employment** • employment and industrial relations • health and safety
Head J – Health and Medicines • xenotransplantation • embryology, surrogacy and human genetics • medicines, medical supplies and poisons • welfare foods	**Head K – Media and Culture** • broadcasting • public lending right
Head L – Justice • legal services • legal aid • coroners • arbitration • information rights • mental capacity • personal data • public records • public sector information • compensation for persons affected by crime and miscarriages of justice • prisons and offender management • family relationships and children • gender recognition • registration of births, deaths and places of worship	**Head M – Land and Agricultural Assets** • registration of land • registration of agricultural charges and debentures • development and buildings

Head N – Miscellaneous	
• judicial salaries • equal opportunities • Antarctica • control of weapons of mass destruction • Ordnance Survey • deep sea mining • time • outer space	

In respect of some of these reservations such as public sector information, equal opportunities and medicines, policy is not entirely reserved to Westminster. In respect of medicines for example, it is the licencing which is reserved, and not matters relating to the use of medicines or the funding of medicines in Wales.

Where there is a difference of opinion about whether a matter is devolved or not, it is usually referred to the Supreme Court for determination.

Who has policy responsibility?

Once you are clear on whether a matter is devolved, the next action is to determine who has responsibility for that policy area. A devolved responsibility will always ultimately lie with one of the Welsh Government Ministers. A list of functional responsibilities is produced after every change of government or major restructure of an administration. Thus, when Mark Drakeford became First Minister in December 2018, he changed not just the personnel of his Cabinet, but the shape of it, and then underpinning that was a list of functional responsibilities.

Some of this is obvious from the title of the Cabinet Minister or their deputy. Using the 2018 allocation of portfolios, you would be right in assuming that the Local Government Minister held responsibility for local government policy, but you would be wrong in thinking that includes policy relating to Council Tax and local taxation, which sits with the Finance Minister. I will return to this topic in Chapter Five: Working with the Welsh Government.

Remember also that determining the relevant Minister is often not enough. Taking local government again as an example, the Minister may just set the broad policy, but it is the individual local authorities that make the policy decisions within their broad competency framework. The same can also be said of Local Health Boards, which also work within broad policy frameworks but apply decisions to the health locality.

TOP TIP: You don't have to be a lawyer to understand legal systems and legal powers. Applying processes, context and information will help you decipher a question around powers. Be sure that one of the first questions asked by officials about any campaign will relate to the legal powers and responsibilities to deliver on it.

3

Stripping Away the Mysteries:
How to target

With a context of both time and function of decision making, it is then possible to work out how to target the right person or people in a successful public affairs campaign. In order to further progress your objectives, it is important to have a clear plan with clear objectives. Every experienced public affairs practitioner will approach this slightly differently – there is no one true path to success – but certain principles remain universally accepted.

Clarity of targeting

Once you have determined who has the policy responsibility, a useful exercise is working out a stakeholder map. At the most basic level, approaching it from the perspective of two factors is an effective measure – who has influence and who has interest. This can be expressed in terms of a grid approach:

		INFLUENCE	
		Low	High
INTEREST	Low	3	2
	High	2	1

Obviously, the key individuals would sit in the box marked with 1, i.e. those having both high interest and high influence. You can brainstorm names using this grid and try and arrange the key players into the overall pattern. The names can then be extracted and turned into a stakeholder mapping grid, including contact details and other information.

To McGeachy and Ballard, this exercise is summarised not as an influence/interest grid but rather in response to a series of mirroring questions which they suggest public affairs campaigners ask themselves before embarking:

- Who has the power to give you what you require?
- Who is able to make the decision?
- Who can directly influence those who make the decision?
- Who are the indirect influences on those who make the decision?[1]

Answering these questions as truthfully and fully as possible should help you populate the grid. However – and this is the critical point – your stakeholder map also needs to be a live document. You can ensure it is live in two ways. Firstly, use it as a base for information storage and build in ways to gather and store meaningful data about interactions with the individuals you are choosing to target. This can log phone calls, emails, face to face meetings and other interactions.

The other way of making it interactive is by recording not just a classification for each stakeholder, but a classification of where you would like them to be. This would allow you to map against a journey rather than it being simply static scoring. It enables you to bring public affairs planning alive in a meaningful way and to turn your stakeholder mapping exercise into a tool for micro targeting.

Alongside this mapping, as McGeachy and Ballard also recommend, you might consider a SWOT (Strengths, Weaknesses, Opportunities, Threats) analysis which 'will enable you to hone down your ideas and will give you an opportunity to look at the barriers you will need to plan to overcome, or accept.'[2]

Clarity of objective

Alongside clarity of target, you also need clarity of your objectives because in a multi-layered campaign you may have a series of different objectives to achieve. Some campaigns never achieve all of their

---

1   McGeachy & Ballard, *The Public Affairs Guide to Scotland*, Welsh Academic Press (2017), pps.4-5.
2   Ibid., p.3.

objectives but settle for key points. As with planning your targets, you need to maintain a flexibility of approach. Ultimately you are in a process of negotiation with decision makers and compromise is at the heart of making this a success.

Having said that, without clarity of objective you will not realise your potential. In terms of correctly framing your objective you need to consider at core what you are actually seeking to achieve. This can take a number of forms.

You could well be looking for the adoption of a brand new policy. A very good example of this would be the introduction of a levy on plastic bag use in Wales. The single use carrier bags charge legislation came into force in Wales on 1 October 2011. Single use carrier bags are no longer given away for free when people buy goods. The policy has been a successful one, and can be summated by the effective outcomes it has produced. The Welsh Government's analysis of the policy impact estimates that:

- Single use carrier bag use between 2011 and 2014 has declined by 71%.
- Between 2001 and 2014 there has been an estimated overall reduction in all bag use by 57%.
- Consumer support for the charge has increased since 2011 from 61% to 74% in 2015.
- From when the 5p charge was introduced in October 2011 to October 2014 additional donations to good causes from the levy have been estimated at between £17m and £22m.

Before the policy was implemented there were several years of campaigning, originating with the Petitions Committee of the Senedd. It was a campaign with a clear new policy objective and which established a principle without getting drawn into the nitty gritty of how it would be implemented. The precise level of charging and the method of introduction was secondary to the clarity of the overall campaign objective and the fact it was implicitly linked to behaviour change. In this example, there was a clear ask of Government to introduce a new policy which then, in turn, had a behaviour change response from the public.

The success of the policy in Wales led to its introduction in England in 2015. This is another important aspect of policy innovation. In an increasingly divergent UK, especially in terms of public policy development, you might well be looking for the introduction of new policy that is already being delivered somewhere else. This can be particularly appealing to UK organisations, which are aiming to get Wales to follow Northern Ireland, for example. A note of practical political caution, however: taking this approach is not without risk and often comes loaded with a party political dimension. You can never take politics out of policy making, and for example urging a Labour Welsh Government to follow the lead of a Conservative UK Government or an SNP Scottish Government comes with implicit politicisation.

Another important aspect that it is wrong to overlook is the extent to which existing policy frameworks can shape the potential for a new policy being introduced. A Government will be committed to delivering its programme and will ultimately view every potential new policy in the light of its existing policy commitments. Indeed, over 90% of any government programme will be set at the start of a term. Other than gestating a policy for possible introduction later, beyond an election, there is often little that can be achieved in the short term to bring forward a wholly new policy. Exceptions to this rule do exist though, such as the legislation to control wild horses brought forward by the Welsh Government in the Fourth Senedd, which was a result of different lobbying from local government and animal welfare organisations. Other examples would include legislation to enact changes following an independent review or a consultation, which would have commissioned by the Government for such as the 2019 legislation on banning wild animals in circuses.

You will note that these examples are often very specific. They demonstrate the point of clarity in objectives in determining policy change. But sometimes it is not policy change or policy innovation that is required. Sometimes it is the actual implementation of a policy. A good friend with long experience of public affairs, said to me at the time of the Fourth Senedd election in 2011 that they hoped the next administration would focus on policy implementation and not on new policy development. They felt there had been enough consultations, enough initiatives and enough policy frameworks for health, their area of expertise. What was needed was a change of approach from evolving new policy positions to actually implementing the ones that existed. This is another reason to be very clear about how your campaign objectives relate to existing policy.

An aligned angle to this, is sometimes the objective is related to the implementation of a policy, where the intention is undermined by unintended consequences. The UK Government's roll out of Universal Credit is a good example of this, where different Ministers have refined the policy implementation to deal with impact concerns. A Wales specific example would be changes to guidance notes issued to local authorities or health boards in terms of how a policy should be implemented. This is often what campaigning organisations want: they do not want something new done, they want it done consistently or done in a certain way. We will discuss later how this can operate in the context of regional and local policy delivery.

The challenge of your objective can also lie with the issue of policy prioritisation. Take the health and social care department as an example. It controls, at time of writing, some 50% of the Senedd budget, with that percentage forecast to increase. Getting policy prioritisation within such a huge policy area can be a real challenge. Sometimes campaigns just seek to shine a light on a particular area of concern, in the hope it will achieve increased attention and prioritisation, without necessarily a policy change following. An excellent example of this sort of impact is the work of the Sepsis Trust around policy prioritisation, detection and treatment. For some campaigners, this increased prioritisation is what they are really looking for.

An equally valid campaign objective could be based around funding. To achieve funding outcomes, you need to be properly aligned with the budget cycle of the Welsh Government, which also will be discussed in more detail later. Your objective could simply be to protect funding or a clear budget line, as was the outcome sought by the organisations defending the Supporting People budget in 2017. Alternatively, it might be about getting a significant budget increase, which is usually the campaign objective of the Welsh Local Government Association during a budget round. Either way, clarity of objective is required.

A truism that stands throughout, however, is that objectives should not just solely pinpoint a problem, they should offer a solution. Again, the plastic bag lobby is an effective example. People had spent years complaining about plastic waste. It was only when this was tied to a direct and discernible action that progress was made. In that instance, clarity of objective and clarity of communication aligned perfectly to produce a policy outcome.

Clarity of communication

Political decision makers are bombarded every day with requests to assist with a wide variety of political objectives. As well as being clear on your overall campaign objective, you also need to be mindful of exactly what you are asking an individual politician to do. Is it ask a question or raise something in a debate; is it to request a meeting or make a representation; is it attend an event, or meet a local group in the constituency; is it send a letter or sign a statement; is it to give a quote for a press release or take part in a protest.

Politicians are precisely programmed individuals, especially if they have been in office a long time. They will always be thinking of ways in which your objectives can be met and integrated with existing political processes. They will thus have an opinion, usually well meant, on how they can help. Sometimes, however, they may not be offering to help in a way that aids you because going to press on something or asking a formal Oral Question is not always the best way to promote a campaign or achieve an objective. However well meaning their intentions, always bear in mind that you have an overall campaign plan which needs to be delivered. By all means work with them to achieve goals, but make sure they are your goals rather than the political goals of the person you are talking to. Often, however, these two things collide and that can be of significant benefit.

In the Senedd, with access to politicians being so immediate and proximate, it is not being able to speak to the right politicians which is often the problem. It is what you do with those opportunities when they present themselves.

The communication tool of the Elevator Pitch can assist with better and more targeted communication. An Elevator Pitch is a brief yet persuasive speech that you use to spark interest in what your organization does. It is a form of communication aimed at creating interest in a project, idea, or product – or in yourself. A good Elevator Pitch should last no longer than a short elevator ride of 20 to 30 seconds, hence the name. Imagine you are in a lift with the person you are seeking to influence and take it from there.

As with everything else in public affairs, context is critical. Structuring an effective Elevator Pitch from a political perspective, there are a number of points of communication which need to be established:

- Who you are: Don't forget the sheer number of representations a politician receives and the number of people they meet every day. You may have a crystal clear recollection of every interaction you have had with that politician – and if you are using a stakeholder mapping grid described above that may be doubly true – but their memory of you and your organisation may be a lot more hazy.
- What you are doing: This needs to be focused around what your organisation is specifically doing in relation to the matter you want to raise, rather than a more general approach. Try and make this as distinctive and focused as possible.
- What you want them to do: Engage them with an ask. The more precise your ask, the better it will be received. If you have had an affirmative response, a key element is then to follow this up with an email or other communication to confirm what you have just agreed and to ensure it translates to action on their part. This is also vital in sharing contact details.

Clarity of context

You create and shape the context in which your campaign objectives are framed. Information is critical. The plastic bag example levy I keep coming back to only became policy when there was a policy impact assessment conducted on its potential effectiveness. Every new policy or new innovation will be processed by Government in this way in order to measure potential courses of action or alternative approaches. This is a standard tool of Welsh Government and will include not just financial impacts, but impacts on other policy initiatives, impacts on equalities, impacts on sustainability, and impacts on very specific cross-cutting policy objectives such as decarbonisation.

In order to shape that context, it is important to have a body of evidence to accompany your campaign objective. You should fully research the potential consequences of a proposed policy and evaluate the positives or negatives of a policy before seeking to float it. Try to look at it from different angles and different impacts to see how best it might be delivered and framed. This will then shape the way in which you seek to take the campaign forward.

It will determine whether you attempt something hard hitting and press led, or involving a wide variety of people and other stakeholders.

It could also lead you to make coalitions with other organisations in presenting your case. For example, the system of presumed consent for organ donation came about after several years of campaigning from a cross section of interested organisations. Kidney Wales may have led the campaign, but it was actively supported by others with an interest in increasing organ donation rates such as the British Heart Foundation and the Cystic Fibrosis Trust. It also gathered support from the British Medical Association, which provided additional gravitas in making the case.

While discussing allies as part of the context, it is also perhaps worth reflecting on who your opponents might be. You might not think you have opponents but every interest group chasing the same pound, or every organisation seeking attention to their policy asks, is potentially an opponent. Even those you might assume to be allies are not necessarily so – UK Transplant was one of the most lukewarm organisations in respect of a policy of presumed consent for organ donation in Wales.

The legislation for presumed consent in Wales which reached the statute book in Wales in 2013 began six years earlier with the building of a coalition and an information gathering exercise. This helped establish the context of the campaign. Data and statistics were gathered, best practice examples were observed in other countries, and a bank of knowledge was created to ensure depth and consistency. From this firm foundation, not only was political action taken, but steps were taken to create and shape the context of a wider public discussion. This included becoming part of Welsh Government working groups, inputting into consultations, and publishing articles in newspapers. All of which elevated the issue and gave it clear context to support the campaign and its key asks.

> **TOP TIP: Make sure you have spent a decent amount of time planning, evidence gathering and sounding out potential allies before you embark on any campaign, especially if it is impactful or high profile in nature. Getting things right from the outset can avoid problems and disappointments later down the line.**

4

Political Monitoring

A critical part of establishing context to achieve success is to have political information at your disposal. To achieve this, you really need to know what is happening in both the Senedd and the Welsh Government. Developing an effective and speedy monitoring service is thus an essential component of enabling you to keep abreast of how your issues are being managed and dealt with within political processes.

There are basically two ways that you undertake political monitoring. The first is to develop that capacity internally, and this chapter points at how this can be achieved. A warning though: monitoring is time consuming and can be laborious, taking some organisations probably two days a week to fulfil. This persuades a high number of organisations to actually buy in an external monitoring service, allowing internal resources to be directed to more active parts of the public affairs and communications agenda. The way in which an external monitoring service works tends to depend on the package you have negotiated, but is usually built around a mixture of daily alerts (including name mentions) plus weekly summaries of key public affairs points.

Some organisations with a UK reach and structure buy multi-nation monitoring from a single source like Dod's or Randalls. They both use automated services to underpin their offering. Dod's marketing emphasises this:

> 'Working as part of your team, we use the latest technology to deliver up-to-the-minute news and information to your desktop or mobile device tailored to your specific demands to ensure you have everything you need at your fingertips.'[1]

---

1   http://www.dodsgroup.com/products-and-services/dods-monitoring

Whether an organisation undertakes the political monitoring itself, or buys it in via an agency or larger lobbying company, is a decision very much based on the balance of available internal human resources of an in-house operation versus the financial costs and speed of provision of buying it in. With a plurality of companies in Wales offering a monitoring service, costs are very competitive to the extent that I would suggest buying-in the service here. In Scotland, as a comparison, one provider seems to dominate the market. Their monopoly enables them to maintain higher prices and as such it may be financially advantageous for our Scottish counterparts to undertake their monitoring in-house. In both nations, though, this is a situation that may change at any time so regularly re-evaluating your position is important.

Irrespective of the in-house or bought-in means of acquiring the information, the true value of monitoring lies in how it is used to promptly identify potentially negative implications for your organisation, and how it guides your activities to prevent those outcomes. How the key information, provided by the monitoring, is identified and acted upon depends upon who is assigned to that role within your organisation. McGeachy and Ballard, using the example of in-house monitoring, make the important point that:

'... to ensure that your organisation makes the most of its parliamentary monitoring, it is important that [it] is undertaken by someone with a strong grasp of your organisation's strategic aims and objectives, its business, the sector in which it operates, and the geographical spheres of operation and influence. Alternatively, the person undertaking the monitoring should be line managed, or provided with clear guidance, by a person in your organisation who is able to exercise such a strategic overview... and ideally report their findings to a person able to exercise such an overview, and who is able to interpret the information to ensure that your organisation responds effectively and strategically.'[2]

Extending this point, you can equally apply it to any monitoring agency that you choose. Many monitoring agencies have subject specialists in their teams and will often be allocated to you in order to take things

---

2   McGeachy & Ballard, *The Public Affairs Guide to Scotland*, op. cit., p.17.

forward and deliver your monitoring needs in a very bespoke way. The same rule of thumb should also be applied to the person receiving the monitoring from the agency so that they have the ability to exercise the same sort of overview on the material received.

It is by effectively using information that you have obtained that your public affairs activity gets the context and response right. Without developing a monitoring service, you are operating in the dark. Good monitoring needs to operate both retrospectively (transcripts of questions being answered, debates or Committee evidence) and proactively pointing to what will happen in the near future (alerts of when questions are tabled, debate topics raised, or what issues Committees will deal with and what witnesses they will take). Basically, done well, a political monitoring service is an alert mechanism and an information archive.

Monitoring the Senedd

The following table, inspired in structure by McGeachy and Ballard, offers an outline of the key elements of monitoring and where they can be found.

Section	Purpose	Potential use
Record of Proceedings	A verbatim account of the proceedings of the Senedd, produced within a couple of hours.	Interacting with Plenary business depends on the type of business potentially being proposed and is covered in Chapter 14. The turnaround for engaging with debates and other matters may, however, be pretty tight and demand significant reprioritisation of workload should a highly relevant motion appear at short notice.
Business Statement	Produced every week the Senedd is in session and sets out Plenary business for the following three weeks.	
Motions and Amendments	These are tabled at the end of the week before the debates are due to take place.	
Written Questions	Lists the Written Questions tabled and the answers when provided. Discussed in detail in Chapter 13.	Worth checking on a daily basis. Answers often take longer than the stated date for answer.

Section	Purpose	Potential use
Statements of Opinion	Indications of political belief relating to a wide variety of issues. Examined in detail in Chapter 15.	Worth checking every week unless you have actually tabled a Statement.
Laid Documents	Documents which are formally placed before the Senedd, including draft legislation, Committee reports, and others as required by law.	These documents are updated periodically. The budget documents will be laid here, so it's an especially useful resource during the budget round period as discussed in Chapter 12.
Deposited Papers	The deposit of papers in the Library usually arises as a result of a Ministerial commitment made in response to an Oral Question, during a Senedd debate or a Committee meeting.	Not an extensive section and, as you can imagine, the deposits are pretty focused. You can use it for additional research purposes.
Committees	Each Committee has its own page on the Senedd website. This will contain details of Members, forthcoming meeting agendas and papers. Transcripts of Committee meetings are published around 3-4 days later.	The monitoring of Committees is often a burdensome task, as discussed in Chapter 9. The range and depth of discussion means it is often the case that things are missed if not covered adequately. This can mean hours of the week taken up in watching multiple Committees. The relatively slow process of publishing verbatim accounts of Committees means this is the part of Senedd business that is often the most challenging to cover. Further, the process of sifting through often lengthy and multiple evidence sessions to gather political intelligence is a laborious one.

Section	Purpose	Potential use
Legislation	The legislation sub-section contains an overview of the legislative system, a database of legislation passed and enacted, and a tracker for legislation currently passing through the Senedd.	One of the most user friendly and easy to find parts of the Senedd web pages is its extensive and informative section on legislation. It covers the legislative process (Chapter 10) but also deals with each Bill in detail, detailing the ways in which it has been or will be scrutinised.
Consultations	Senedd and Committee consultations are located in a set consultation section.	If you're properly tracking the Committees most relevant to you, then most of the content here will already be known to you.
News	This will contain details of press releases issued by the Senedd and its Committees	Not an extensive section and is often linked, as with consultations, to the work deriving from the operation of Senedd Committees.
Research Service blogs	The Research Service will from time to time publish detailed policy blog posts and research briefings here.	No rhyme or reason lie behind the topics chosen, but the content can often be really informative and engaging. Drafted in a very accessible style, and especially useful for learning about a subject area which might not be central to the one in which you work.
Papers to Note	This can be letters to Committees from Ministers and vice versa and other bodies / organisations. Can include information not previously known.	Some valuable information can enter the public domain through this method, for example, in the summer on 2019, a letter from Vaughan Gething to the Health Committee announced that responses to healthy weight consultation as to be published shortly, the first time this information was made public.

Section	Purpose	Potential use
Senedd TV	The Senedd TV service broadcasts live streams of Plenary and Committee meetings.	Allows access to Plenary and Committees as live.

Monitoring the Welsh Government

Section	Purpose	Potential use
Consultations	The Welsh Government's website has an easily navigable consultation section. It is covered in more detail in Chapter 8.	You can look up current or previous consultation documents, summaries of responses received, and can segment your search to subject areas.
Announcements	The announcements section includes press releases, news stories, Written Cabinet Statements, and transcripts of speeches made by Ministers.	Operates in the same way as the consultations section.
Decision Reports	These are short summaries of decisions taken by Ministers in respect of policy changes or funding decisions.	Very brief summaries, but they are valuable to understanding the decisions of government and who is benefiting from them.
Cabinet meetings	Brief minutes are published two to three weeks after a meeting has taken place.	Useful as a pointer but little else. The level of detail is usually very minimal.
Statistical releases	Statistical information which is released without spin.	A very rich source of information which is maintained historically, allowing different aspects to be cross referenced and examined.
Documents Laid	Government responses to Committee reports and recommendations are laid before the Senedd.	Can sometimes contain useful information.
Publications	Welsh Government policy, strategy and guidance documents are published on here, as are official reports and responses to FoI requests.	Again, there can sometimes be gems of information here.

TOP TIP: Keep a log of when your organisation is favourably mentioned or referenced. You can then use these quotes in your campaign material, annual reports or marketing material to demonstrate some of the impact that you are making.

5

Working with Welsh Government

Now that you have a plan in place, supported by the appropriate information within a political sphere to track its progress, the next step is to begin to implement it by engaging with key policy makers. In many cases this will directly be the Welsh Government. Even if it is not, it is likely that the Welsh Government will be setting the remit and direction of the policy, such as in respect of local government services or local health boards, discussed later in Chapter 21.

The apex of influence and achievement in Welsh public affairs lies with the Welsh Government, by which I mean both the Ministers and Deputy Ministers but also the civil service and special advisers that support them. Together they form a single entity called the Welsh Government, which is the body that ultimately runs Wales.

Forming a Welsh Government

At the end of a Senedd election, the new Senedd is formally convened and the first actions are the election of the Llywydd/Presiding Officer and their deputy. This brief process is governed by some basic rules. Candidates must be proposed and seconded, but cannot make speeches. The ballots to decide the winners, if there is more than one candidate for a post, is done in secret. The most significant rule, however, is that the two officers must be drawn from both 'sides' of the Senedd Chamber – one from the Government side and one from the opposition. This is intended to achieve some sort of balance, since both of these will not ordinarily vote in any Senedd proceedings, and therefore cancel each other out. If, however, both Llywydd and Deputy Llywydd end up on the same side of the chamber, then a motion can be passed to suspend this rule, which requires two thirds of Members to vote for it in order to pass. Such a suspension has only been invoked once. In May 2011, Dafydd Elis Thomas (then a Plaid Cymru Member) became Llywydd for the third time; while Rosemary Butler from Labour, which was to form a minority government, was elected unopposed as his deputy. Two months later, Plaid Cymru came to the One Wales Agreement with Labour and entered government as a junior partner. The Senedd subsequently voted to suspend the relevant rule for balance, with both Presiding Officer and Deputy Presiding Officer being from the governing side. Since two thirds of Members of the Senedd were also from the governing side at this time, the opposition parties were happy with this arrangement, recognising that all their energies would be required seeking to hold the new coalition government to account when it had such a substantial majority in the Chamber.

Once the Llywydd and their deputy are in place, a vote is then held to elect a First Minister, who will in turn form a government. Again, only nominations are required and not speeches, but unlike the election of the Llywydd, if there is a contest then the ballot for First Minister takes place in public. It follows the pattern of a roll call, with each Member being able to name the candidate for First Minister they wish to back. The most memorable example of this was the roll call in 2016 between Carwyn Jones and Leanne Wood which resulted in a tie at 29 votes each. The matter was resolved by the following week, when Plaid Cymru did not put a candidate forward, having come to a deal with Labour over aspects of the government programme, and thus Carwyn Jones was elected unopposed.

It is not just at the start of a new Senedd that this process can take place. If a First Minister has resigned, it is up to the Senedd as a whole to find their successor. This occurred when Carwyn Jones was first elected in 2009 (unopposed) and when Mark Drakeford was elected in 2018 (opposed by both Adam Price and Paul Davies).

Once a candidate has secured a clear nomination, the Llywydd then conveys their name to the Queen, who formally appoints the candidate as their First Minister in Wales. Once this appointment has taken place, the First Minister can then appoint the Ministers to their government. There is a limit under law of 14 Ministers, excluding the First Minister, who has free hand in creating and allocating portfolios. The First Minister can, at their own discretion, appoint fewer Ministers than this number, as Carwyn Jones did initially in forming his third administration in 2016. All Ministerial appointments must also be accepted by the Queen, since they are also Ministers under the Crown.

However, the Senedd plays no role in the appointment of Ministers other than the Counsel General, the Welsh Government's law officer, who must be approved also by the Senedd by simple majority. This is because it is the one office that can be held by someone other than a Member of the Senedd and the Senedd must therefore be given an opportunity to have an opinion on the appointment. At the time of writing, only one Counsel General has actually come from outside the Senedd, Theodore Huckle QC, who held the office between 2011 and 2016.

Generally, if there is an agreement with another party to enter a coalition or support a government, they will receive some of the available Ministerial portfolios. The size of the allocation will be down to the actual negotiation between the First Minister and the other parties or individuals entering the Welsh Government. It is perhaps worth pausing at this point to reflect on the shape of every Welsh Government since coming of devolution to see its size and shape. This in itself tells many tales about how governments are formed in Wales. The constant is Labour – it has been the perpetual majority party of government – so that factor needs to be included when interpreting the table.

	Dates	Shape of Government	Labour & partner seats	Ministries allocated to junior coalition partner	Opposition seats outside government
First Senedd (May 1999-April 2003)	May 1999	Minority Labour	28		32
	October 2000	Labour/Lib Dem	28 + 6	2 Cabinet, 1 junior[1]	26
Second Senedd (May 2003-April 2007)	May 2003	Labour	30		30
	April 2005	Minority Labour[2]	29		31

1   For most of this period, Mike German AM was temporarily excluded from Cabinet while under investigation for suspected expenses fraud. When he was cleared, he resumed full Cabinet duties.
2   Following the decision by Peter Law AM to leave the Labour Party and become an independent.

	Dates	Shape of Government	Labour & partner seats	Ministries allocated to junior coalition partner	Opposition seats outside government
Third Senedd (May 2007-April 2011)	May 2007	Minority Labour	26		34
	July 2007	Labour/Plaid	26 + 15	3 Cabinet, 1 junior	19[3]
Fourth Senedd (May 2011-April 2016)	May 2011	Labour	30		30
Fifth Senedd (May 2016 – April 2019)	May 2016	Labour + 1 Lib Dem	30	1 Cabinet	30
	October 2017	Labour + 1 Lib Dem + 1 Ind.[4]	31	1 Cabinet, 1 junior	29

This table illustrates many things, not least the fragile hold that Labour has often had on power. On three occasions it has led a minority government and both times it has had a technical majority without a coalition partner it has actually held the same number of seats as the combined opposition. At no point has Labour ever had an outright majority on its own. Taking May 2019 as an analysis point, exactly twenty years into devolution, the proportions of time divided between the different types of government is as follows:

	Number of months
Labour technical majority (30/30)	23 + 48 = 71
Labour in coalition	41 + 48 + 36 = 125
Labour in minority government	17 + 25 + 2 = 44

---

3   Became 20 when Mohammad Asghar AM defected from Plaid Cymru to the Conservatives.

4   Dafydd Elis Thomas AM joined the Government. He had left Plaid Cymru in October 2016 and was following the Labour Whip informally for a year before joining the Government.

This table shows that over the 240 months of the Senedd's life, for 125 of those Labour was in some sort of formal coalition deal with others. That appears, from the first two decades of devolution, to be the most 'natural' form of government in the Senedd.

For public affairs professionals, this has a particular significance for two clear reasons. Firstly, it is a clear indicator of a co-operative culture in the Senedd, certainly amongst parties of the centre-left. This is an important shaping factor in how the Senedd tends to work, and also a key to the type of tone you should be using when seeking to influence not just the Senedd but also Welsh Government itself. The longest serving Minister of devolution, Jane Hutt AM, has played a key role throughout much of this period in reaching out to the 'natural allies' in Plaid and the Liberal Democrats. Her approach is by no means unique. She is characteristic of a style of politics which has sought to stabilise devolution by bringing other parties who are ideological partners along on the same journey. Even when Labour has had a technical majority, it has still reached out to others in order to get its budgets through or legislation passed. Sometimes it has done this more grudgingly than other times. As Carwyn Jones recognised on being made First Minister for the third time in May 2016, his Labour government did not have a monopoly on good ideas:

'No one party has a monopoly on good ideas, and I want this Assembly to be more open and more confident than the last.'[5]

A second aspect that should be critically important to public affairs professionals is that this balance of types of government, sat alongside the tendency of Labour to often reach out, and the chances of a non-Labour government in the future, means that it is simply not good politics to just focus on and work with Labour during party manifesto compilation periods. These processes are looked at in more detail in Chapter 20, but it is worth noting here that facts show that over half the time Labour has governed with the clear support of others. Indeed, part of the pledge by Carwyn Jones referred to above was not just about including Kirsty Williams in government, but also reaching out

---

5   National Assembly for Wales record of proceedings, 18 May 2016.

to Plaid Cymru to provide ongoing support for the government on its legislative, financial and policy programmes.[6]

What do governments do?

This reference to the importance the Welsh Government attaches to its legislative, financial and policy programmes pretty much sums up the core work that any government does. Essentially its activities can be divided between passive and active. The passive would be the routine things it does such as fund agricultural payments, deliver certain grants, grant licences, or anything that basically means it behaves in exactly the same way that it had done in the previous year. Essentially these services are passive because they do not change. That does not mean they could not change, but without a policy change or a funding change, essentially they are passive, replicating acts which do not require political action. The natural state of governance, regardless of who is governing, tends to be such passive behaviour.

Active government is a different matter. The translation of a manifesto into a programme of government occurs once a First Minister has been appointed and a government formed. Working with officials, this government then works up a document for public consumption which sets out the areas in which they will operate in an active way.

Essentially, the designation of a policy area within a programme of government means that it becomes part of the active process of governing. There is also an unofficial hierarchy within government of how such active government operates:

*   **Legislation**: As a later chapter will demonstrate, legislation is the most complex and time-consuming approach that a government can take to a policy area. To say that legislation is only introduced as a last resort may be over egging the pudding, but usually officials will examine other ways of achieving a policy objective rather than legislating. It is not a last resort, but neither is it the first response. Take for example the legislation being taken through the Senedd on wild animals in circuses. This had been knocking around

---

6   A formal agreement agreed between Labour and Plaid to this effect between May 2016 and October 2017, without Plaid actually joining the Welsh Government.

from a policy perspective for years and was only committed to as legislation when other options had been exhausted.

- **Funding**: Again, as a later chapter will demonstrate, funding decisions are directly related to the amount of money available. During the years of plenty of the first decade of devolution, when the Welsh Government budget grew from £8 billion to £15 billion, obtaining funding was a relatively straight forward matter. Even if you went to the government and asked for legislation or policy change, you usually came out with money. Governments can do that, and they use resource actively to solve problems (or to paper over problems with twenty pound notes) or to designate priorities. For example, when Carwyn Jones became First Minister in 2009 he did so on a platform of increasing by 1% the amount of the Welsh budget spent on education. This personal commitment was then integrated into the annual budget setting process of the Senedd and Welsh Government.

- **Policy**: A change in direction or a new policy innovation can also be set out in a programme of government, without legislation or money being required. Indeed, the bulk of the commitments in a programme of government probably fall into this category. Significant policy change is often accompanied by a consultation exercise, allowing further input and shaping. Indeed, policy commitments can often be written up in a very superficial way in a programme of government. The important thing is that a commitment of some sort is made, even if the detail looks to be lacking.

- **Policy prioritisation**: A designation of something in a pre-election manifesto and subsequent programme of government can also be an indicator of policy prioritisation, which is essentially a signal that something has moved from an area of passive government to an area of active government. Even a relatively weak mention can suffice. Once something is referenced in a programme of government, it is given a new sense of priority and purpose that then marks it out for attention within government as an area of prioritisation. Sometimes policy prioritisation can be particularly difficult to achieve, especially if there are major over arching policy challenges at the same time. Brexit is an obvious case in point, both in Wales and Westminster. Indeed, Alan Milburn resigned as Chair of the Social Mobility Commission in December 2017 because it did not 'seem to have the necessary bandwidth to ensure the rhetoric of healing social division is matched with the reality.'[7]

The development of a programme of government can often be a complex undertaking. If there is a coalition government, then the document that is worked to will not be drawn from a single party but will be a hybrid of the manifestos of the governing parties. Think of it in terms of a Venn diagram – the bigger the intersection between the circles, the more commonality there is, and the more manageable the process of coalition policy making is.

I am told this was a pretty straightforward exercise when the One Wales Agreement was developed in 2007 between Plaid Cymru and Labour. When the two manifestos were compared, over half the government programme could be agreed easily since there were easily interlocking policy suggestions in both of them, albeit they had been written in slightly different language or with different emphasis. The re-wording of the common policy areas was relatively straightforward. After that, Labour got about 25% of the programme from the distinctive elements of its manifesto and Plaid Cymru some 15% from its own party programme. Both of these elements had to have the agreement of the other party too, in order to ensure that there was buy in and coherence. Though framing rejection as a veto might be harsh, this is effectively what happened. The whole package was then taken to special party meetings of both Labour and Plaid to get their buy ins too. That way the programme of government was protected against revision or rejection further down the line, and stability was brought to the coalition.

A similar, though less detailed, story was played out when Kirsty Williams joined the Welsh Government in the education portfolio in 2016. On this occasion the deal was between her and Carwyn Jones not between parties. Thus, she drew up a list of education priorities only – not those impacting on other departmental areas – and these were discussed as a basis of enabling her to take up a post in the government and deliver on that list alongside the background policy of Labour's general programme for education. The agreement was then formalised and incorporated into the general programme of

---

7   Resignation letter of Alan Milburn as Chair of the Social Mobility Commission, December 2017.

the Labour government. Note that in this instance it was a personal agreement between Carwyn Jones and Kirsty Williams that was made and neither party was asked to endorse it. Since Kirsty Williams had already stood down as leader of the Welsh Liberal Democrats, she was in a much freer position to do so. This approach worked so well it was made again with Mark Drakeford on the same basis in 2018 when he became leader of Welsh Labour.

From a public affairs perspective, this is not a dead period. If you have worked with a minority party that is negotiating an entry to government, this is an ideal opportunity to try and ensure that their negotiating points are taken into discussions. This can be done both by quiet lobbying (perhaps with party policy officers or potential special advisers, a group of people who will be explained shortly) or by media activity around your themes or hoped for pledges, in an effort to make sure they are not disregarded or overlooked. This may be critically important during the formation of a coalition because remember that even though Labour or Plaid got a notional 85% or 75% of their manifestos included in One Wales, there was still some 15% or 25% that wasn't included. Getting your ideas carved out at that stage, when you have succeeded in getting them in one or other manifestos, is not a good outcome.

In a non-coalition scenario, public affairs professionals can of course make their voices heard in the period between the forming of a government and the publication of that government programme. Again, this will be about persuading Ministers and special advisers those around them to prioritise your areas and ensure your asks are committed to. Just because something has been referred to in the manifesto of a winning party, does not mean it will necessarily find its way meaningfully and with emphasis into the programme of government.

Ministers and responsibilities

Once a government is formed, the First Minister will then take time to allocate specific policy responsibilities against each portfolio. This will be published in a list a few weeks after a government is formed, providing a full breakdown of responsibilities. It is worth familiarising yourself with this because functional responsibilities do not always completely mirror expectations. For example, in Mark Drakeford's first Cabinet in December 2018, Julie James became Minister for Housing and Local Government but her responsibilities are way more extensive than this, taking in the voluntary sector, welfare reform and aspects of the justice agenda too. Additionally, she was given responsibility not only from planning (previously in the environment brief for many years) but also the National Infrastructure Commission (which had sat with Ken Skates since the inception of NICW). These examples prove the rationale of reading the list fully.

The first Drakeford government also demonstrates two styles of allocating responsibilities. The Julie James portfolio mentioned is also shared by her deputy Hannah Blythyn, with either of them able to exercise responsibility over policy areas. Compare this with the approach in the department for Health and Social Services, where Vaughan Gething and Julie Morgan were given distinct responsibilities as Minister and Deputy Minister for Health and Social Services. Both approaches are completely legal and, as this example illustrates, can easily sit alongside each other. It is basically a question of leadership style and also, if required, the preference of the senior Minister as to which model is chosen.

A final word on Ministerial responsibilities. These can also be changed during reshuffles. Sometimes a First Minister wants to do more than just refresh the faces in a team, they want to restructure departments and responsibilities too. A good example of this was the September 2014 reshuffle when Leighton Andrews returned to government and a new Public Services ministry was created for him.

The role of a Minister

It is Ministers who decide. Exercising the power granted to them under law, they make the types of decisions outlined earlier in this chapter. Ultimately responsibility rests with them and it is the role of a Minister to make decisions and be accountable for them. If you look at the nature of political decision making in Wales, it is Ministers who sit at the apex of this. They exercise the power to make those decisions under law. Thus when it comes to a major decision like the M4 Relief Road, ultimately whether to build it or not was a Welsh Government decision rather than a Senedd. The Senedd could debate it, vote on it, even oppose it, but the final decision maker was always going to be the Welsh Government. Of course, there would be a hugely significant political fallout if the Welsh Government were to directly reject a motion passed through the Senedd, but so be it.

Ministers come to decisions in a variety of ways. The most important of these is the collective decision making of Cabinet. The most significant policy issues of the day are usually taken to Cabinet, which meets once a week under the stewardship of the First Minister. Its deliberations are confidential, though a sanitised and headline version is published in the public domain. A flavour of these minutes can be had from this rather anodyne entry on a significant issue in May 2019:

'Item 7: Any Other Business
7.1 The Minister for the Environment, Energy and Rural Affairs informed Cabinet that she had declared a climate emergency earlier that day.'[8]

Welsh Government Ministers also meet periodically in Political Cabinet, from which civil servants are excluded, to map out political decisions and their ramifications. These meetings are not minuted, and they usually occur in advance of election campaigns or for more major strategic concerns. A source from within a previous Welsh Government estimates one political Cabinet used to happen every term, with an emphasis on the strategic rather than the political.

Beneath Cabinet, there are also cross-cutting Cabinet sub-committees drawing in the relevant Ministers to make collective decisions. Monitoring these is even more opaque. But both Cabinet and its sub-committees operate by a convention of Cabinet collective responsibility, which is a feature of government in most western democracies. Cabinet collective responsibility, also known as collective Ministerial responsibility, is a constitutional convention in Parliamentary systems that members of the Cabinet must publicly support all governmental decisions made in Cabinet, even if they do not privately agree with them.[9] It is built on principles of both confidentiality (not leaking what happens within collective decision making) and solidarity, whereby

---

8   Minutes of Welsh Government Cabinet meeting, May 2019.
9   Wikipedia definition of Cabinet Collective Responsibility.

Ministers defend each other from motions of no confidence or from other forms of criticism. It essentially means that a government speaks with one voice, and if a Minister cannot agree to do this they must resign (which former Welsh Government Minister Huw Lewis did twice). On a UK level, the Cabinet collective responsibility principle has occasionally been suspended (such as during the 1975 and 2016 European referendums, when Members were allowed to take sides opposing the official government view).

Most decision making is at a much more individual level. Only the big issues are escalated to Cabinet or Cabinet sub-committees. In most instances, Ministers make decisions themselves. These can be around policy, issuing a consultation, making a funding decision or, in respect of secondary legislation, simply signing a piece off. (This process is examined more fully later). All Ministerial decisions are supposed to be publicly reported in a log. Back in 2015, the Welsh Government decided to suspend the publication of Decision Reports. The author spearheaded a short campaign which succeeded in getting this policy reversed.[10] There remains, however, a force within government which is determined to do away with the openness inherent in Decision Reports.

In making decisions, Ministers will be especially advised by two other parts of government, the officials who make up the civil service or perhaps special or specialist advisers. Both of these merit attention.

Civil servants

The government is predominantly composed of civil servants or officials, who keep the system functional and deliver the administration of policy. There are a multitude of books written about the functioning of the civil service in the UK and the officials within. An important point to keep in mind is that the officials are permanent – they do not change with a change of administration – they are career appointments. Yes, they can change departments, and many of the more capable and ambitious ones often do, but they work for Ministers within the Welsh Government, not for individual political parties. Indeed, even where

---

10 "Transparency in Welsh politics a 'tick-box exercise'", BBC Wales report, 4 November 2015.

one party has been in power for two decades, this rule must apply for the civil service to have meaning.

Their job is to implement policy decisions from Ministers though this is certainly not always the actuality. They are explicitly banned from party political involvement including conferences, dinners or any form of manifesto compilation. However, in the run up to the Senedd election, the most senior officials including the Permanent Secretary of the Welsh Government, are available to advise and check the costs of policies for all potential governments.

Officials must walk a thin line. They operate in a political environment but cannot be political. Their role is to advise Ministers, and then to implement decisions. Martin Donnelly, the Permanent Secretary of Department for Business, Innovation and Skills (BIS), expressed this well online in 2014 when writing about the role of officials:

'... policy officials have to work wholeheartedly for the government of the day. They should not be looked to as a brake on politically divisive policy, nor expected to brief those outside government about policy disagreements. If voters do not like outcomes the answer lies in the ballot box, not in expecting permanent officials to take on a political role.'[11]

Returning to the twin roles of advice and implementation, both are done in a supposedly impartial way. In the matter of advice, before a Minister makes a decision they will receive a briefing paper from officials which sets out the ways in which that decision might be implemented. Sometimes the range of options is fulsome on other occasions the options presented can be very narrow and exclude any options that officials deem to be either difficult to implement and administer, will divert resources from other departments or carry a higher than usual degree of risk. The options paper will be structured around a series of potential options. One of these will usually be a 'do nothing' option. The options will contain a clear recommendation for a preferred course of action. This will invariably be the choice the Minister ultimately makes, though they can choose another option or refer the paper back for more work. In presenting policy options, the officials will also have

---

11 Speech on The Positive Neutrality of Civil Servants by Martin Donnelly, the Permanent Secretary of Department for Business, Innovation and Skills (BIS), October 2014, which is stored of the UK Government webpages.

measured them through a series of integral impact assessments on measures like decarbonisation and environmental impact, social justice impact, Welsh language impact and other matters of equalities. Such an approach mainstreams key over-arching policy objectives within the decision making process for Ministers.

In matters of policy implementation, officials are then under an obligation to ensure that political decisions from Ministers are carried out. This is the bulk of the business of government. If a policy is not being implemented adequately or achieving the objectives set out when it was introduced, then it can be subject to review. The Senedd can sometimes provide a key interest in policy implementation. The Public Accounts Committee is structured just for this purpose, while the policy reviews undertaken by Committees are intended to inform and assist this process. Sometimes Committees will also examine how their reports are being implemented if a government has agreed to implement their recommendations. Indeed, by agreeing to implement recommendations, the Welsh Government is under a clear obligation to actually do so. Ministerial agreement with recommendations in a report means they will also be brought within the scope of government policy.

The civil service has been structured in a very particular way. Think of it in terms of a pyramid, and the base is the strength upon which the rest is built. The civil service is rigidly structured to give effect to this approach and works on the basis of gradings which can briefly summarised as follows:

- **Grade One**: Permanent Secretaries (departmental heads in Westminster or the head of the Welsh Government in Wales).
- **Grade Two**: In Wales, the Deputy Permanent Secretaries who look after a number of different government departments.
- **Grade Three**: Director of a department.
- **Grade Four and Five**: Divisional directors and assistant directors.
- **Grade Six and Seven**: Team leaders, policy heads.

There is an in-built expectation that all officials will engage externally subject to their level of responsibility. In many cases you will be working officials whose primary role is simply delivering policy in a specified area, some of whom have considerable and detailed policy expertise. They are usually the Grade Sevens, and are described as follows on an explanatory website for the civil service:

'The key grade is Grade 7. Grade 7s are expected to know all there is to know about their policy area, and to know all the key players, pressure groups and so on. In a well run department, you will find that senior officials listen very carefully to their Grade 7s, and tend to operate in a way which supports their Grade 7s, rather than vice versa.'[12]

In both policy development and policy implementation, as well as any other functions an official undertakes, you will note their absolutely pivotal role. For many public affairs professionals, building up strong and ongoing relationships with officials, especially at Grade Seven, is as important as with Ministers.

Without becoming too critical, there is also a persistent criticism of Welsh Government that there is a huge variability in the quality of officials and the advice they provide. As one former political operator told me when I began writing this section, 'There is of course widely varying quality of officials at all grade levels? I've worked with brilliant officials who are superb at what they do – but conversely I have worked with incompetent, obstructive and duplicitous officials that I wouldn't pay in rusty washers.' Perhaps this comment is best left unattributed, but it is certainly not atypical of attitudes to the quality of civil servants in Wales.

Special Advisers

Special Advisers, or SpAds, are a small number of political civil servants appointed by the First Minister to serve their administration. Governments have for many years used SpAds to supplement the support available from the permanent but apolitical civil service. These can be brought on board either through direct personal recruitment by government or via advertisement. They are generally limited within Welsh Government to ten to twelve people, and not every Minister or department gets its own SpAd in Wales. (The number of SpAds is governed by the Government of Wales Act) This is a matter for the First Minister to decide, and they will structure the SpAd team accordingly. If a First Minister resigns, the whole SpAd team will also

---

12 Civil service grades and roles https://civilservant.org.uk/information-grades_and_roles.html

be considered to have resigned, and would be subject to reappointment or otherwise by their successor.

As with officials, there is a clear structure with a SpAd team in which several different roles are played:

- **Chief SpAd**: The team leader and co-ordinator, working directly to the First Minister. This role has been held most notably by Mark Drakeford, Jo Kiernan and Matt Greenough. Under Mark Drakeford as First Minister there are now two senior SpAds, one is almost a SpAd to the First Minister, and the other a Chief of Staff.
- **Communications SpAd**: a cross-cutting role which at different times has been held by Julie Crowley, Jo Kiernan, Steve Jones, Matt Greenough and Madeleine Brindley amongst others.
- **Policy SpAds**: These are the bulk of the SpAds, working to set Ministers on different areas of policy and their deployment generally either reflects the priorities of government or areas of specific policy challenge.
- **Specialist Advisers**: A smaller number of people who are experts in their own right in policy areas and behave less politically, with a focus on policy development and delivery. Notable examples in Welsh Government have been Ian Butler dealing social services and children under Rhodri Morgan, Tamsin Stirling on housing, and Gareth Williams on Brexit policy.

SpAds are a critical lynchpin within the functioning of government, employed as temporary civil servants. They act as an essential lubricant in the process of government. The UK civil service summarises their functioning as follows:

'They are exempt from mainstream civil servants' obligation of political impartiality, they can assist Ministers on any aspect of departmental business, they can convey to officials Ministers' views, instructions and priorities, they can ask officials to prepare and provide information and data, including internal analyses and papers, and they are allowed to engage in limited political activities outside the office, such as telephone canvassing.

But ... they cannot engage in public canvassing such as for Parliamentary candidates in constituencies, they cannot line manage regular civil servants, nor may officials' advice be transmitted to Ministers via Special Advisers. And SpAds may not formally represent the Government or their Minister, not commit the Government in any way.'[13]

In discharging their duties, SpAds act as the closest political confidante of their Minister. They are able to offer candid advice and support in decision making, which sits alongside the impartial advice from civil servants. Indeed, the expectation is that they will bring a political analysis to bear, and share it in a trusted way. This is a critical counterpoint to any Minister.

More broadly, SpAds also undertake work that is overtly political. They can maintain their own links and networks within political parties, for example. This can often translate through into advice on injecting political elements to speeches, or the drafting of out and out political speeches, something officials cannot do.

SpAds are also the eyes and ears of their Minister, both within government and outside it. They can provide a good political antennae for their Ministers. Indeed, there is an expectation that they will reach out and connect with key public affairs professionals. Building up a solid relationship with SpAds is an important part of public affairs work, along with knowing when exactly to work with them. This can be around sharing good news stories as well as around negative coverage.

A good SpAd has little public persona and should not be the subject of headlines. On occasion this has happened in Wales, most notably in a complaint upheld in 2004 against then special adviser Cathy Owens,[14] but more often it is a feature on a UK level. Those interested in this area from a Westminster perspective can find out more from a publication by University College London.[15]

---

13 Special advisers https://civilservant.org.uk/spads-homepage.html

14 In December 2004, the trade union Prospect received an apology from the Welsh Assembly Government after complaints about Cathy Owens' allegedly hectoring manner towards civil service press officers based in Cardiff Bay. https://www.walesonline.co.uk/news/wales-news/media-doctor-gets-herself-spin-2359899

15 UCL's Constitution Unit in 2013 published Research Note: Special Advisers and Public Allegations of Misconduct 1997 - 2013.

Meetings with Ministers and Ministerial invites

From time to time, especially if you are from a large organisation or one with a particular contemporary concern, you will look to engage with Ministers directly. It will be at the Minister's decision and discretion whether such invitations are accepted or meetings are offered.

Sometimes this may not happen, due to the complexities of diaries or the decisions of Ministers not to meet with certain organisations.

All approaches for formal Ministerial meetings need to be done formally through the system of contacting the appropriate diary secretary, which you can find listed on the Welsh Government website. Provide as much information up front as possible and, if you have a relationship with the relevant SpAd, you can also work through them to maximise your chances of a meeting taking place.

If the request is one for a simple meeting and it is accepted, then the diary secretary will come back to you and suggest a time and a location. They will also want to know more about the purpose of the meeting as well as who will be present. The Welsh Government keeps and publishes a log of all such formal meetings. In some cases, the Minister will refer you to officials for a meeting, instead of directly with them. Don't necessarily be disappointed if that happens, providing it is the right officials, and also providing that an outcome note from the meeting is passed on to the SpAd or the Minister.

Note also that recent rule changes mean that agency public affairs staff are now prohibited from attending such meetings in support of clients, as the author found out having attended such a meeting in error.[16] Despite this, the general rule of thumb has been that public affairs agency professionals have never particularly attended such meetings, choosing instead to brief their clients to speak effectively for themselves. Indeed, in my experience, in the handful of such meetings I have attended, the invitation has often come from the Minister to do so. This included some engagement with Carwyn Jones when he was First Minister during the 2011 referendum, and it was he who introduced the rule change to prevent this from now happening.

In respect of invitations to speak to conferences or set piece events, involving speeches or prize givings in a Ministerial capacity, if a

---

16 BBC report, Rules tightened after Minister Ken Skates met lobbyist, 11 March 2019 https://www.bbc.co.uk/news/uk-wales-politics-47530623

Minister accepts then their private office will want a great deal of information between acceptance and attendance. This will generally be around wanting more detail of the event in terms of location, parking, agenda and timeframe, and general purpose of the event. It will also drill down into the actual logistics of the event, such as who will introduce the Minister, who will meet them on arrival, and who are the key people in attendance (a very strong requirement if the Minister is on a panel). The questions involved in setting up a meeting may sometimes feel overly laborious and intrusive, but they are intended to make sure that the Minister is well briefed and knows what to expect.

TOP TIP: Building up strong and trusted personal relationships within government is a key part of the work of a highly functioning public affairs professional, be they Ministers, Deputy Ministers, officers, or special/specialist advisers. The trust element of such relationships is absolutely critical.

6

Working with Members of the Senedd

General rules can be applied to working with Members of the Senedd, but these come with the health warning that Members are people, and all people are different. Therefore, the first rule is to always remember this and not treat elected representatives as if they were a single flock of sheep: the more personalised and context-rich your approach, the higher the likelihood of success.

Indeed, Members of the Senedd sometimes actively dislike being approached in a blanket way. While general event invitations, for example, should be issued to all Members, you are well served by taking personalised approaches to get them there (discussed more fully in Chapter 18). The same principle should be applied to the way in which you work with Members of the Senedd more generally.

Engaging with different types of Members

In Chapter 3 we examined how to target Members and the development of a stakeholder matrix. Making value judgements about who to include in this matrix is part of the skill of public affairs. Party political concerns will obviously be a factor, but there are others too which need consideration as you develop an engagement strategy around a particular campaign or objective.

The most obvious defining type is geography. If you are a small, single centre organisation then you will need to cultivate a particularly strong relationship with your local directly elected Member. You can also use this approach with a number of Members if you are an organisation with a presence in a number of constituencies, be they third sector shops or points of service delivery. Remember of course that regional Members should also be included as they have equal status as political representatives in your area and can also be good advocates. Indeed, if you have a campaign or an issue that is particularly politically charged, then engaging with as wide a geographic pool as possible is advantageous since it will maximise the number of Members naturally inclined to agree with you.

Local engagement and utilisation of Members can be extremely effective even if you are not seeking to deal with something that is particularly politically charged. For example, Community Pharmacy Wales, the umbrella body for high street pharmacies, makes good use of its extensive pharmacy network and invites Members to visit ones in their locality in order to become more familiar with the range of services provided there. Other organisations hold meetings on a local and regional basis and can invite Members along to coffee mornings or during action weeks, such as Macmillan or Parkinson's UK, allowing the Member to engage meaningfully with a specific group. You may not hear much from that Member for the rest of the year, and they may not become a regular champion, but they can be relied upon to offer specific and targeted support and publicity for a set activity.

Further to this point, your organisation should also ensure that it does not overlook developing local contacts with any Member who also serves in the Welsh Government. They might not be able to publicly campaign alongside you (former Minister Leighton Andrews had to resign in 2013 for campaigning to save a local school while at the same time acting as Education Minister), but they will be able to exercise influence on their government colleagues behind the scenes. If you want to contact the responsible Minister though, and they happen to be the local Member too, it is best to engage using official channels as, in that scenario, they will generally prefer the Ministerial approach rather than being primarily regarded as just a local Member. The rule is this: if you want to contact the Member in their Ministerial capacity, go through their private office in the Welsh Government; if you want to speak to them in their representative role, approach them through their constituency office.

Also important are two categories of politician outside government but holding key roles. The first of these is the lead spokesperson for each of the opposition parties, which is covered in detail in the next chapter. Equally important is the person who leads the Subject Committees or committees covering your policy area. These politicians are absolutely critical, along with their committee colleagues, and suggestions for relationship building with them are a key focus of Chapter 9.

Another distinct 'type' of politician is the extent to which they have a strong affinity with your organisation and interest in its issues. Indeed, some Members are very aligned to certain issues or causes to the extent they can be seen as particular natural champions. Good examples of this would be Lorraine Barrett, who was a consistent voice for animal welfare in the first three terms of the Senedd; the way Helen Mary Jones has become a regular voice for carers and piloted previous legislation on their behalf is also notable; David Melding is the go-to person on children in care; and a consistent voice of rail users has been Hefin David. While it is true to say that these types of Members have many varying political interests, the fact that they are the most vocal and consistent champion for specific issues makes them key individuals to target. Some Members have also been very strong champions of and synonymous with different issues and causes at different causes, such as Bethan Sayed, who has been vocal on many things including eating disorders, steel pensioners, Cystic Fibrosis medicines and street art at different times.

A useful illustration of what can be expected of a champion is presented by the influence curve depicted below. Champions are often on a journey to a point where, at the end, they feel a shared sense of ownership, an ownership often shared with the organisations working in the same field of interest and usually working to the same ends as the champion.

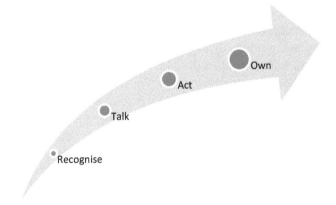

The point with champions is that you do not need many of them. They just need to be vocal and effective. To do this, they often rely on detailed and regular briefing relating to those specific subject areas and develop a strong reliance on the organisations operating in those subject areas. This can sometimes be manifest also in their work with Cross-Party Groups, as described in some detail in Chapter 17.

Champions usually emerge based on existing levels of interest or constituency/regional concerns. A clever move at the start of the Fifth Senedd was undertaken by the Species Champion initiative taken by Wales Environment Link. This campaign randomly allocated paired Members with individual species. This well noticed initiative gave political representation and awareness to wildlife under threat, allowing Wales Environment Link to directly inform Members on population developments and habitat initiatives. Examples of the Species Champions were Labour's Hefin David on the adder and Rebecca Evans on the black beetle, and Conservative Angela Burns on the horseshoe bat. Around 40 out of the 60 Members actively took up the challenge of being species champions.[1] Wales Environment Link's campaign enjoyed such political engagement and profile that it was then replicated by its sister organisations in the other legislatures of the UK.

Champions can also sometimes focus on relatively small aspects of policy which catch their eye and which they then pursue vociferously before getting a result. Helen Mary Jones is a good example of a serial campaigner who sometimes focuses on things which seem small but can have a big impact. Back in 2007, she championed the campaign by the Fostering Network, Voices from Care Cymru and the Bryn Melyn Group, in the 'This Is Not a Suitcase' campaign to encourage Welsh councils to ban the use of bin bags when moving looked-after children's belongings. Ultimately this campaign, with its champions, resulted in local authorities buying suitcases for all looked-after children so they could better protect their possessions and engender a sense of dignity when facing difficult circumstances.

Another defining factor, and one that is rarely thought of, is the consideration of the campaign 'type' of Member that you are seeking to engage with. Politics or geography are not key here, it is about the way in which a Member conducts themselves and engages with

---

1   https://www.waleslink.org/species_champions

outside organisations. In short, it is the extent to which a Member can be perceived as an active campaigner, and every political grouping has Members who appear particularly campaign orientated. In the Fifth Senedd you can see Darren Millar in the Conservative group, Leanne Wood in Plaid Cymru, Julie Morgan or Jenny Rathbone in Labour, or Neil McEvoy as good examples of politicians who see the Senedd as vehicle for campaigning and often prefer to engage with campaigners outside its confines. Others tend to operate more strictly within the confines of the Senedd itself but can be equally powerful advocates, such David Melding for the Conservatives or Joyce Watson from Labour.

Some Members favour certain courses of action within the Senedd too – we will discuss in Chapter 13 how the Conservatives are more prone to use Written Questions, while Labour backbenchers seem to particularly favour the backbencher debates method outlined in Chapter 14. There is no right or wrong way of approaching this. The point is that each Member has a different style and approach, which needs to be identified and understood, and needs to be approached accordingly.

Different types of activities

The local visit, as suggested, is a strong hook for informing and influencing, which should be followed by effective engagement to build on that visit or interaction. As Chapter 3 demonstrated, there is real value in being explicit about the next stages of activity. This should be related to your campaign planning and the way in which you have decided to target an individual and to what end.

Chapters 9 to 18 provide an important overview of the different types of activities an elected Member can deliver on your behalf. As was set out at the start of this chapter, it is critical to take a personalised approach to this process and to work with them in respect of different types of your proposed activities.

One area of engagement, which is not covered in the more formal parts of interacting through Senedd business, is mass campaigning: a strategy with different options and variations but they all have merits. The main types of this activity are summarised in the table below, along with reflections on possible advantages and disadvantages.

Type of mass activity	Positives	Negatives
Demonstrations	• Good way of generating media interest. • One of the best ways of involving a large number of people. • Appeal to campaign orientated politicians, allowing them to add their voices and stand alongside you.	• Often take a great deal of organisation and planning. • Can look weak if there is a lower than expected turnout. • Can be hijacked by extreme groups or factions.
Protests at the Senedd	• Often a very effective media hook since the activity takes place in easy reach of most media outlets. • Similarly, it is easy for politicians to connect and join with you and make speeches of support.	• The same negatives apply as per demonstrations, plus the danger of the event alienating the Government.
Lobbies inside the Senedd	• The Senedd is an open space and members of the public can enter as individuals who will have contacted their elected Members to meet them to discuss individual concerns. • This approach works best when tied to a debate or other activity within the Senedd.	• This approach has to be supported and co-ordinating, linking individuals with their local or regional Members, which can be very time consuming.
Direct action protest	• Can be highly impactful at drawing media attention or making a powerful point.	• Can often be seen as disruptive, borderline illegal, or extremely negative. • Many politicians take a dim view of anything that intimidates or threatens themselves, their staff or their constituents.

Type of mass activity	Positives	Negatives
Petition launches	• The gathering of petition signatures will obviously have been a mass activity; • This is also a hybrid activity which sees a mass gathering form to hand in a petition into the Senedd processes (which are covered in detail in Chapter 16).	• Fewer than other forms of direct action, though does involve organisation and preparation.
Email, postcard or letter campaigns	• Relatively easy method of interaction which was particularly popular between 2001-11. • Allows people to become involved in an open access form of lobbying and campaigning without travelling to do so. • Can emphasise depth of feeling, especially when representations are clearly personal and constituency related.	• Contact can be grouped together if there is a generic message: politicians are often wary of mass communication they believe has been almost auto generated. • Reliant on self restraint on the part of those making the communication.
Online campaigning such as direct messaging on social media tools	• Open access forms of lobbying and campaigning where politicians are contacted online. • Works best where there are set campaign themes/links and hashtags to demonstrate a unified approach (see also Chapter 24).	• Little control over what is said and how interaction takes place, leading sometimes to confrontation and counter productive lobbying verging on abuse and bullying. • May be conducted by people who aren't constituents, which may again alienate an elected politician.

It is sometimes suggested that popular mobilisation into the form of a demonstration or protest can be counter-productive and should be avoided. Experience shows that this is far too blunt an analysis. As well as demonstrating range and strength, which can exert particular pressure on decision makers, the use of mass campaigns may also play a vital internal role. If yours is a mass membership campaign, the campaigners will be looking for a way to show their commitment, to actively participate and to exert influence. Depriving them of avenues to add their voices, often with very personal concerns, will risk alienating your most passionate advocates and supporters. Disregarding any form of action on a mass campaign can, bearing in mind most people do not understand the subtleties and intricacies of a wider public affairs campaign, sometimes lead organisations to be accused of being too 'top down' or out of touch in their approaches.

Direct action on its own, however, is not going to achieve the desired outcomes. Usually it has to be tied in to some form of managed political action within your public affairs planning.

TOP TIP: Stratify and personalise your approach and remember to treat different Members as people rather than just names of a list.

7

Working with Political Parties

As in the previous chapter, it is important not to take a one size fits all approach to working with either politicians or political parties. Two later chapters deal specifically with two of the most important forms of political interaction, namely Party Conferences (Chapter 19) and Manifesto compilation (Chapter 20). This chapter will assess other party political interaction, excepting that of Welsh Government which has already been analysed and discussed.

Working with Government backbenchers

This group of Senedd Members is often numerous but can be challenging. Essentially a government backbencher is there to support the government, and they have been elected to the Senedd on that basis. Breaking the whip and voting against the Welsh Government is therefore a pretty big step to take. Indeed, it happens more rarely in the Senedd than the other legislatures of the UK. During the writing of this book, when the Brexit war was raging in the UK Parliament, groups of Labour and Conservative backbenchers would take to the airwaves on a daily basis to indicate their intentions to either support or oppose the position of their respective leaderships.

This phenomenon has been mostly absent from the workings of the Senedd. Perhaps the main reason for this is the tightness of the political arithmetic. Excluding the Labour-Plaid Cymru coalition of 2007-11, governments in the Senedd have usually had a relatively small majority. The following table illustrates this point:

	Government vote	Opposition vote
First Senedd: Labour only 1999-2000	28	32
First Senedd: Lib Dem-Lab coalition 2000-2003	34	26
Second Senedd 2003-2007	30 became 29	30 became 31
Third Senedd 2007-2011	41	19
Fourth Senedd 2011-2016	30	30
Fifth Senedd 2016-2017	30	30
Fifth Senedd: with Dafydd Elis Thomas supporting the government, 2017-date	31	29

The 'normal' pattern, 75% of the time since devolution, is for the Government to command 28-31 seats and, in such circumstances, there is little room for rebellion amongst government backbenchers as on a significant issue it could result in a vote being lost.

Government backbenchers can, however, make their views known on issues. Much of the time this is done privately, with Members effectively lobbying Ministers on a personal level behind closed doors to achieve concessions. Obviously Whips and Ministers prefer to deal with business in this way as it avoids any form of media spotlight but, on other occasions, disagreement can be pretty public and lead to open displays of opposition. Mike Hedges (Labour, Swansea West) was, for example, very vocal in criticising the Welsh Government for phasing out the Communities First programme in 2016, but ultimately did not vote against the budget. Also, in 2007, Lynne Neagle (Labour, Torfaen) led a cross-party campaign to secure more funding for disabled children, which won a concession of some £20 million from Welsh Government without a single vote having to be taken. In the Fourth Senedd, Julie Morgan (Labour, Cardiff North) and Christine Chapman (Labour, Cynon Valley) led a campaign for the Welsh Government to legislate on ending the ability of parents to physically chastise children, which was so challenging and powerful that it resulted in a commitment to that effect in the 2016 manifesto.

Indeed, public and private pressure can result in government backbenchers sometimes being more robust with government than they otherwise would have been. It is also true that that pressure is sometimes applied without any external stimuli. Independently-minded backbenchers like Alun Davies (Labour, Blaenau Gwent) have, when they are outside government, proven to be the most challenging and effective critics of their own side.

Some might suggest that backbenchers who have been Ministers are perhaps the best critics of all, since they understand processes of government, know 'where the bodies are buried', and might also be settling scores once they are outside of administrations. All of which should help give you a context in which you can gauge how to work with government backbenchers. They may be inclined to work with you to get concessions and achieve wins, but more often than not if they do so it will be behind the scenes rather than in the glare of publicity: one aspect of traditional political culture that is lacking in the Senedd is outright rebellion.

Working with lead opposition spokespeople

The value of lead opposition spokespeople cannot be understated. This book will refer to how they can make a difference in a number of ways, particularly around how you can successfully engage with the legislative process (Chapter 10), the financial process (Chapter 12) and in tabling Oral Questions (Chapter 13).

Being the lead opposition spokesperson on an issue does give a Member kudos and status. It means they are virtually guaranteed to be called in debates and statements on that policy area and also as part of question sessions, and when they are not it is always because someone else in their party group is taking the lead by mutual agreement. What they have to say is usually therefore the most important parts of any debate other than the government's own position.

It is therefore critical that at the top of your public affairs target list should be the lead opposition spokespeople. Cultivating strong and respectful relationships with people covering your policy areas is an absolute must if you wish to ensure that the policy spokespeople are not just aware or your organisation, but also have a useful working knowledge of its mission and activities. The sign of a good working relationship, and of mutual respect, is when the party spokespeople welcome further engagement on other policy areas and perhaps even approach you, formally or informally, for your organisation's views and input.

This advice may appear to be obvious but it is essential and must be well understood by every organisation seeking to influence Members. A consequence of following this approach is that new opposition policy leads tend to get inundated with requests for meetings. Nick Ramsay tells an amusing story about feeling totally bombarded when he briefly became health spokesperson for the Conservatives because of the sheer number of organisations that suddenly approached him. He felt overwhelmed and time poor in a way he had never experienced when shadowing the previous portfolios of local government, finance or economic development.

In working with opposition parties, however, never lose sight that they are working to a political agenda. In most cases they will want to score points against the government. This is why they are often seeking external organisations to come up with ideas for opposition debates in the Senedd. Should you choose this road, remember that it is usually not one that leads to policy change. Very few opposition debates are won on the floor of the Senedd, despite the slender majorities pointed to above.

Even where an opposition party is in broad agreement on a policy which has strong cross-party and expert support, they will still want to pick at weaknesses. A good example of this is the Welsh Government's introduction of a new curriculum for Wales. Leading for Plaid Cymru, Sian Gwenllïan honed down on specific aspects of the proposals relating to Welsh language and Welsh history teaching. This fitted well with her party commitment on these issues and allowed the opportunity to pick at the detail of the proposal rather than attacking it whole scale.

Indeed, the best approaches from opposition parties often come from where they take targeted and focused approaches rather than attacking a policy as a whole. This sort of approach often puts the government under more pressure since it is forensic and, most dangerously, can appear more reasonable. It is much easier to change the views of an administration on small aspects rather than whole policy initiatives. Some of the best external collaboration with opposition parties works on this basis.

These same party groups will also have several meetings a week. Sometimes, especially amongst opposition parties, it may be possible to come in and present to those groups. There are examples where this has been done solely to staff and not politicians, especially in relation to non-contentious but complex issues. Occasionally this has offered valuable platforms to organisations.

Working with party staff and researchers

Politicians in the Senedd tend to have two types of political staff. The first is their personal staff, probably case workers, researchers and media officers, who work with them in their Senedd offices or work locally on their behalf. The other type is less well known, and these are the party group staff. These are not staff working in the party's headquarters, but rather staff paid for by the taxpayer to support the work of Members' political groups in the Senedd.

Each party will organise its group staff slightly differently, but some general rules apply. They will usually contain at least one communications/media officer, and the bulk of them will be focused on policy research. It is worth examining the party group staff structure for each party in order to work out who best to target and build up relationships with.

In undertaking this exercise, don't forget that the governing party also has group staff. Most of the examples in this volume tend to focus on working via the opposition to raise an issue, and many external organisations are locked into this way of working. It doesn't always pay dividends. Even where organisations engage with group staff, they might usually just focus on opposition parties. This disregards the potential of tapping into government group staff. They are political, they are not civil servants, and they will be looking for ways to assist government-supporting Members to contribute to statements or debates. They might also be looking for content to generate press coverage. If your organisation agrees with the government's policies, why not feed into them with examples and quotes which can then be used by supportive backbenchers in speeches and their media work.

Across all parties, though, working with the group staff can often be a productive and time effective way of raising your profile and projecting your policies to a wide range of potential allies. This can be particularly vital when dealing with legislation or the budget process, which tend to be planned on a group basis, certainly by opposition parties.

Another important angle is how you work with such staff members during the compilation of party manifestos in the run up to an election period. This form of working is so distinctive that it has been afforded a totally separate analysis in Chapter 20.

> **TOP TIP: Be focused and targeted when working with political parties. Try and avoid getting into scenarios with opposition parties where you totally oppose the government, but rather try and focus down on key weaknesses and areas of improvement in a policy or a piece of legislation.**

8

Responding to Consultations

Done well, political consultation is more than just a tick box exercise. This applies both to the body which is consulting – be it the Welsh Government or a Senedd Committee – or yourselves as the body which is responding to the consultation exercise. They are mechanisms to gather opinion or test a policy hypothesis and are deeply ingrained in the way that both Government and Senedd work.

Consultation periods usually extend from around ten weeks to a maximum of four months. There is a general rule that consultations are not launched during Senedd recess periods, though this is not an absolute rule, and an effective monitoring system will alert you to consultations when they are published, allowing you to input and engage. Further, there is often a 'heads up' that consultations are forthcoming via statements made by Ministers indicating their willingness to consult in due course before the introduction of a new policy or a new proposal for legislation, or might be visible from the agreed forward work programme of a Committee (of which, more in the next chapter.)

Usually the most important consultations are those issued by the Welsh Government. They take the form of online documents to which, usually, any organisation or individual can respond. The Senedd also issues regular consultations, which can be on behalf of the Senedd as a whole on a major constitutional development, such as changing the number of Senedd Members or changing the name, or they can also be issued by individual committees of the Senedd, and from time to time all committees consult.

Other bodies you'd need to keep on your public affairs radar are departments of the UK Government such as the Wales Office, or committees of the House of Commons such as the Welsh Affairs Select Committee. Be aware, however, that these consultations may sometimes be very similar to the ones run through Wales-based political institutions. There was a case a few years ago where both the Welsh Affairs Select Committee and the Economy Committee of the Senedd ran consultation exercises on marketing Wales and organisations submitted responses to either, or both, consultations.

Similarly, there are arms length Welsh bodies such as Public Health Wales which will run consultation exercises from time to time; and local health boards often use a combination of public meetings and written consultations to gauge the public's view before coming to a position on local service reconfiguration.

Nevertheless, for most public affairs professionals in Wales, the focus tends to be either on Welsh Government or Senedd Committee consultations and it is worth detailing the consultation processes for both of these, before examining some common themes to ensure your consultation responses matter and have an impact.

The Welsh Government consultation process

The Welsh Government tends to consult on between 15 and 25 issues at any one time. These are spread out across the different portfolios and responsibilities of government. During the summer of 2019 there were 16 consultations ongoing.

The Welsh Government consults in three ways. The least used is a pre-legislative consultation, when they float an idea for legislation, almost in the style of a White Paper, and ask for comment and input. It can be done to try and add flesh to the bones of an idea or an intention. Examples of this sort of approach would be the consultations, conducted in the fourth and fifth terms of the Senedd, concerning a potential Public Health Bill for Wales when issues related to public toilets and intimate piercings were included and road tested with the public via the consultation exercise.

The second type of consultation relates to major over-arching policy related to the programme of government and is intended to solicit opinion and ideas. During 2019 a number of broad topics were consulted upon:

- **Healthy Weight, Healthy Wales**: reducing the obesity problem in Wales.

- **Improving public transport**: proposals for bus services and the licensing of taxi and private hire vehicles in Wales.
- **Draft climate change adaptation plan for Wales**: testing opinion on a broad range of 32 potential adaptations.
- **Action on disability: the right to independent living**: proposals to develop and improve access to help, advice and services for disabled people in Wales.
- **Reform of fire and rescue authorities in Wales**: proposals to reform how fire and rescue authorities (FRAs) in Wales are governed and funded.

The remainder of the 2019 consultations (around two thirds of the total) related to detailed secondary legislation and applied to the development of statutory instruments, regulations, codes or guidance on specific topic areas, namely:

- Draft professional standards for assisting teaching.
- Code of practice on the delivery of autism services.
- Draft guidance to challenge bullying in schools.
- Reform of fire and rescue authorities in Wales.
- A494 River Dee Bridge improvement scheme.
- Draft Additional Learning Needs Code.
- Changes to student finance from academic year 2019 to 2020.
- Draft national violence against women, domestic abuse and sexual violence indicators – to agree and produce the indicators as set out.
- Guidance to school governing bodies on school uniform and appearance policies.
- Extending financial administrative penalties (FAPs) within fisheries.
- Code of Practice for the welfare of cats.
- Updating Welsh food law in preparation for Brexit - consulting on corrections to Welsh statutory instruments derived from EU law. These relate to food marketing standards, labelling and school milk.

This list relate to areas where the Welsh Government is already exercising powers and is seeking to clarify, change or amend the ways those powers are exercised. In most cases, there is a strong technical element to these consultation exercises. This split between over-arching consultations and those pertaining with the detailed application of law or regulations always tends to follow this pattern, so there are usually a lot more of this latter type of consultation at any one time.

Welsh Government consultations, especially the over arching ones or those aimed at vulnerable groups, also tend to come in easy read formats to encourage engagement. Some organisations use these to engage with their own stakeholders before submitting a more detailed response through the more advanced consultation process.

Welsh Government also organises consultation events from time to time, which are open meetings of the kind you also see at Local Health Board level. These are structured to test opinion with sections of the population who might not ordinarily have submitted evidence to the formal consultation process. You can think of them maybe as local focus groups, which tend to be a mixture of the informed and those seeking more information. Before introducing legislation of presumed consent for organ donation, the Welsh Government used this consultation technique extensively, and their importance cannot be understated.

It is imperative that your organisation attends, and fully engages with, Welsh Government consultations. The information gleaned from these sessions, as to how the proposed measure is to be implemented and its potential impact, is invaluable and they also enable you to commence your engagement with the Government from a very early stage.

Being aware of, and participating in such consultations illustrates how hard-wired into political systems is the practice of using interactive tools to gather opinion and shape policy, hopefully for the better.

The Senedd consultation process

Senedd Committees conduct a variety of consultation exercises, often simultaneously. For example, in January 2019 the following Committee consultations were live:

- **Children, Young People and Education Committee**: School Funding.
- **Climate Change, Environment and Rural Affairs Committee**: Microplastics; Rethinking Food and Drink in Wales; Biodiversity Public Goods Scheme.

- **Culture, Welsh Language and Communications Committee**: Supporting and promoting the Welsh language; The role of arts and culture in addressing poverty and social exclusion.
- **Economy, Infrastructure and Skills Committee**: Compulsory purchase; Electric vehicle charging in Wales; Research and Innovation in Wales; Barriers facing small home building firms; The future development of Transport for Wales.
- **Equality, Local Government and Communities Committee**: Public Services Boards; Diversity in Local Government; Voting Rights for Prisoners.
- **External Affairs and Additional Legislation Committee**: The Withdrawal Agreement: Implications for Wales; Wales' future relationship with Europe and the World.
- **Health, Social Care and Sport Committee**: The wellbeing of Carers; Hepatitis C.

The term 'live' signifies that the committees were either taking written evidence or had begun the process of open hearings on at least one of the consultation topics. How these are chosen is covered in Chapter 9.

The other standing committees of the Senedd also undertake consultations on policy, although not so frequently. The Standards Committee has looked at lobbying and at the time of writing is re-examining the Code of Conduct of Senedd Members in relation to complaints; while the Constitutional and Legislative Affairs Committee is dealing with the UK Trade Bill; and the Finance Committee will look at the future provision for structural funds for Wales through the proposed Shared Prosperity Fund. You will see that these committees tend to only undertaken one inquiry, with associated consultations, at any one time. Additionally, the Petitions Committee's work is tied directly to the petitions it receives but can also undertake a style of policy inquiry, linked to an ongoing petition, which closes when the petition period ends.

In addition to the myriad of policy consultations, every committee can also have legislation remitted to it by the Senedd. During the summer of 2019, the Legislation (Wales) Bill before the Constitutional and Legislative Affairs Committee, and the Ombudsman (Wales) Bill before the Finance Committee were the only two ongoing consultations, but this is atypical as there are usually three or four Bills passing through committees at any one time. Each one will usually have a Stage One consideration based on a policy consultation on the remit of the Bill.

In reflecting on legislative consultation from Senedd Committees, it is important to remember the Senedd is a distinct organisation from the Welsh Government. You may therefore have already submitted evidence on a topic to the Welsh Government at the pre-legislative phase before it is subsequently taken up by a committee but you will still need to make the same arguments again when a Stage One consultation is launched by a Senedd Committee. It is vital therefore to never assume that Senedd Members will have already read the evidence you had submitted previously: assume no prior knowledge of your lobbying position.

The length of time a Senedd Committee will look at Stage One of a Bill is usually no more than a few months. Indeed, when the Bill is formally remitted to a committee, there will be a set date by which that committee has to respond with a formal report but the committee's deliberations may offer more opportunities for influencing Welsh Government policy than the original Government-led consultation. Other issues around engaging with committees on legislation are also covered in the chapter on legislative processes.

As far as policy inquiries are concerned, the length and level of detail of a Senedd Committee inquiry can vary enormously. Some exercises are very focused, with maybe just a day of hearings and a small number of organisations invited to contribute oral evidence. Others can last for months and deal with a very broad policy area, such as an energy policy inquiry that once lasted over two years.

The clerks of the relevant Senedd Committee will decide which organisations to call in to give evidence during consultation exercises and may, as noted above, often involve the larger, more established organisations rather than a full cross section of evidence givers. The actual oral evidence process might well have begun while the written consultation period is ongoing, so ensuring your evidence gets the maximum level of exposure might necessitate asking Committee Members, or even the Chair directly, to include you in the oral evidence process.

When Senedd Committees take oral evidence, though, they generally bring a range of organisations together at the same time to present opinion. This brings both opportunities and challenges. It can bring the opportunity of aligning with other organisations alongside you, but also brings a danger of both public disagreement and, more pointedly, you may well find yourself crowded out from saying too much by the others who are presenting at the same time. As a rule of thumb, it is generally best to give evidence alone, though in most cases this option will not be available to you if you are lucky enough to be called to give oral evidence.

A final word on Senedd Committee processes. If the consultation relates to legislation, both the Finance Committee and the Constitution and Legislative Affairs Committees will also look at the Bill and take hearings, though usually only from the Government and, where it is Backbencher legislation, from the proposer of the Bill.

Making your consultation response stand out

As consultations can sometimes generate tens, perhaps hundreds of submissions, the skills, experience and ingenuity of the public affairs professional are required to ensure that your organisation's response attracts attention and its policy stance wins support.

You do, nevertheless, have one immediate advantage. Responding on behalf of an organisation rather than as an individual automatically brings some weight to bear, and not all responses are equal or treated equally. Sometimes identical responses from individuals issued against a set template from a co-ordinating campaign mean that those responses are treated as one bloc. Campaigning organisations such as *Cymdeithas yr Iaith Gymraeg* (The Welsh Language Society) have fallen foul of this approach in the past, where hundreds of respondees have been grouped together and counted as just one response: quality, not quantity, counts.

Good public affairs means that if something is worth saying, it is worth saying for effect, but if you approach a consultation exercise as simply a tick box exercise, then don't be surprised if the receiver of your response treats it in that way. As with any other aspect of public affairs, consultation responses are enriched with data and examples.

Having an opinion is one thing, being able to back it up gives it veracity and gravitas.

Another way of adding credibility to a response is by aligning it with the responses of others. A good way of doing this is by circulating your response to other organisations who might share your views, concerns and perspectives and encouraging them to do likewise. You may also belong to a network of organisations, such as Wales Environment Link, which might also be constructing a response. In that case there is no problem with working in that network to shape its response but also submitting your own and referencing the joint response too.

Further, there is absolutely no problem with referencing the opinions of others in your response – or even constructively criticising the responses of others that might be in the public domain. This is particularly true when it comes to Senedd Committee consultation responses. Often the committees will start to take oral evidence before completing their written consultation exercise and usually it's the key organisations or players that get invited first. For health and social services, for example, that would usually be the biggest stakeholders like the NHS Confederation, the British Medical Association, the Royal College of Nursing and the Association of Directors of Social Services. Their intention is to shape the consultation exercise just like you, so don't be afraid of challenging their opinions and perspectives, in writing, and always in a respectful way.

On the issue of oral evidence, if you are offered the opportunity to give evidence to a committee, always take the chance to do so, and you should make clear in the preamble or summary of your consultation response that you are willing and able to do so. For most consultations though, your input will only be in writing. Most consultation documents can be completed online, and it may be easier to do it this way, but you also can choose to submit a bespoke response in writing. Some organisations prefer to take the latter option, often because that allows them to develop a narrative or because it enables them to circulate their responses more easily.

An important principle in consultation responses is to work with the officials dealing with those consultations. If it is a Welsh Government consultation there will be a lead official whose role it is to be the point of contact for organisations, and they will be the person at the end of the email who receives the submission. The same principles apply to the committee clerks who gather evidence during Senedd Committee consultations. They are there to help and advise as well as gathering the information and views of stakeholders. If you are uncertain of something, don't be afraid to ask. Some organisations have even managed to secure extensions to submission deadlines providing they have engaged early enough with the relevant officials in Government or Committees.

That Welsh Government official or committee clerk will also be working to produce a meaningful and informative outcome to the consultation exercise. To do this, they will use a grid system in which they log all the answers. It will follow this sort of pattern:

	Question 1	Question 2	Question 3	Question 4
Organisation 1				
Organisation 2				
Organisation 3				
Organisation 4				

The point of this approach is to allow the meaningful analysis of responses. You should never, ever respond to a consultation without responding in the form of answers to the set questions because that is the way the responses are measured and evaluated. Therefore, no matter how frustrated you feel by the questioning structure, you need to keep to it. If questions are repetitive, your answers can be too. If some questions are irrelevant or you do not have an opinion, you just need to leave those answers blank. Your objective must be to share information in as persuasive a way as possible, and in order to do that you must fit into this grid approach.

You should also never lose sight of the ability of consultation exercises to make a genuine difference. Back in 2008, the then Health Minister Edwina Hart issued a consultation on restructuring the NHS in Wales which received over 800 responses. Her original proposals discussed keeping a split in services between structures for planners and providers within NHS Wales, but such was the weight of opinion that she accepted the view of the overwhelming number of consultees that the distinction should be ended and the new Local Health Boards should be empowered to do both these functions. Indeed, it cannot be stated too strongly that a robust and structured approach to consultation exercises is one of the most important things a public affairs practitioner can do.

Follow-up actions

If something is worth saying, it is worth saying loudly and often. You should therefore also consider sharing your consultation responses in other ways too, such as turning them into online or printed media articles. Just submitting a written response via email to a clerk is not always enough. You need to be shaping the context in which that response is digested.

Sometimes, especially in relation to major policy consultations, the Welsh Government will publish some sort of analysis of the responses received. On highly critical matters this would take the form of written or oral statements, perhaps on a regular basis as options are worked though, as was done in the case of the wholesale health reforms undertaken by Edwina Hart in 2008 noted above.

Once a consultation process has ended, it is important that you do not see that as the end of it, particularly with reference to Senedd Committee consultations. The committees will always produce reports at the end of their inquiries and these will be structured around set recommendations. Also, the Welsh Government will always have to produce a response to these reports, detailing its opinion of each recommendation. Sometimes the report and the response end up on the floor of Plenary, especially if it is a contentious matter. All of this period can be viewed as an opportunity for further engagement and follow-up actions around making your voice and your perspective heard.

An increasingly popular technique is also getting Senedd Committees to do short follow-up enquiries into areas they have previously consulted upon in depth. This has the advantage of allowing for informed scrutiny of Government to check whether anything has changed or been implemented in the light of committee reports. Usually such inquiries are short and sharp, do not involve further consultation, but can be supported by the organisations who previously submitted to the full inquiry providing further evidence or data.

TOP TIP: Don't forget that consultation responses can also be useful in profile raising for your organisation. If you are taking the trouble to submit a response on something that is important to you, why not also circulate copies to other organisations to shape their responses; or draft an article for the press or an online blog site where you can set out your case to a wider audience. All of this will help you stand out and shape a debate more thoroughly.

9

Influencing Senedd Committees

The committees of the Senedd are its engine house and, done well, can be its most impressive and effective assets. There are two types of committee that operate in the Senedd – the Standing Committees which are defined under the standing orders and have to exist to fulfil certain functions – and the Subject Committees which can and do change after every Senedd election.

The Standing Committees of the Senedd are:

- **Petitions Committee**: receives external petitions, the process for which is covered in a separate chapter.
- **Finance Committee**: oversees the budget process of the Senedd, examines the future spending and raising of monies, has oversight of the Welsh Treasury.
- **Public Accounts Committee**: receives reports from the Auditor General for Wales, conducts inquiries based on the findings, and analyses the way money has been spent and administration has been done in the past in order to shape future decisions and practice.
- **Constitutional and Legislative Affairs Committee**: examines primary and secondary legislation passing through the Senedd, playing a key role in the legislative process described in the next chapter.
- **Standards Committee**: acts as the disciplinary committee of the Senedd, based on Standards Commissioner reports, and reviews matters related to the probity of Senedd Members.

There is also a **Business Committee**, which decides the business of the Senedd and is comprised of the Llywydd/Presiding Officer and also the Chief Whips of each party group. It tends to meet on a Tuesday morning. Every recognised party (groups that total three or more Members) is represented on the Business Committee, usually by the respective Chief Whips. The Business Committee seeks consensus but if that is not achieved, every Member is allowed to cast a weighted vote proportional to the size of the members of the group – though in respect of non-government business, the size of the governing party's vote is cut to just the backbenchers, allowing opposition parties to have a say. A relatively recent innovation is that the agenda of the Business Committee is now made public on a Monday, allowing independent Members outside party structures to engage and make representations via the Chair. Also, the committee's minutes are published the following week, another innovation intended to make proceedings more transparent. Public affairs professionals, however, rarely engage with the Business Committee as it is internally focused.

The Subject Committees of the Senedd mirror distinct government portfolios which are grouped together. As of 2016, there are seven of them, though the number can change:

- **Children, Young People and Education Committee**
- **Climate Change, Environment and Rural Affairs Committee**
- **Culture, Welsh Language and Communications Committee**
- **Economy, Infrastructure and Skills Committee**
- **Equality, Local Government and Communities Committee**
- **External Affairs and Additional Legislation Committee**
- **Health, Social Care and Sport Committee**

As a general rule, most public affairs activity tends to be focussed on the Subject Committees of the Senedd.

Committee membership

The Chairs of each Committee of the Senedd are democratically elected in a secret ballot at the start of each Senedd term. The Business Committee agrees the remit and the number of the Subject Committees and then does a calculation based on party size so that each political party in the Senedd is allocated a number of Committee Chairs based on its relative size. The Business Committee also agrees which party will Chair the Committee. After that, any Member of the Senedd from that party group may stand for election to be a Committee Chair. If there is a contest, a secret ballot is held across the Senedd as a whole to determine who is elected Chair. Committee Chairs are paid an additional salary and tend to sit on fewer committees than other Members to reflect their additional workload. They also play a key role in determining committee business and setting the general direction of a committee.

The Business Committee also determines how many members each committee should have. The Subject Committees, the Finance Committee, and the Public Accounts Committee tend to have between six and eight members, while the Constitutional and Legislative Affairs, Standards and Petitions committees will usually have four Chairs each. Committee memberships are split between parties on a proportional basis, with the already elected chairs included in that calculation.

From time to time a committee may also create a sub-committee, formed from a smaller cross section of its membership, to deal with a specific issue. For example, at one point in the Fifth Senedd, there was too much business before the Equality, Local Government and Communities Committee, so it created a sub-committee for the purposes of scrutinising a new piece of legislation on Registered Social Landlords.

No member of the Welsh Government may sit on any of the committees, with the result that backbenchers from the governing party or parties can each sit on one, two or three committees unless the governing party or parties has a huge majority (which, to date, has only happened in the Third Senedd following the agreement of a Labour Plaid Cymru coalition).

Most Committees meet once a week. The exceptions to this rule are, at the time of writing, the Petitions Committee (fortnightly) and the Standards Committee (meets when required). All Committee Chairs also come together, once a term, to sit as a Committee of Scrutiny of the First Minister. This committee tends to move around Wales and will usually be structured in two parts. The first, and more detailed, will take a theme for questioning, and when this is completed, a chance will be offered to Members to raise urgent or contemporary issues.

From time to time, committees can meet in joint sessions to discuss matters which cut across the remit of more than one, but this process is the exception rather than the rule.

Committees do not exist in a vacuum, however. and more than any other formal business of the Senedd, they are geared to try and capture external opinion, especially in their scrutiny functions. Some even do specific outreach work to connect better with stakeholders, with a 'speed dating' approach taken by some in the past at the start of a new Senedd in order to build up relationships between key external stakeholders and the Committee Members. With initiatives such as this, you should be able to work more closely with key relevant committees than any other part of the Senedd structures.

Forward work programme

Led by the Chairs, the Committees then set their general pattern of work which can be reviewed and updated periodically. Some committees do this every term and it is easy to consult the committee pages of the Senedd website to see what priorities the individual committees have. Some of them update these every term (three times a year) and produce clear and concise documentation, which are extremely helpful for external engagement.

Generally, the pattern of work undertaken by committees falls into five categories:

- **Legislative scrutiny**: Stages 1 and 2 of a Bill being taken in committee (as will be described in Chapter 10).
- **Budgetary scrutiny**: (as will be described in Chapter 12).
- **Scrutiny of the Minister**: evidence sessions and open questioning.
- **Scrutiny of public bodies**: which fall under the remit of the committee.
- **Committee inquiries**: using consultation as a means of gathering evidence (previously described in Chapter 8).

The work programme will pay attention to all these five elements in the hierarchy in which they are described here. However, if a committee is remitted a piece of legislation to scrutinise, it must prioritise that work. Similarly, during the autumn term, budget scrutiny will also dominate other meetings. As the Ministers and public bodies are not brought in very regularly, this actually leaves a great deal of time for committee inquiries. In the case of Subject Committees, where they do not have a piece of legislation before them (which can dominate proceedings for up to six months) the focus is very much on inquiries, despite its place in the pecking order given above.

Some committees also set out themes for their work over the five years of a Senedd. The most obvious example has been the External Affairs and Additional Legislation Committee in the Fifth Senedd, which has prioritised its work on Brexit.

Committee inquiries

The previous chapter dealt with committee inquiries from a consultation perspective, offering pointers on engagement, but how do committees decide which topics to pursue? The answer lies in the suggestions made by Committee Members, along with the input of the Chair or clerk. A strong Chair will have a clear series of topics already planned but no Chair will ever be able to dominate an agenda over a whole five-year period, and best practice is to seek ideas for inquiries from other Members. These may often be very topical in nature – such as winter pressures in the NHS or a specific government decision concerning a major project, for example the Circuit of Wales or the M4 relief road. Individual Members can also use committees to push pet areas of interest, or sometimes link them to the work and outputs of cross-party groups (dealt with in more detail in Chapter 17.)

A strong rule of thumb, though, is that suggesting topics for discussion, especially when you are meeting with individual Committee Members as part of your general public affairs work, is often worth doing. The different lobbying organisations linked to health have a strong track record of this. Indeed, if you can persuade two or maybe three Committee Members of the validity and appropriateness of a committee inquiry, then you are usually home and dry. Remember, however, that committees do tend to move quite slowly and it can be some months from when a committee agrees a topic for an inquiry to the point at which it actually starts to take evidence. Factors that will influence the timing are not just the existing workload (be it legislation, financial scrutiny or existing and ongoing inquiries) but also the depth of preparation that the committee has to undertake before commencing.

Central to deciding the precise remit and structure of an inquiry will be the committee clerk, who works just to that committee and shapes all aspects of its delivery. They will play the pivotal role in setting out what the inquiry will aim to achieve, how it will run and who will be involved and consulted. They might even steer the committee to outreach visits, in which case you might have the opportunity to host such a visit. They will also consult with the Members' Research Service (MRS), which is an independent research resource available to Members and clerks. The MRS has an extensive library of research and should always be a repository of your published research and policy papers.

Cultivating good links with the committees is therefore crucial. Take time to get to know not just the elected Members but also the clerk and the relevant member of MRS staff. If you are launching a policy paper, prioritise inviting all of these to attend. A good relationship with this group of people is absolutely vital in terms of improving your public affairs outcomes.

The length of a committee inquiry will also vary dependent on the depth of its subject matter. When an inquiry concludes, the committee will meet in private session to consider a draft report prepared by the clerk. Once this has been agreed – and this usually happens without an inquiry being reopened for more evidence or to call back a witness – the committee will formally publish its report. Sometimes this is done in an outside venue in the hope of attracting media attention. It has even been done outside Wales: the Economy and Transport Committee during the Fourth Senedd purposefully launched a committee report on the Wales and Borders rail franchise in Hereford. The key point for you is that if you have been heavily involved in creating and shaping a committee inquiry, then you could suggest or offer a venue for a committee report launch.

Once a report has been published, that is not the end of the process as the report then goes to the Welsh Government to express a view. All inquiry reports contain a series of recommendations and each one will command a response from the Welsh Government. The Welsh Government then produces a response report in which it will detail its opinion on each recommendation, and do one of three things with each of them: Accept, Accept in Principle, or Reject.

The most significant or contentious committee reports, along with the responses of the Welsh Government, will then go to a full debate on the floor of Plenary. Should this occur, then it offers an additional opportunity to engage with the debate and offer briefings to Members in the same way you would with an ordinary debate in the Senedd (covered in detail in Chapter 14).

> **TOP TIP: Build up a relationship with the clerks of the committees of the Senedd that you are seeking to engage with. They are the gatekeepers to committees in all of its work.**

10

Engaging with the Legislative Process

A core function of any legislature is, of course, to pass legislation. This function was significantly enhanced following the 2011 further powers referendum, since when the Senedd has passed Acts in devolved areas, and the ability of organisations to raise awareness and influence legislation and change laws for the better, for a particular group or for society as a whole lies at the very apex of public affairs activity. It is the *raison d'être* of the public affairs professional.

This perspective was certainly shared by Kidney Wales at the time of the change in organ donation law, by environmental charities when the plastic bag levy was introduced. Yet while the number of organisations who can claim such victories is surprisingly small, it is the potential for, rather than the actuality of, community and voluntary organisations to initiate and shape legislation which is so impressive.

In Wales, the local government sector has, by far and away, been the best at organising public affairs activities which have impacted meaningfully on the legislative process, and the Welsh Local Government Association (WLGA) that has the most impressive record in promoting ideas that have led to legislation, shaped legislation, or dissuaded the government from legislating.

The picture is not quite the same for the community and voluntary (third) sector which, in comparison to local government, has smaller pockets and fewer public affairs specialists to promote its views. However, the outlook certainly isn't bleak. Indeed, it is a struggle to think of any pieces of legislation which have affected the third sector where their voice has not been heard and their lobbies have not been vocal. The issue might be one of the range, rather than the number, of organisations that are engaging and, hopefully, one of the desired outcomes of this book might be that a wider range of smaller organisations are able to engage with the legislative process once they have a clearer understanding of how it works and, therefore, what potential there is for them to really engage.

As part of that desire to widen the number of participants within the public affairs arena from the third sector, let's start with some of the basics when it comes to legislation. Perhaps the first helpful explanation in respect of legislation is to distinguish between Bills and Acts. A Bill is a proposal for a new law or a proposal to change an existing law. It only becomes an Act once it has passed through all the stages of consultation and scrutiny, and received the monarch's signature, known as Royal Assent. These same general rules apply whether a Bill is being introduced as legislation in Westminster, Holyrood or the Senedd.

Sometimes you might also hear about something called a Draft Bill, or the Welsh Government might indicate a consultation is being introduced in order to support future legislation at a later point. If this is the approach being undertaken, then try and follow the general advice set out in Chapter 8 around responding to consultations. Draft Bills are not infrequent, but neither are they as embedded as once promised. For example, addressing Plenary in July 2011, the then First Minister Carwyn Jones pledged:

'We will work with others in the development of policy and legislation and, where appropriate, will seek to publish draft Assembly Bills for consultation.'[1]

Experience since then has shown that although around half of Bills are consulted on in some form, certainly a formal pre-legislative consultation approach to every Bill has not been followed with any rigour or consistency.

The focus of this chapter will be engaging with Bills in the Senedd. To make sense of this, you firstly need to be familiar with the general principles of the legislative cycle. Then we can look at examples of the scale and pace of legislation. After that, the focus will switch to

1   Record of the Proceedings of the Senedd, 11 July 2011.

understanding the stages a Bill passes through before it becomes an Act and therefore law.

The legislative cycle

Most legislation is introduced to the Senedd by the Welsh Government. The best clue as to what legislation to expect comes from a reading of the programme of the Welsh Government (outlined in Chapter 2) or in an annual legislative statement which is delivered by the First Minister in either July or September. This statement has two parts. Firstly, it will look back at the legislative Bills introduced in the previous year, including the ones which have not yet completed their passage, and secondly will announce which pieces of legislation the Welsh Government will bring forward in the following year. There are usually four or five of these, but there is no hard and fast rule. The First Minister may also indicate whether consultations or Draft Bills might be being introduced.

Similarly, the First Minister might be deliberately evasive in their descriptions in a number of ways. For example, the way in which they describe the Bill might not drill down into the totality of the legislation but just be a clue as to content. An example would be the Health Bill promised in September 2018 which would be framed around patients' rights and a duty of candour. Those were the only clues presented as to the Bill's content. The First Minister is usually also quite evasive around the timings of when Bills might be introduced. In the absence of a chronological list, phrases like, 'in due course', 'in the autumn term' and 'next year' (i.e. beyond Christmas) are often used as markers of a very rough timeline for introduction.

In the final year of a Senedd, however, it is unusual for more than one or two closing Bills to be introduced. These are usually ones that are limited in scope, and they are then sped through the process in order to be completed before the session finishes ahead of a Senedd election.

Although public pronouncements on the timing and structure of legislation may be deliberately ambiguous, there is much more information available within government itself. There will be an overall legislative timetable for a full five years which increases in detail as the term progresses, so the public ambiguity is designed to give the government more flexibility in the preparation of Bills. In the Fourth

Senedd, the First Minister had offered a total five year outline with annual updates on the legislative cycle, but this level of candour now seems to be a thing of the past. In respect of clarity of the legislative cycle, there has been a marked decline in public information between the Fourth and Fifth Senedd terms, the only two which could exercise full legislative powers. In 2011 the Senedd Members' Research Service provided a publicly available document listing 20 bills scheduled over five years, with significant detailed content against each one, including, where available, some sort of timings. By 2019 this would be virtually impossible to do if you were not within government itself.[2]

It is also not unheard of that a piece of legislation promised by the Welsh Government is withdrawn before being introduced to the Senedd. In the Fourth Senedd, a promised Bill on Statutory Third Sector Compacts was never introduced; while in the Fifth Senedd the plans for a Welsh Language Bill were dropped. There is also a small amount of legislation, the Control of Horses Bill for example, which is introduced as an emergency measure.

Scope of legislation

The best way to get an idea of the scope and pace of actual legislation is, without being too obvious, to actually look at the scope and pace of actual legislation. The following table sets out the remit, scope and pace of all of the legislation which completed its passage through the Senedd during the first eight years of devolution with law making powers (May 2011 to May 2019).

Title	Date introduced	Date completed	Length of passage	Approximate Size
Renting Homes (Fees etc.) (Wales) Act 2019	June 2018	April 2019	10 months	17 pages
Childcare Funding (Wales) Act 2019	April 2018	January 2019	10 months	7 pages

---

2   Welsh Government's Legislative Programme 2011-16, Members Research Service, July 2016.

Title	Date introduced	Date completed	Length of passage	Approximate Size
Public Health (Minimum Price for Alcohol) (Wales) Act 2018	October 2017	August 2018	11 months	19 pages
Regulation of Registered Social Landlords (Wales) Act 2018	October 2017	June 2018	9 months	18 pages
Law derived from the European Union (Wales) Act 2018	March 2018	June 2018	4 months	26 pages
Abolition of the Right to Buy and Associated Rights (Wales) Act 2018	March 2017	January 2018	11 months	15 pages
Additional Learning Needs and Educational Tribunal (Wales) Act 2018	December 2016	January 2018	13 months	93 pages
Trade Union (Wales) Act 2017	January 2017	September 2017	9 months	4 pages
Landfill Disposals Tax (Wales) Act 2017	November 2016	September 2017	11 months	66 pages
Public Health (Wales) Act 2017	November 2016	July 2017	9 months	97 pages
Land Transaction Tax and Anti-avoidance of Devolved Taxes (Wales) Act 2017	September 2016	May 2017	9 months	249 pages
Tax Collection and Management (Wales) Act 2016	July 2015	April 2016	10 months	99 pages
Historic Environment (Wales) Act 2016	May 2015	March 2016	11 months	66 pages
Environment (Wales) Act 2016	May 2015	March 2016	11 months	77 pages

Title	Date introduced	Date completed	Length of passage	Approximate Size
Regulation and Inspection of Social Care (Wales) Act 2016	February 2015	January 2016	12 months	149 pages
Renting Homes (Wales) Act 2016	February 2015	January 2016	12 months	200 pages
Local Government (Wales) Act 2015	January 2015	November 2015	11 months	29 pages
Qualifications (Wales) Act 2015	December 2014	August 2015	9 months	59 pages
The Planning (Wales) Act 2015	October 2014	July 2015	10 months	100 pages
Violence against Women, Domestic Abuse and Sexual Violence (Wales) Act 2015	June 2014	April 2015	11 months	18 pages
Well-being of Future Generations (Wales) Act 2015	July 2014	April 2015	10 months	56 pages
Higher Education (Wales) Act 2015	May 2014	March 2015	11 months	39 pages
Housing (Wales) Act 2014	November 2013	September 2014	11 months	109 pages
Agricultural Sector (Wales) Act 2014	July 2013	July 2014	13 months	12 pages
Education (Wales) Act 2014	July 2013	May 2014	11 months	44 pages
Social Services and Well-being (Wales) Act 2014	January 2013	May 2014	16 months	189 pages
Control of Horses (Wales) Act 2014	October 2013	January 2014	4 months	6 pages
National Health Service Finance (Wales) Act 2014	September 2013	January 2014	5 months	4 pages
Further and Higher Education (Governance and Information) (Wales) Act 2014	April 2013	January 2014	9 months	13 pages

Title	Date introduced	Date completed	Length of passage	Approximate Size
Active Travel (Wales) Act 2013	February 2013	November 2013	10 months	11 pages
Human Transplantation (Wales) Act 2013	December 2012	September 2013	10 months	18 pages
Local Government (Democracy) (Wales) Act 2013	November 2012	July 2013	9 months	55 pages
Public Audit (Wales) Act 2013	July 2012	April 2013	10 months	59 pages
Food Hygiene Rating (Wales) Act 2013	May 2012	March 2013	10 months	16 pages
School Standards and Organisation (Wales) Act 2013	April 2012	March 2013	12 months	110 pages
Local Government Byelaws (Wales) Act 2012	November 2011	November 2012	13 months	26 pages

In terms of pace, you can see that the usual time it normally takes for the passage of a Bill, from introduction to Royal Assent, is about ten months. Virtually every piece of legislation fits into that pattern.

A few of these pieces of legislation are also atypical for the same particular reason, insofar as they're all examples of emergency legislation which were fast tracked through the Senedd:

- **The Control of Horses (Wales) Act 2014** was passed so quickly it never featured in a long term legislative programme, as mentioned above.
- **The Law derived from the European Union (Wales) Act 2018** was emergency legislation and was speedily passed though never enacted.
- **The Agricultural Wages Act** went through the Senedd in just a month but was then delayed by a legal challenge from the UK Government before its devolved status was eventually confirmed by the Supreme Court, a year later.

In terms of scope of legislation, you will note from the table above that the vast bulk of legislation is well under 100 pages, with most

Acts not reaching 50 pages. There is also a variable correlation between size of legislation and time of its passage. This is because some straightforward legislation is often the most politically charged. The Trade Union (Wales) Act 2017 took nine months of consideration before it was passed despite being only four pages long; while the Senedd simultaneously considered the Public Health Act 2017 and took just as long to do so, despite it being a much more complex Bill and without being politically contentious. Indeed, this latter Bill had previously been considered in the Fourth Senedd and fallen at the final stage, so virtually every element was uncontroversial when it passed through the Senedd for a second time.[3]

The table below shows the number of Bills introduced every year. Taking the same data, we can also display the Bills by the year of origin:

Year	Number of Bills introduced	Bills per Senedd
May 2018 – April 2019	3	13 in 3 years
May 2017 – April 2018	4	
May 2016 – April 2017	6	
May 2015 – April 2016	3	25 in 5 years
May 2014 – April 2015	8	
May 2013 – April 2014	6	
May 2012 – April 2013	6	
May 2011 – April 2012	2	

The table is illustrative of two things. Firstly, it hones down to the number of Bills being introduced every year and gives you an understanding of how much legislation a government is procedurally able to process. The second aspect is that it shows that in the Fifth Senedd there has been substantially less recourse to legislation than there was in the Fourth Senedd, which perhaps pinpoints something absolutely critical to bear in mind when thinking about legislation: the Welsh Government only permits or introduces Bills when it has to. In Wales, legislation is the last recourse of government when something

---

3   The Senedd rejected the Public Health Wales Bill 2016 at closing stages following a breakdown in agreement of its content during the final sitting day of the Senedd before the Bill was passed in March 2016. A near identical Bill was introduced later that year, minus a section on vaping restrictions which had been the most contentious part of the legislation but had not been the cause of the disagreement.

needs to be done, rather than the first reaction. The next chapter will make this point again when it deals with backbencher legislation.

Amending legislation

You will have noted that Bills can vary in length, but in general, the scrutiny of Bills follows a set process. These are defined in the Senedd's Standing Orders and pretty much hard wired into the work of any public affairs professional. It follows a set pattern based on:

- **Stage One**: laying the legislation and its consideration in Plenary and Committee from an 'in principle' basis.
- **Stage Two**: Scrutiny in committee on a line by line basis with amendments.
- **Stage Three**: Scrutiny in Plenary with amendments, usually done in a single afternoon.
- **Stage Four**: Approval of the final text of the Bill

Incidentally, it should also be noted at this point but these stages are not equal in length. Each one gets shorter and shorter until usually there is no more than a week or a fortnight between Stages Three and Four.

Essentially the Senedd's legislative process is a structured process which actually mirrors that in Scotland and is based on the twin principles that there should be open consultation before legislation is introduced; and that Members of the Senedd are given multiple opportunities to amend the legislation once it has been laid for consideration.

Although the opposition may not be that successful in formally amending Bills, parliamentary actors can and do exert influence in the legislative process, which then results in the government amending their own legislation. Indeed, it is important to note that changes to a Bill don't just come from the opposition parties. Furthermore, it is often more difficult for an opposition Member to win through and amend a Bill than a government backbencher.

The Welsh Government, like all governments, tends to believe they have a monopoly on being right and will usually defend the intention of a Bill against any criticism, however constructive and well meant. Evidence shows, however, that it often drafts its own amendments. Of the sum total of 3,289 amendments which were agreed to for the 34 government Bills analysed for this book, 3,075 (93.5 per cent) were moved by the Welsh Government itself. This equates to an average of 83 government amendments per government Bill introduced.[4] To a large extent, therefore, opposition attempts to amend Bills are much more likely to fail than the Welsh Government's own amendments, regardless of when or how they are proposed.

Stage One scrutiny

The process and complexity of Stage One scrutiny is both logical and complex. A Bill can only be introduced when the Senedd is sitting. It is laid, usually on a Monday, and then formally introduced to the Senedd by means of a statement the following day. This will always be delivered by the lead Minister who has been charged with overseeing the passage of a Bill. Barring reshuffles, the same Minister will take the legislation through all its stages, though the long and complex legislation that became the Well Being of Future Generations Act 2015 uniquely passed through a wide range of sponsoring Ministers.[5]

In 2019, the Welsh Government published a new Bill to outlaw the physical chastisement of children. Unpicking the introduction of this Bill gives a good case study on how it is introduced and what is required. The Children (Abolition of Defence of Reasonable Punishment) (Wales) Bill was thus unveiled on Monday 25 March and then introduced formally the following day, Tuesday 26 March 2019, to the Senedd. The purpose of the Bill is to abolish the common law defence of reasonable punishment so it is no longer available in Wales to parents or those acting in *loco parentis* as a defence to assault or battery against a child.

The sponsoring Minister, Julie Morgan AM, as Deputy Minister for Health and Social Services, had been a long term campaigner on this

---

4   Research undertaken by Dafydd Huw Wrennal, employee at Positif Politics.
5   The Well-being of Future Generations (Wales) Act 2015 was introduced to the Senedd in July 2014 by Jeff Cuthbert AM, Minister for Communities and Tackling Poverty. Prior to that the Bill had been handled at various times by both John Griffiths AM and Alun Davies AM, and both had helped shape its early basis. It was eventually passed in April 2015 under the stewardship of Carl Sargeant AM, who had inherited the legislation in a Cabinet reshuffle in September 2014.

issue. She used the opportunity of her speech on introducing the Bill to do a number of things. As well as placing the Bill in a historical context, she referenced international best practice and also spelt out in strict legal terms what the Bill would do and would not do. She also pointed to the pre-legislative consultation undertaken on the Bill before it was introduced and explained there would also be a public awareness campaign if the Bill is passed but before it is enacted (becomes enforceable law), promising that the enactment date would not happen until that had occurred.[6] The value of detailing the content of the statement is to demonstrate the approach that the Government takes when it introduces a Bill: it is a mixture of political and legal explanation, influenced by evidence gathered both nationally and internationally.

Every time a Bill is introduced, the Welsh Government also publishes an Explanatory Memorandum. This sets out the rationale of the Bill and answers basic questions from a layperson's perspective. For a public affairs professional, the Explanatory Memorandum is perhaps the most accessible and useable of the documents that are produced when a Bill is laid. Indeed, it is hugely more understandable than the legalese of a Bill, and should be a very good starting point for any form of engagement.

Explanatory Memorandums tend to follow the same format and, taking Julie Morgan's Bill as an example, there are a range of content elements which make a Bill more understandable:

- **General Description**
- **Legislative Competence**: explains the legal basis on which the legislation is being brought.
- **Policy Objectives and purpose and intended effect of the Bill**: essentially the same material used by the Minister in the introductory remarks.
- **Consultation**: details how the proposal has been consulted upon.
- **Power to make subordinate legislation**: a description of the way in which laws might be made under the proposed law (this is explored in more detail later).
- **Regulatory Impact Assessment**: examines the way the proposed legal change will work in respect of policy and delivery, and its cost potential.

---

6   National Assembly for Wales Record of Proceedings, 26 March 2019.

- **Options**: setting out succinctly the case for the legislation as opposed to not legislating.
- **Costs and benefits**: a detailed analysis, forming the meat of the document.
- **Impact Assessments**: every Bill is accompanied by policy impact assessments in respect of the defined policy pillars of: Children's Rights; Equalities; Rural Proofing; Privacy; Welsh language; Biodiversity; Climate change; natural resources; health impact; and justice.
- **Post-implementation review**: sets out the intended approach for monitoring and reviewing the effect of the legislation.

As will be abundantly clear from this breakdown, for a public affairs professional it is the Explanatory Memorandum which is the key accessible document in terms of fully understanding the legislation and, quite naturally, Explanatory Memoranda are usually much longer than Bills.

It is now worth looking at the process by which the Senedd responds formally to any legislation laid by the Welsh Government. It starts with the Llywydd/Presiding Officer making a written determination that the Bill is within the competence of the Senedd to discuss: just a technical tick box exercise. The more significant discussion happens in the Business Committee of the Senedd before the legislation is introduced, and it decides which of the Senedd's committees should deal with Stage One and Stage Two scrutiny of the Bill.

The other important thing that the Business Committee does is to set a timetable framework for the legislation at Stages One and Two. With the legislation having been introduced on 25 March 2019, the Committee set a deadline of 18 July 2019 (four months later) for Stage One to end; and 8 November 2019 for the end of Stage Two (approximately two months if the summer recess period is naturally discounted since the Senedd will not be in session). In the case of this example, the Business Committee revised the timetable slightly in light of feedback, showing it is also able and willing to reconsider timetabling issues.

Stage One of the Bill was, therefore, to be conducted in committee over a maximum four month period and the clock will start ticking when the Children, Young People and Education Committee begins a process of consultation and issues a call for evidence. Chapter 8 details how this happens and offers advice on making the most of consultation opportunities in relation to Committees. In essence, however, in conducting scrutiny and consultation, a committee will be mindful of three things:

- The aims/policy objectives of the Bill;
- Whether a legislative approach is necessary to achieve those aims/ objectives; and
- Whether the Bill, as drafted, is capable of achieving its stated aims/objectives.

This will be the focus of Stage One and will lead to the publication of a report which states whether the Committee agrees or disagrees with the legislation. It will also summarise the evidence received and detail any concerns raised in the process of evidence gathering.

Two other committees also play a role at Stage One. The Finance Committee will examine the cost of the legislation, usually in one sitting, and will present a report, while the Constitutional and Legislative Affairs Committee will also examine the legislation to test its effectiveness and aspects like the balance between the detail on the face of the Bill and what secondary legislation might be required.

Before the end of Stage One, the reports of the three relevant committees would be referred back to Plenary of the Senedd for a full-scale debate. In this debate the sponsoring Minister will respond to the matters raised in the reports and may seek to accommodate them, pledging to amend any legislation in line with points of agreement. During the debate, most of the other contributions will come from the members of the main scrutiny committees, along with, usually, also the Chairs of the Finance Committee and the Constitutional and Legislative Affairs Committee.

At the end of the debate on Stage One, a vote is taken on whether, in light of the report, the general principles of the Bill are accepted. No motion on the general principles of a piece of Welsh Government legislation has ever been rejected at Stage One, and no Stage One report has ever recommended that a piece of government legislation should not proceed. (This is not the case in respect of backbencher legislation, as detailed thoroughly in Chapter 11 later).

Stage Two scrutiny

At the start of Stage Two, the Llywydd/Presiding Officer becomes involved again and determines whether a financial resolution is required for a Bill. The motion simply asks the Senedd to agree in principle to the possible financial consequences of the Bill. Throughout Stage Two, if a financial resolution has been deemed as required, because of the size of the financial impact of a Bill, it becomes a central part of the discussion. Indeed, until a financial resolution has been produced by the Government and approved by the Senedd, Stage Two scrutiny cannot proceed. If a financial resolution is required, but is not agreed within six months of the completion of Stage One, the Bill falls.

As indicated, the Business Committee will have set out a timescale for Stage Two scrutiny at the time that a Bill is introduced. The same committee which undertook Stage One will also be trusted to undertake Stage Two scrutiny. The focus of Stage Two is on the wording of the Bill and it is discussed on a line by line basis within the timeframe set out for the Bill. Some Bills clear in just one or two hearings, others take far longer, usually directly related to the length and complexity of the Bill in question.

In examining the Bill, any Member may table amendments at Stage Two, and there is no limit on the number of amendments that may be tabled. The clerks servicing the relevant committee are able to provide or arrange confidential procedural, legal and tabling advice to Members in relation to amendments. All amendments are public and all get a number according to the order in which the amendments were tabled. Generally, amendments tabled at Stage Two are disposed of in the order in which the sections and schedules to which they relate arise in the Bill, unless the committee decides otherwise.

Voting on amendments in committee is done 'on the nod', unless any Member objects. The Chair will put the question that an amendment be agreed and, unless there are any objections, that amendment is deemed agreed and the Bill is amended. Where any Member objects, the committee is asked to vote on the amendment in question. Voting is by show of hands, and a simple majority in favour of an amendment is required for that amendment to be agreed. If there is a tie, the Chair gets an additional casting vote which must always be used to vote against amendments at Stage Two.

Following the completion of Stage Two proceedings, an 'as amended at Stage Two' version of the Bill is prepared and published. The Explanatory Memorandum has to be updated too, by the Minister, if a substantive amendment has been passed.

Any amendments which are made in committee at Stage Two go forward to Stage Three in Plenary as part of a revised Bill. A government with a majority in Plenary (but not on Committee) can use the transition period to reverse any changes made in Stage Two at Stage Three.

Not everything is as black and white as winning or losing amendments at Stage Two. Even if a Bill is not successfully amended at Stage Two, a Minister can sometimes give an undertaking to accept the views of the Committee and amend it when it gets to Stage Three. Instances of such successful opposition-initiated 'strands' in the Senedd are not unprecedented. For example, when the Additional Learning Needs and Education Tribunal (Wales) Bill reached Stage Two, opposition Members sought to insert amendments in relation local authority workforce capacity and Welsh-language workforce planning.[7] Having sought legal advice, the Minister invited the Members to withdraw their amendments and gave an undertaking to work with them on an agreed amendment for Stage Three. On that basis, both amendments were withdrawn, to be dealt with at Stage Three.

Stage Three scrutiny

Stage Three starts on the first working day after Stage Two is completed, but 15 working days must be allowed to elapse between the start of Stage Three and its formal debate, to allow Members to consider and table amendments. Such amendments must be tabled no fewer than five working days before the Plenary session at which they are to be considered. Amendments must usually be tabled no fewer than five working days before the meeting at which they are to be considered. Unlike Stage Two proceedings, where any admissible amendment is able to be moved and debated, the Llywydd/Presiding Officer may

---

7   Davies, A. 2017. The Record of Proceedings, 12 October, Additional Learning
     Needs and Education Tribunal (Wales) Bill: Stage Two Proceedings.

select those amendments which are to be taken during Stage Three proceedings. In practice, however, all amendments are usually debated.

For each Stage Three meeting, a Marshalled List and a Groupings List are prepared and published.

These lists set out the order in which amendments will be debated and disposed of during proceedings. Generally, the lists will follow the pattern of the Bill, with the amendment numbers relating to the allocation made to the individual amendments.

Again, voting on Stage Three amendments in Plenary is 'on the nod', unless any Member objects. The Llywydd/Presiding Officer will put the question that an amendment be agreed to and, unless there are any objections, that amendment is deemed agreed. Voting is then done by the normal Senedd electronic vote, and a simple majority in favour of an amendment is required for that amendment to be agreed. At this point, if the vote is tied, the Llywydd/Presiding Officer must vote against any amendment.

At Stage Three, there tends to be two types of amendment made to a Bill. The first, and the most numerous, are the Welsh Government's own technical or linguistic amendments, which are intended to clean up a Bill before it becomes an Act. The more of these you see, the poorer the original drafting of the Bill tends to have been. Because every word is law, it is important each word is precise and correct. Chris Warner, former Head of the Policy and Legislation Committee Service at the Senedd, recalled the 60 single-line amendments to the Social Services and Well-being Wales Bill at Stage Three, and expressed concern about the implications thereof for the scrutiny of more substantive alterations.[8]

The second type of amendment would be where the Government has genuinely been persuaded of the case for something, usually by its own backbenchers or based on dialogue and persuasion from an opposition politician. In such a scenario the Government will sometimes table its own amendment to effect the change rather than relying on the wording supplied by others. A good example would be the changes to the Additional Learning Needs and Education Tribunal (Wales) Bill referred to above in connection with Stage Two scrutiny. At Stage Three, the Cabinet Secretary brought forward

---

8   Warner, C. 2014. Oral evidence from the Head of Policy and Legislation Committee Service to the Constitutional and Legislative Affairs Committee's Inquiry on Making Laws in Wales, 24 November.

amendments which 'respond[ed] directly to a commitment made by the former portfolio holder at Stage Two',[9] and these were agreed without objection.

Stage Four and beyond

Stage Four scrutiny is a simple formality. It is a process by which the final text of the Bill, as amended at previous stages, is presented to the Senedd for ratification. It cannot be amended, it must either be accepted or rejected. A simple majority in favour of the motion is required for the Bill to be passed. If the vote is tied, the Llywydd/ Presiding Officer must vote against.

Stage Four is usually a simple opportunity for the sponsoring Minister to speak about the journey of the legislation, to reflect on changes made and input received, to restate the policy aims of the legislation and tends to take no more than 15 minutes. The Bill is then voted upon and, if passed, its journey through the Senedd is over.

The Clerk of the Senedd then writes to the Secretary of State for Wales, the Counsel General and the Attorney General to inform them that a Bill has been passed by the Senedd, and of the date on which the period for approval expires. At this stage the Secretary of State for Wales can refuse to refer the Bill to the monarch for signature, or the UK Attorney General could refer the Bill to the Supreme Court if it is deemed outside the competence of the Senedd to have passed it. The Supreme Court then has the power to refer the Bill back to the Senedd. There is a complex legal process around this which need not concern a public affairs professional. If a Bill has reached such an impasse then it will be the work of lawyers, not lobbyists, to investigate a way forward.

If no objections are received, the Bill is then referred to the monarch for Royal Assent. Once this has been done, the Bill becomes an Act and is law in Wales.

---

9   Williams, K. 2017. The Record of Proceedings, 21 November, Debate: Stage Three of the Additional Learning Needs and Education Tribunal (Wales) Bill.

Subordinate legislation

Most legislation is not primary legislation, like an Act, but rather subordinate legislation termed as Orders or Regulations. Other forms of subordinate legislation can include codes of practice, rules, schemes or guidance. These are made in a variety of ways as stipulated in the Act that allows Ministers to make them, and subordinate legislation therefore can only be made if primary legislation confers a power to do so. The primary, enabling, act is key therefore because it allows the subordinate legislation to be subsequently made. In Wales, the Welsh Government's Ministers make subordinate legislation using powers given to them in enabling acts which are not just Acts of the Senedd, but can also be Assembly Measures (the system used in 2007-11) or Acts of the UK Parliament. The latter category of Acts may include Acts made before the devolution of powers to the Senedd in 1999, or any UK Acts after that date which specifically confer powers to Welsh Ministers (usually these would require the consent of the Senedd through a Legislative Consent Motion, the process and purpose of which is described in Chapter 14).

Subordinate legislation is also often referred to as delegated legislation or as secondary legislation or as statutory instruments. The key body of the Senedd in relation to this type of legislation is the Constitutional and Legislative Affairs Committee, which has the power to judge the legality of such legislation, to examine whether it fulfils the objectives of the over-riding Act, or is of a politically contentious nature. Most subordinate legislation sails through against these criteria, but if the committee is not content it will issue a report. This is not a veto, but can trigger wider debate and scrutiny.

All subordinate legislation must be laid before the Senedd, and therefore the Constitutional and Legislative Affairs Committee, at least 21 days before it comes into effect. If this rule is breached, the Welsh Government has to explain the reasoning in the form of a letter.

It is worth noting that the subordinate legislation made under some Acts comes under a lot more scrutiny than others. All subordinate legislation made under the EU (Withdrawal) Act 2018, for example, was subject to rigorous sifting.

Subordinate legislation procedures

The subordinate legislation section of the Senedd website helpfully sets out in some detail the variety of procedures for dealing with different examples of such legislation.[10] An abridged version of the main processes is duplicated below:

- **Subordinate legislation subject to the negative procedure**: The negative procedure provides that, after the Welsh Ministers have exercised their power to make subordinate legislation, they must lay the subordinate legislation. The Senedd then has a period of 40 days to object to the subordinate legislation. If the Senedd objects by means of a vote, then the subordinate legislation is annulled. Most subordinate legislation made by the Welsh Ministers follows this procedure.
- **Subordinate legislation made by the Welsh Ministers and UK Ministers acting together**: Sometimes, the enabling Act will say that subordinate legislation must be made jointly by both the Welsh Ministers and UK Ministers acting together. This kind of subordinate legislation must be laid before both the Senedd and the UK Parliament.
- **Subordinate legislation subject to the affirmative procedure**: The affirmative procedure provides that the Welsh Ministers cannot exercise their power to make subordinate legislation unless the Senedd has passed a resolution approving a draft of the subordinate legislation. This procedure is often reserved for more significant subordinate legislation.
- **Commencement Orders**: Some subordinate legislation does not have to be laid before the Senedd. Commencement orders (i.e. subordinate legislation that specifies a date when primary legislation comes into force) are an example. Ministers simply notify the Committee of commencement orders.

---

10 The Senedd website has an extensive section of subordinate legislative procedures found in the Legislation sub-section.

TOP TIP: The earlier the better is the general rule when seeking to influence legislation. The further down the track toward the final destination a piece of legislation has progressed, speed and momentum pick up, and it is pretty impossible to flag down and get on a moving train.

11

Non-Government Legislation

Not all legislation comes from Welsh Government. Although the vast bulk of legislation originates from this source, there are also three other vehicles which can be utilised to bring forward legislation: the Senedd Commission; committees of the Senedd; and non-government Members also have access to a limited process to bring legislative ideas forward.

Procedure for non-Government legislation

Once a Bill originates from any of these three sources, the Senedd – in the first instance – gets a chance to debate the principles of that Bill. Following the debate a vote is then taken on whether a Bill can proceed further. Sometimes Bills fall at this stage, especially if the Welsh Government is opposed to the Bill and a whip is issued to their Members to vote against it at this stage. If the Senedd votes to let a Bill proceed, responsibility for leading it is given to the Member who proposed it, or a Member designated as the lead by the Commission, or the relevant Subject Committees. Whoever is appointed the lead Member then has 13 months to develop and lay the legislation before the Senedd.

This item of legislation, like Government Bills, must then be formally laid in the Senedd and accompanied by an Explanatory Memorandum. This Memorandum must contain the following elements:

- An explanation of the purpose of the Bill.
- A view on why it is within the legislative competence of the Senedd.

- A statement on whether alternative ways of achieving the policy objectives were considered and, if so, why the approach taken in the Bill was adopted.
- A summary of the consultation undertaken.
- An assessment of financial impact, be it additional costs or cost savings.
- Present environmental and social benefits, and disadvantages, arising from the Bill.
- A judicial impact assessment.

A vote is then taken on whether the Bill can proceed. If that happens, the Bill moves into the formal stages of consideration. The stages for each of these three types of Bills mirror the legislative stages 1 to 4 in the process relating to Government legislation.

All legislation of this nature lapses if it has not completed all its stages by the end of the Senedd term in which it was introduced.

Legislation brought forward by the Senedd Commission

At the time of writing, despite the Senedd having had primary law-making powers since 2011, the Senedd Commission has only passed one piece of legislation brought forward in this manner. This was the first ever Act passed by the Senedd and was intended to regulate the provision of bilingual services on a statutory footing. Despite being very precise in focus, and having cross-party agreement, it still took ten months to be passed, from introduction to assent.

A second example was the Bill to rename the institution following its enhanced constitutional status, and to change the qualifications for its electoral system. The Commission agreed to consult with the people of Wales on the issue following a unanimous Senedd vote in July 2016 and, once the consultation was completed in the autumn of 2018, the Llywydd/Presiding Officer, Elin Jones, reported back on the outline of the Bill and made recommendations in relation the legislation being taken forward. It was eventually introduced in 2019 and it was a constitutional Bill it required 40 Members (66 per cent) rather than the normal 30 (50 per cent) to be passed by the Senedd.

As far as public affairs professionals are concerned, a golden rule is to focus on engaging in the consultation exercises around Bills from the Commission rather than seeking to promote the idea of a Bill with the Commission. The same rule also applies to the next form of legislation, those matters brought forward by Senedd Committees.

Legislation brought forward by committees

Legislation by committee is also pretty rare. The only current example is the Public Services Ombudsman (Wales) Act. A previous version of this legislation was considered by the Fourth Senedd, but reintroduced in the Fifth Senedd. Its progress, however, was remarkably slow considering there had been cross-party consensus around much of its content and, despite being previously being consulted upon by the Fourth Senedd, the Stage One process was enforced again. Bearing in mind the length of time it took to proceed with the Act, it does not seem a particularly popular route for external organisations to take to pursue legislation through a Committee.

One additional process point: the committee which introduces the Bill, cannot be the one to give it scrutiny at Stages One or Two.

Legislation brought forward by backbenchers

The Llywydd/Presiding Officer must, from time to time, hold a ballot to determine the name of a Member, other than a Member of the Government, who may seek agreement to introduce a Member's Bill. Not all eligible Members enter the ballot, but they are all entitled to do so and to bring forward a single legislative idea – with the exception that no Bills concerning taxation may be proposed – which is then subject to the four formal, different stages of scrutiny.

Members enter the process by submitting a title and a very brief outline of the intention of the legislation and after a Ballot is held, just one option is chosen from amongst the eligible options.

The 'from time to time' element of the process for backbencher legislation gives a great deal of leeway to the Llywydd/Presiding Officer in calling such ballots. The following table sets out the detail of all such ballots held in the eight year period between May 2011 and May 2019.

Date of Ballot	Winning Member and Topic	Outcome
14 November 2018	Darren Millar – Older People's Rights Bill	Defeated on floor of Senedd at first introduction stage
28 March 2017	Paul Davies – Autism Bill	Defeated on floor of Senedd at Stage One report stage
25 January 2017	Dai Lloyd - Protection of Welsh Historical Place-Names Bill	Defeated on floor of Senedd at first introduction stage
11 December 2013	Kirsty Williams - Minimum Nurse Staffing Levels Bill	Reached the statute book as an Act of the Senedd
17 July 2013	Bethan Jenkins - Financial Literacy Bill	The Bill was withdrawn at the end of Stage One following assurances from the Welsh Government
24 April 2013	Darren Millar - Holiday Caravan Park (Wales) Bill	The Bill passed Stage One but the Bill fell at the end of the Fourth Senedd due to lack of time
21 November 2012	Mark Isherwood - Community Care (Direct Payments) (Wales) Bill	Withdrawn at introduction stage
11 July 2012	Darren Millar - Chewing Gum Levy (Wales) Bill	Defeated on floor of Senedd at first introduction stage
21 March 2012	Mick Antoniw - Asbestos (Recovery of Medical Costs) (Wales) Bill	Passed Stage Four but blocked at post-legislative phase and fell at the end of the Fourth Senedd
29 November 2011	Peter Black - Regulated Mobile Home Sites (Wales) Bill	Reached the statute book as an Act of the Senedd
29 November 2011	Mohammad Asghar - Enterprise (Wales) Bill	Defeated on floor of Senedd at first introduction stage
19 October 2011	Ken Skates - Continuity from Care into Adult Life Bill	Bill given leave to be introduced, but not passed because the Member withdrew the proposal

This table demonstrates a number of things. Firstly, it shows very clearly how few Bills taken through this route actually make it to legislation. In the eight year period, only two have managed it. Secondly, it shows that the number of ballots and therefore Bills slowed quite considerably between the Fourth and Fifth Senedd terms.

Indeed, the process and opportunity for securing the passage of a Bill through this route is not as busy as it once was. The realisation that simply having an worthwhile concept in the ballot does not offer good odds on being chosen, let alone getting a Bill through every stage, means that fewer external organisations now target this process for legislative change.

That is not to say that organisations should not utilise this process, but rather you should be realistic and measured in your hopes of success should you decide to do so. Further, just getting a Member to take forward your Bill into the ballot achieves absolutely nothing unless it is drawn or the ideas therein are taken up in another way.

In terms of suggested Bill topics, Members are able to add a new topic or to withdraw Bill ideas at any time. Members do so if they enter Government, change their mind on the legislation they wish to bring forward, or their idea may have been taken forward in some other way by the Welsh Government in its own legislative programme. For example, Labour's Mike Hedges as well as the Brexiteers Gareth Bennett and David Rowlands all withdrew proposals for Bills supporting the abolition of letting fees when the Welsh Government brought legislation forward in this area. Additionally, if a Member has been successful in a ballot, they cannot enter more ballots in that Senedd since it is deemed they have had their chance. (This is a recent change since the Fourth Senedd when, as you will see from a close examination of the ballot results, Darren Millar won the ballot twice).

The non-governmental route to changing legislation is, essentially, not a practical one. The tendency of the Welsh Government is to avoid legislating unless it really has to; and the tendency of the Welsh Government is to generally kill off legislation that originates from other places. Having said that, Members legislation does sometimes work. Both Peter Black and Kirsty Williams triumphed with backbench legislation in the Fourth Senedd, and both of them relied extensively on external organisations both for support in ideas, drafting and lobbying for that success.

TOP TIP: If using the backbench legislation method, don't get your hopes up. The ballot is a lottery, and even if your topic is chosen, the Welsh Government generally doesn't like them, and very few make the statute book and become law.

12

The Financial Process

Alongside legislation, it is worth understanding the financial process by which the Welsh Government secures its budget through the Senedd. This process has been developed over a number of years and has been refreshed and refined particularly with the advent of tax raising powers by the Welsh Government in March 2019. One thing that can be confidently predicted is that this system, like its counterpart in Westminster, will continue to be tweaked and refined.

Having said that, there is a fundamental financial relationship that will not change which can be expressed in the following four part table:

Income	Spending		
	Approves budget	Recommends & spends budget	Delivers on income received against Welsh Government policy
Welsh block grant	Senedd	Welsh Government	Welsh Government
Taxation revenue from Income Tax and other taxes			Health Boards
Reserves			Local Government
Borrowing powers			Other agencies

Within this pattern of operation, the key thing to remember is that the Government tables the budget but the Senedd has to approve it.

Every Welsh Government budget will be in two distinct parts. There is the Welsh Government's revenue budget, which is the money that it plans to be spend on delivering and maintaining public services; and there is the capital budget, which is about infrastructure spending and maintenance, be it new roads, the NHS estate or the funding of new infrastructure projects.

In this chapter we will look specifically at the revenue raising side, depicted as the first column of the table. The chapter will be structured firstly to look at how the Welsh Government has traditionally received its money through the Welsh Block Grant. We will then look how the Senedd and Welsh Government financial processes have evolved to deal with the process of setting a budget.

We will then move on to look at the other sources of Welsh Government funding: taxation, reserves, and borrowing powers. No area of Welsh public policy is undergoing more of a churn and more of a change than fiscal policy in Wales. Income Tax powers have recently been enacted, and the Welsh Government has, for the first time, the power to suggest Wales-only taxes. In writing this chapter, I have been careful not to be too prescriptive, conscious that much can change quickly in an area that is rapidly evolving, leaving guidance and expert opinion dated all too quickly.

Nevertheless, to my mind, the potential opportunities for public affairs professionals from engaging creatively with the fiscal and financial side of policy making are arguably even bigger than in respect of legislative powers, especially since public affairs professionals have, to date, paid the money side of politics far less attention than the law making side.

The Welsh block grant and the Barnett Formula

The majority of Welsh Government income comes from an annual block grant which is provided by the UK Government. This is a portion of UK Government income allocated to the Senedd to determine its use by the Welsh Government. The block grant is mainly unhypothecated, meaning the Welsh Government has discretion how it allocates this funding. This means that the funding priorities of the Welsh Government and the UK Government can differ considerably – the Welsh Government is not tied to the priorities in England or the rest of the UK, but the funding formula used is totally reliant on the UK Government's spending priorities.

It is important, however, to make a distinction between public spending in Wales managed through the Welsh Government in devolved areas and public spending in Wales managed through the UK Government in non-devolved areas. The Welsh Government controls approximately £18 billion annually but the total estimated public expenditure in Wales is closer to £38 billion (around 5% of total UK public expenditure). Thus, although many public services have been devolved to Wales, the UK Government still controls over half of public money spent in Wales: welfare spending is the biggest element but other significant UK spends relate to defence, foreign affairs, and some aspects of transport.

Our focus here, however, will be on how the block grant is calculated and spent. When setting the UK budget, the UK Government treats the devolved administrations in a similar way to the way it treats UK governmental departments, but unlike, for example, the Department of Health or the Department for Education in England, the UK Government is not free to change at will the overall amount allocated to Wales. A mechanism known as the Barnett formula exists to apportion government spending across the UK and is used to calculate the annual change in the block grants of the three devolved administrations, including Wales. The basic rule is this: if the UK Government makes spending changes in England to areas that are fully or partially devolved, the block grant for Wales has a consequential change. Thus increases, or decreases, in funding to departments like Health or Education do have a consequential result for Wales and the other devolved administrations in terms of the overall money available to Welsh Government. It is important, however, to stress they are not directly linked because of the lack of hypothecation. This was particularly vividly illustrated in 2011-13 when the Welsh Government, faced with increased consequential revenue, prioritised local government spending over health spending leading to a higher, and much publicised, rise in health spending in England compared to Wales.

Thus, the biggest variability in Welsh Government funding has always been, until now, how much is spent in England, which defines the Barnett consequentials and the size of the block grant. In 1999, the block grant was around £8bn but, by 2010, it had grown to around £16bn as a direct result of higher public spending in England, in those areas devolved to Wales. During the austerity period from 2010, the block grant has not increased significantly because public spending by the UK Government has been under tight control. This is basically the reality of what politicians refer to as austerity, in terms of the Welsh block grant: the money has not kept pace with either previous increases, or as some would argue, kept up with public service demand. The Welsh Government's own estimate is that £4bn has been 'lost' from the Welsh Block Grant between 2010 and 2019.

As the former Finance Secretary Mark Drakeford wrote in October 2018:

'... (I)f spending on public services had kept pace with growth in GDP since 2010-11, the Welsh Government would have an extra £4bn to spend on public services in 2019-20. Figure two also shows that if the budget had grown in line with the long term trend in public spending the Welsh Government would have around £6bn extra to spend on public services next year.'[1]

Within the Barnett Formula, there is a weighting given to each of the different parts of the UK. In 2017, it was calculated that relative funding per person in Wales is around 120% of that in England using the Barnett Formula. For historical and political reasons, the weightings given to Scotland and Northern Ireland are somewhat higher.

The Welsh Government and UK Government have also managed to negotiate a better funding formula for Wales, and a new Fiscal Framework introduced a needs based factor to the application of the Barnett formula in Wales for the first time. From 2018-19, increments passed onto the Welsh budget from the Barnett Formula are now 5% greater than they would have been under the previous formula. If, in the future, this falls below 115%, then the needs based factor will be changed to 115%.[2] This is what is known as the Barnett Floor and provides, for the first time, long term financial security for the Welsh Government in terms of how much core or baseline public money is received.

The Barnett Floor is not an abstract concept, it is of real fiscal benefit. As the Welsh Government itself conceded in October 2018:

---

1   Welsh Government Budget Narrative document, October 2018, paragraph 2.3.
2   Figures provided from the budget web pages of the National Assembly for Wales, as of April 2019.

'The funding floor has so far delivered an additional £70m for Wales and will deliver a further £271m over the next five years, as a result of the Barnett consequential for the UK Government's NHS spending announcement.'[3]

The UK budget process is therefore critical to any determination of amounts awarded to the Senedd to pass to the Welsh Government, once the Barnett Formula and the Fiscal Framework have been applied. The UK Government decides a detailed Autumn Budget each year that sets out any adjustments to spending and tax and borrowing requirements including information relating to previous budget initiatives, the UK Government's financial position and potential future budget proposals. Any changes to departments with responsibilities devolved to Wales will likely result in a change to funding provided via the Welsh Block Grant. This is explored in more detail toward the end of the next section.

The Senedd's budget setting process

In the autumn, the Welsh Government lays a draft budget in the Senedd which is open for analysis, amendment, debate and discussion. Taking the 2019-20 budget as the most recent example at the time of writing, the budget was actually laid in two stages:

- The outline draft Budget published on 2 October 2018 represents the first stage. It includes detail on the financing, taxation and Main Expenditure Group (departmental) level allocations.
- The detailed draft Budget was published on 23 October 2018 and set out detailed portfolio spending plans, tied to each Welsh Government department.

The Welsh Government funding process is divided into a number of Main Expenditure Groups (MEGs). There are currently, as of April 2019, six MEGs: Health and Social Services; Local Government and Public Services; Economy and Transport; Education; Energy, Planning and Rural Affairs; and Central Services and Administration. The Budget will be always be built around these MEGs as base building blocks. When you examine the outline draft Budget it will be split in

3   Welsh Government Budget Narrative document, October 2018, paragraph 3.1.

terms of MEGs and allocation, along with other data showing increases or decreases in spending within a particular MEG.

These figures aren't just introduced as cold spreadsheets. They are accompanied by a Budget Narrative document, which explains funding priorities and provisions. The two budgets are also introduced formally to the Senedd by the Finance Minister, who explains the process and uses the same narrative to explain why some decisions have been made.

Before either of these documents was produced, the Welsh Government's Finance Minister would have spent the summer working with different Ministers, departments and public bodies to agree the overall headline sums and the detailed allocations. This process is always lengthy, discursive and complex. Thus, even at the point the outline draft budget is laid, considerable work has been undertaken. Previous Finance Ministers have said to me the room for manoeuvre is always tight, especially with the lack of increased funding since 2010, and the wiggle room perhaps amounts to less than 2% of the overall budget.

Early budget setting can also involve other political parties. For example, between 2016 and late 2017, an agreement on budget setting was made between Labour and Plaid Cymru, allowing the latter considerable influence on the budget allocations from outside government. Similarly, in the Fourth Senedd, Plaid Cymru and the Liberal Democrats collaborated for two years in jointly negotiating with Labour, so that they could not be played off against each other. Proving the point above, no negotiation with another political party has ever resulted in more than a 1%-2% shift in overall spending.

The period between October and December is then one of intense pressure and negotiation, both formal and informal, in the hope that the Welsh Government will produce a final budget which reflects the pressure and lobbying it has received, both formally and informally. No Welsh Government budget has ever been passed by the Senedd without at least some changes between first draft and final version.

The Welsh Government needs to get its budgets through the Senedd in order to govern effectively. A failure to do so means it cannot spend public money. Opposition parties know this, so they use the budget period to lever as much pressure as they can on the Welsh Government, especially if it does not have a majority in the Senedd. Indeed, in the winter of 2006 the Budget proposed by the Welsh Government was actually defeated, and only later passed when further concessions had been made to demands from Plaid Cymru.

This is the only example, so far, in the history of devolution where a budget proposal has actually been defeated. In retrospect, it demonstrated two things. Not only did it signal the willingness of Plaid Cymru to make deals with Labour (paving the way perhaps for the One Wales coalition the following year), but it also demonstrated in graphic and stark terms the ability of the Senedd to control the Welsh Government. The vote on the final budget, along with votes for a First Minister or a vote of no confidence in a First Minister, are the only times this brutal power can actually be used to full effect. Any Welsh Government knows this, so it is always seeking to reach out to make sure its budget actually gets through.

Party political negotiation is usually done behind closed doors. It can provide a good opportunity for forcing concessions, which are often better agreed in private and then announced in public, rather than being publicly negotiated and agreed. A good example was contained within the Budget Narrative document produced by the Welsh Government in 2018:

'Last year, we reached a two-year agreement with Plaid Cymru on a number of specific measures where we have shared policy priorities. The outline draft Budget 2019-20 reflects the second year of this agreement. We have also agreed an additional capital allocation of £2.75m to upgrade the Urdd camps at Glan-llyn, near Bala and Llangrannog … (and) £5m capital has been earmarked in 2019-20 to take forward the results of some of the feasibility studies commissioned. We will continue to discuss with Plaid Cymru the funding options and further details will be provided at the final Budget, subject to the outcome of the UK Government's Autumn Budget.'[4]

Like so much of other Senedd business, however, these set piece budget statements are not where the real action takes place. Indeed, even within the formal structures of the Senedd, it is much more likely that the committee scrutiny processes will make a real difference than any debate in Plenary because once the Detailed Budget has been

---

4   Welsh Government Budget Narrative document, October 2018.

introduced, the committees of the Senedd really kick in with their work. The Finance Committee meets every week during the budget round, sometimes twice a week, and produces a very important report at the end of the process which is intended to put pressure on the Welsh Government from the perspective of whether the budget actually meets and reflects policy obligations and priorities. Naturally, the debate and discussion can often range beyond this, as can the recommendations of the report, but the important focus of the Finance Committee work has to be on whether the Welsh Government is actually delivering financially on its political commitments, rather than seeking to set out alternative political commitments in an alternative budget – that is what the set piece Plenary speeches are for.

When considering its report, the Finance Committee will take evidence from a range of interested parties including the Chairs of the different Subject Committees of the Senedd. It will also have conducted detailed scrutiny of the budget with members of the Welsh Government and will have produced their own reports or letters setting out any concerns or any room for improvement. All of these inputs will be considered by the Welsh Government as it structures its final budget proposals.

When it comes then to the more formal budget negotiation process, an increasingly important player is the Future Generations Commissioner. This arms length position, created during the Fourth Senedd, has played a powerful role in the budget rounds during the Fifth Senedd in offering a serious critique of Welsh Government spending as compared to its obligations under the Future Generations and Well-being Act. The significance in the 2018 budget round was perhaps best demonstrated by the emphasis in scrutiny on preventative spend in health and social care, as opposed to ongoing traditional patters of spending, something the Welsh Government took on board.

A good specific example is also contained in the 2018 Budget Narrative, reflecting on steps taken since the previous year to better accommodate the views of the Future Generations Commissioner:

'Our budget preparations have also sought to strengthen the steps we are taking to embed the Well-being of Future Generations Act into the budget process. This is an evolutionary process and has been a core consideration during the Cabinet's discussions about budget planning and has featured in each of the budget meetings between the Cabinet Secretary for Finance and Cabinet Secretaries and Ministers. We continue to develop a systematic and incremental approach to ensure the Act has a growing impact to inform spending plans and maximise opportunities to join-up activities across portfolios and align resources.'[5]

All of this scrutiny then feeds into the final budget which is tabled in December. The final budget will also take account of any changes made to the funding of the Welsh Government by the UK Government during its Autumn Statement. In the 2018 budget round, these changes were quite substantial:

'On 29 October, the Chancellor of the Exchequer presented the UK Autumn Budget. As a result of the UK Government's spending decisions, Wales received Barnett consequentials of £554.3m between 2018-19 and 2020-21. This comprises an extra £485.9m revenue; £59.9m capital and £8.5m of financial transactions capital.'[6]

The bulk of this additional money was spent on increasing the resources available to most local authorities in Wales. This directly linked to the lobbying and representation made to the Welsh Government through the Finance Committee and other Senedd Committees, as well as through the media. Indeed, the major changes between draft and final budget all related to how this additional income was to be prioritised and spent and was directly in line with representations made during the budget round.

The Welsh Government was also able to make a number of other spending commitments as a result of this additional cash, not least to the supporting of businesses through 'An extra £23.6m to enhance our current high street rates relief scheme with an additional £2.4m for local authorities to provide discretionary rates relief.'[7] This spending was derived directly from additional spending in the same area on the same budget priority, though delivered on the ground in a different way, and is a good example of where even with devolution in place the same budget priorities can emerge. That it did so, is partly down to the effective lobbying of the Federation of Small Businesses (FSB)

---

5   Welsh Government Budget Narrative document, October 2018, paragraph 1.23.
6   Final budget 2019-20 explanatory note, paragraph 2.1.
7   Final budget 2019-20 explanatory note, paragraph 3.3.

Wales and others in the economic development lobby, arguing that additional spending in Wales should mirror additional spending in England in this respect.

Lobbying during the Budget process

For a public affairs professional, the budget process therefore presents a critical opportunity for influencing and seeking to either secure more income or protect existing income and budget lines. From the examples of the 2018 budget round, the following opportunities seem to stand out within the budget process:

- Working to influence the Welsh Government directly at an early stage so that the overall draft budget reflects your interests.
- Applying pressure through the negotiation process via other political parties, which was clearly the strategy of the Urdd in securing additional capital funding to its centres via the negotiation priorities set out through Plaid Cymru.
- Making your case through the relevant Subject Committees of the Senedd during the budget process.
- Persuading the Future Generations Commissioner to big up your case during the budget round. Providing your suggestions and your intentions are congruent with the future development and well-being goals, this approach is possible, and you could be cited as a case study or an example of a service worthy of investment.
- Applying a large scale lobbying campaign across all parts of the Senedd alongside a media campaign during the budget round. This was the successful strategy of the Welsh Local Government Association in 2018 – they were literally everywhere every time the budget was discussed – and got results. From the time of the draft budget onward, the Welsh Government pledged to increase local government funding if it was able to do so, and when the additional funds became available, it was committed to making this the top priority.
- Looking at any increases made to budget lines in England during the Autumn Statement, and using this as a lever to make sure that any consequential funding is applied to the same budget heading in Wales, as did FSB Wales.

The choice of which technique to use is of course in the hands of the public affairs professional. Sometimes you may not even be trying to increase resources, but seeking to protect existing spending. This was the case in respect of the Supporting People grant, which was scheduled to disappear as a distinct budget line. In 2017, the 2018/19 budget proposals attributed £124.4m to the Supporting People programme but this was not in the 2019/20 outline. Instead, the scheme appeared to have been merged with other initiatives – Flying Start, Families First, Communities First and an employment grant scheme – under the banner of the 'Early Intervention - Prevention and Support Grant' with a budget of £252 million. Defenders of Supporting People, led by the charity Cymorth Cymru, argued the changes would mean funding would be cut by £13 million. As a result of concerted campaigning during the 2017 budget round, distinct protection and funding guarantees were offered to the Supporting People programme.

In examining which techniques and approaches to use in lobbying over the budget, the same general rule of thumb as legislation applies: the earlier you can get into the budget setting process, the more likely you are to be able to influence successfully.

Supplementary budgets

During the course of a financial year, the UK Government may introduce additional financial statements or budgets. This is often done after a crisis or a UK General Election, but can occur simply on a routine financial planning basis too.

They can also be triggered simply by internal changes of priority within Welsh Government. A supplementary budget, in February 2019, was presented to explain, in fiscal terms, the changes to portfolios that had happened during the Welsh Government reshuffle the previous December when Mark Drakeford became First Minister and altered the architecture of government. Other changes in Supplementary Budgets can come about because of adjustments to resources and capital baselines, transfers between Ministerial portfolios and allocations from reserves.

Supplementary budgets are usually not radical and significant, and usually represent only very small amounts of money, but they can be an opportunity for public affairs professionals to exercise an influence. For example, they can be used to make calls to mirror spending in England which may have triggered the Supplementary Budget, or they can be used to make the case for emergency funding, perhaps on a one off basis.

Reserves

The Welsh Government also has access to financial reserves, reflecting accrued unspent income, which can be used in respect of any emergency.

The Wales Reserve was introduced in April 2018 as part of the fiscal framework arrangements to deal with possible volatility arising from tax revenues by retaining unspent resources for use in future years. It replaced the previous budget exchange process between UK Government and Welsh Government, and permits the Welsh Government to hold up to £350m and drawdown up to £125m for revenue spending and £50m for capital spending. There are no annual limits for payments into the reserve.

In real money terms, at the start of 2018-19, £325m was held in the reserve: £274m revenue and £51m capital.[8] The Welsh Government now accounts for the use of these reserves as part of its annual budget setting process.

Welsh rates of taxation

The relatively recent enacting of powers to raise Wales-only taxes has meant, for the first time, Wales has been able to set its own taxation policies, albeit in just a small number of areas. Without going through the hoops and hurdles that have led to the current situation, including the Holtham Commission[9] and the Silk Commission[10] and the original

---

8   Welsh Government Budget Narrative document, October 2018, paragraph 3.38.

9   In 2009, an Independent Commission on Funding & Finance for Wales was established by the Welsh Government, Chaired by Gerry Holtham. It produced a report, *Fairness and Accountability: a new funding settlement for Wales (2010)*, which considered possible alternative funding mechanisms including the scope for the Welsh Government to have tax varying powers as well as greater powers to borrow.

10   The Commission on Devolution in Wales was established in 2011 as a commitment in the UK Government's Coalition Agreement, and Chaired by Paul Silk. It published two reports which reviewed the financial and constitutional arrangements

need for a referendum before introducing income tax powers for Wales,[11] actual fiscal devolution has happened relatively quickly in Wales.

Rates paid by commercial property users were fully devolved to Wales in April 2015. This is the first tax stream to be controlled by the Welsh Government, which is responsible for setting the taxable rate and redistributing the total revenues to local government. The Wales Act 2014 introduced to Wales the power to reform Stamp Duty and Landfill Tax. Both of these were then replaced in Wales by new but equivalent taxes in 2016-17.

For the first time, the Welsh Government was responsible for levying its own taxes and setting its own tax rates, becoming accountable for both raising money as well as spending it. The historical significance was well illustrated by Mark Drakeford:

'The devolution of non-domestic rates and the introduction of land transaction tax and landfill disposals tax – the first Welsh taxes in almost 800 years – means £1.4bn of the 2019-20 Budget will have been directly raised in Wales. This autumn, we are setting the first Welsh rates of income tax, which will be introduced in April 2019 and are expected to raise £2.1bn in the first year, further strengthening the link between revenue raised in Wales and funding spent on public services and the accountability of the Welsh Government to the people of Wales.'[12]

Through a process of negotiation, this money is now managed through a distinct Welsh Revenue Authority which contributes to the Welsh Government income alongside the Welsh Block Grant. As part of the negotiation with the UK Government over this new income stream, the Welsh Block Grant was cut over a phased period, meaning that the

---

in Wales. *Empowerment and Responsibility: Financial Powers to Strengthen Wales published by Silk Commission (2012)* recommended the devolution to Wales of Stamp Duty, Land Tax, Landfill Tax, Aggregates Levy, Air Passenger Duty (long-haul) and Non-Domestic Rates.

11 The Wales Act 2014 said income tax powers in Wales could only be introduced after a referendum. This need for a referendum was dropped in the Wales Act 2017.

12 Welsh Government Budget Narrative document, October 2018, paragraph 3.2.

Welsh Government will become increasingly responsible for raising more of its own income.

From April 2019, the Welsh Government also acquired powers to directly raise a portion of income tax equivalent to the first 10p of every pound taxed, regardless of the rate of taxation. The Welsh Government can now change those rates of income tax at will but has said it will not do so until after the next Senedd election in 2021. Income tax devolution is forecast to constitute 16% of the Welsh Government's total budget. Consequently, this has required an adjustment to be made to the Welsh block grant. The then Finance Minister also discussed this in the 2018 budget round and gave an illustration of how the negotiation between Welsh Government and UK Government was operating in respect of Income Tax:

'In the UK Autumn Budget on 29 October, the UK Government announced the personal allowance for income tax would increase to £12,500 in 2019-20 from £11,850 in 2018-19. This increase was bigger than assumed in the draft Budget forecast and has a negative impact on the revenues from the Welsh rates of income tax (WRIT). The forecast for WRIT in 2019-20 has fallen from £2,099m at the outline draft Budget to £2,059m in the final Budget, largely because of the personal allowance change. However, the block grant adjustment for income tax will be reduced in the same way as it is the first year of the new Welsh rates and there will be no net impact on the Welsh Government's budget in 2019-20.'[13]

Obviously, the ability to vary the rates of taxes – especially Income Tax – has a huge potential for the Welsh Government but also for those working in public affairs. The 2021 Senedd election will be the first where this plays a role. Not only will political parties be developing distinctive plans for spending, but there is the potential for those lobbying to call for increases in taxation pegged to specific spending pledges. This will potentially revolutionise the way that public affairs professionals engage with the fiscal powers and responsibilities of the Senedd and the Welsh Government.

---

13   Final budget 2019-20 explanatory note, paragraph 3.3.

Welsh taxation

Recent devolution has also given powers to the Welsh Government to propose its own distinct taxes, though these would also need to be agreed by the UK Government. In 2017, the Welsh Government suggested four possible areas where it could introduce a new tax on a Wales-only basis, namely land banking to dissuade developers from holding on to undeveloped land which had planning permission, a levy to fund social care, a tax on disposable plastics and a tourism tax. In February 2018 the Welsh Government said it would be proceeding with scoping up a land banking tax, while keeping options on the other three potential taxes open.

In suggesting this tax, the then Finance Secretary Mark Drakeford said the Welsh philosophy around new and distinct taxation was not about raising money but changing behaviour, adding that the Government would not introduce legislation if it would end up costing more money than it raised. However, he also said a recent sample survey of land set aside for development showed no progress had been made in 25% of cases and that the tax would never be intended to capture people who 'are making every effort to carry out the development they have committed to doing'.[14]

The UK Treasury has to agree the new tax before it can be introduced and negotiations commenced in 2018. The sticking point seems to be that the UK Government wants more of an illustration as to what rates might be set, rather than simply discussing the idea of a tax on land banking.

Nevertheless, we can be sure that the development of additional tax powers for Wales will shape the work of public affairs professionals quite profoundly. As yet, apart from the think tank the Bevan Foundation, very few charities or other organisations have engaged in any sort of meaningful or creative way with the evolution of new taxes. This will undoubtedly change.

Borrowing powers

Now that the Welsh Government has the power to raise money through taxation, it also has the ability to borrow money, since it can use the

---

14 BBC Wales online reporting, 13 February 2018.

taxation to pay back what it has borrowed. Limited borrowing powers were initially agreed between the Welsh Government and UK Treasury back in 2012, and have now been expanded to around £1 billion for the construction of major infrastructure projects: raised through the issuing of bonds. Until now, the entire issue of Welsh Government borrowing powers was dominated by the M4 Relief Road debate. The UK Government even agreed to allow the Welsh Government to increase its borrowing requirement if it were to spend the money on this single project, though this move was also criticised back in November 2018 for implying the UK Government was seeking to dictate to the Welsh Government how it actually used its new borrowing powers and, during the summer of 2019, the Welsh Government decided against the Relief Road project.

From a public affairs perspective, the ability to lever spending through borrowing for capital projects is an exciting opportunity which might be used in policy formulation by those working in the construction, civil engineering and transport sectors. Indeed, as the debate on borrowing powers moves on, it is likely to be less fixated on one localised project and may well take more of a national approach.

TOP TIP: With the advent of tax raising powers, public affairs professionals need to become more adept and more creative in thinking about the way money is raised and not just how money is spent. Campaigns can be evolved that use taxation as a positive incentive for behavioural change, or income tax increases can be linked directly to funding concerns.

13

Oral and Written Questions

The Welsh Government is primarily held to account by a process of questions tabled through the procedures of the Senedd. Both types of question are different, but both types of question offer opportunities to put your issues on the record and to attempt to get meaningful answers from Welsh Government Ministers. Indeed, those same Ministers are more wary of their Oral Question times than perhaps any other part of Senedd business. As Mark Drakeford reflected during his campaign to become Welsh Labour leader in 2018, the 'bear pit' of Senedd Question Time was a rather unappealing part of the job: "If you didn't have a bit of nerves about it you wouldn't be doing the job in the right way."[1]

Oral Questions

Oral Questions are tabled each week to be answered in Plenary by the First Minister (FMQs); and every four weeks for answer by Welsh Cabinet Ministers, Deputy Ministers, the Counsel General and the Senedd Commission.

Questions are submitted three working days in advance for FMQs and five days in advance for all other Ministers and the Senedd Commission. Questions must be in the form a single sentence and framed to actually ask a question rather than make a statement.

A maximum of 12 questions are permitted, providing 12 have been submitted, which is rarely the case for the Senedd Commission, but usually happens for the First Minister and the other questions sessions. Putting aside First Minister's Questions, which are set specifically for

---

1   Media coverage before Mark Drakeford's first appearance at First Minister's Questions, 8 January 2018

one designated person, the other questions are asked about the work of a department. Thus, both the Cabinet Minister and, if they have one, their deputy can answer. Functional responsibilities (as described in Chapter 2) are split between Ministers if there is more than one in a department, and the person taking the functional lead will usually field the answer to the question.

After the question has been asked the Minister will read a short response from a script prepared by officials. The questioner is then permitted to ask a supplementary question. This takes the form of up to three or four sentences which seek to build on the initial question, often setting out opinion as well as eventually reaching a question. If the supplementary question is too long the Chair, usually the Llywydd/ Presiding Officer for this part of the Senedd business, will intervene to speed things along. The Minister then provides a fuller response, often with more detail or by being more politicised if it is a challenging question from an opposition Member or, sometimes, a challenging question from their own side.

Once this is done, further supplementary questions are permitted from other Members, usually respecting party balance. These supplementary questions take the form of a single question (usually contextualised within a couple of sentences) followed by a response from the Minister, who will not usually be aware, beforehand, of their content.

However – and this is the real challenge for public affairs professionals when it comes to oral questions – the responses from Ministers depend upon a range of factors, the most obvious being, of course, the official government line as reflected in the drafted response. The more contentious the policy area, the more rigid the approach from the Minister will be. Similarly, the political angle will also play here since a more politically charged question or a more politically sensitive topic will also elicit a rigid rebuttal. The skill is in phrasing the question to tease out a more meaningful response.

Often the best way to do this is working with a government backbencher to table a non-confrontational question, involving putting something significant on the record, or inviting the Minister to a visit in order that they experience the issue being raised. This then helps deepen understanding and works best if the Minister has been briefed in advance of what to expect by the Member asking the question. If you have a good relationship with the Minister or the officials briefing them, you may also be able to take part in the briefing exercise.

It need not, however, be a Member from the governing party who asks the question. Edwina Hart, when Health Minister in the Third Senedd, had such a strong relationship with her Plaid Cymru and Conservative counterparts – Helen Mary Jones and Jonathan Morgan – that she would often respond in this way to pre-planned questions from them. There were even rumours that she would give them material for questions in order to expose the failings of officials or health boards to implement policy to her satisfaction.

This approach is very different from the normal exchanges between a Minister, including the First Minister, and the Members who shadow them. Questions from opposition party leaders to the First Minister, and from the lead opposition spokespeople to other Ministers, do not have to be notified in advance. This generally creates a more probing and challenging environment for that particular part of question time, which is probably what Mark Drakeford was alluding to in respect of a 'bear pit'.

Further, when opposition party leaders question the First Minister, or opposition front benches question the Government front bench, they are allowed two supplementary questions each, and this makes for an even more challenging time for the person being scrutinised. This is partly because of the opportunity for the opposition's chief spokespeople to put their government counterparts on the spot: the Oral Question sessions of the Senedd can be described as the fulcrum of its business.

Certainly, the viewing figures for this part of Senedd business are the highest of the week, and the Welsh media often pays more attention than at any other time. This is an important consideration when you are thinking about interacting with the Senedd through the tabling and supporting of Oral Questions: the audience is far bigger than just the Members in the chamber or the observers in the gallery above.

Treat First Minister's Questions on a Tuesday afternoon in terms of the way that people and the media tend to engage most with Westminster: namely Prime Minister's Questions each Wednesday. So, to maximise the impact of a question, choose it carefully and maximise the media engagement.

This calls for a well-planned public affairs strategy to maximise the impact of a potential question or questions. By getting a question right in this forum you instantly raise the profile of an issue and push it up the political agenda. There is also, of course, the potential downside to consider: that the Minister whom you are trying to pressure may not welcome this particular form of escalation and scrutiny. That consideration, therefore, tends to be part of the strategic thinking you need to go through when you work to get an oral question tabled.

Indeed, the pre-planning of an Oral Question is critical. As well as party allegiance and 'closeness' to the Minister, when tabling a question you might also have chosen to work with a Member who has particular policy expertise in the area in question or is very familiar with your organisation.

Above all, do not lose sight of your original objective when working to table a question and the extent to which it fits in with your overarching public affairs objectives. Done well, your intervention and support will have helped to raise your profile and the campaign you are working on; or will have gathered additional information in the public domain for you to utilise in planning and moving forward with your objectives. It is often useful to touch base with the Member who asked the question for you, or someone who came in with a supplementary question, to work out how best to use the response to the question in moving forward.

The sizes of Ministerial briefs are not equal and this can also impact on the nature of a question time. The First Minister can be asked anything from any departmental portfolio in their government, so clearly they have the broadest remit. Expecting any First Minister to know the ins and outs of any policy area is not realistic, so a First Minister under pressure relating to something obscure (and potentially un-briefed from Cabinet colleagues absent from the topic folder in front of them) will often provide a holding answer in the shape of a promise to write or, worse still, a political diatribe on a tangential topic.

There is also an imbalance regarding the size of the briefs of individual Ministers expected to field questions across the whole of their portfolio. The Health and Social Services department is huge and often contentious, other ministries are not, especially if the Minister has a narrow range of subject responsibilities. Getting a question asked to the latter type of Minister is usually much easier, since the chances of a Member being drawn in the 12-question lottery is much higher.

Within the allocated time limit most Ministers usually answer at least eight out of the 12 tabled questions. Some Ministers, to put it charitably, answer more fully than others so there can be quite a bit of difference in the length of answers. If all the questions tabled for Plenary are not answered within the allotted time, the remaining questions are answered in writing and published as Questions not Reached (QNR). They are, in effect, are transformed into Written Questions.

Written Questions

Members can also table Written Questions. Answers to Written Questions are sent directly to the Member who tabled the question and are subsequently published in the Senedd's official Record. The rule is that Written Questions are supposed to be answered within one week, though responses can take much longer, especially if the question has inadvertently been asked to the wrong Minister and has to be transferred.

As with Oral Questions, Written Questions must be framed in a single sentence and drafted as a question. The response will be drafted by an official but has to be signed off by the Minister to whom the question is addressed. They generally, therefore, have a very focused structure and are less political than oral questions. Indeed, Written Questions work well for technical points or information gathering for use during a campaign. Sometimes, however, Written Questions elicit curious responses, especially if the Minister being asked takes a very 'hands on' approach. There was an example of one question which asked how many responses had been received to a government consultation receiving the response, 'a number', while on another occasion a question about UFO sightings received a response that had been drafted in Klingon!

Such answers are, however, the exception rather than the rule. The answers to Written Questions are usually dry and factual, and they can often be not very helpful at all. If targeted at data on a local health board level, which is often the way with Written Questions linked to the health portfolio, they can get a response that explains the information is not held centrally. Another evasive tactic used by government is to indicate the information requested would be too costly to obtain.

To date, Written Questions have not been used consistently or particularly often. Some Members make more use of this technique than others, and it is particularly favoured by the Members in the Conservative group as a way of information gathering. Most organisations tabling Written Questions use them for that purpose too, and it is not unusual for a single Member to table a range of questions at the same time, all seeking different pieces of information. Taken together, these grouped outputs might be extremely valuable from an information perspective. As ever, the input and advice of the Member tabling the questions is likely to be valuable.

Topical Questions and Emergency Questions

In stark contrast, Topical Questions and Emergency Questions can get a great deal of media attention and interaction. Both these types of question usually come from a Member shadowing a Government Minister on the policy area in question.

Members may ask Topical Questions to a member of the Government if the Llywydd/Presiding Officer is satisfied that the question relates to a matter of national, regional or local significance where an expedited response is desirable. Topical Questions have, since 2016, formed part of the set Senedd business on a Wednesday afternoon.

Members may also ask Emergency Oral Questions which are taken without notice. Emergency Questions may only be asked if the matter is judged by the Llywydd/Presiding Officer to be of urgent national significance. These rarely happen but when they do it is usually on a Tuesday, and can be aimed at any Minister, including the First Minister.

In both cases, the question will usually be one of high public interest on an issue which will already have been the subject of media attention before being asked. They need not be on a matter for which the Welsh Government is responsible, just that the issue is pertinent to Wales. Sometimes the Welsh Government has used this sort of question to set out a policy position in relation to the UK Government.

The Llywydd/Presiding Officer does not allow many Emergency Questions to be asked. Between June and December 2017, for example, permission to ask an Emergency Question was sought 15 times but granted only once. In 2018, there were 33 attempts to ask Emergency Questions, only one of which was granted. The full list of Emergency Questions, both those permitted and those declined, is published on the Senedd website as an aid to political transparency.

From a public affairs perspective, Topical Questions and Emergency Questions happen so quickly and without notice that it is impossible to pre-engage. However, if your organisation is intimately involved in the matter being raised then there is a good likelihood of the Member asking the question either getting in touch with you beforehand, or being willing to receive a succinct briefing containing your perspective on the matter. Similarly, your position, backed up by relevant data and examples may also be welcomed by the Welsh Government, passed through special advisers or lead officials.

> **TOP TIP: Make sure you brief the person asking the question to also ask a supplementary, and if you want a meaningful and constructive answer from the Minister make sure they know the substance of the supplementary too.**

14

Other Senedd Business in Plenary Session

Plenary sessions happen on Tuesday and Wednesday afternoons. They usually begin at 1.30pm, normally close around 6pm, or later depending on the length of the agenda, and are the responsibility of the Senedd's Business Committee.

Plenary sessions are generally Chaired by the Llywydd/Presiding Officer or the Deputy Presiding Officer. If they are unavailable, there is a panel of other senior Senedd Members who are permitted to officiate. By convention, neither the Llywydd/Presiding Officer nor Deputy Presiding Officer vote during Senedd proceedings, thereby cancelling each other out.

The general shape of Plenary sessions is divided between government business and non-government business. As a general rule, the business on Tuesday is in the hands of the Government and most of the time on a Wednesday belongs to the opposition parties, backbench Members and Senedd Committees: a far more generous division of time than would be found in most legislatures. The following table shows the range of items that are raised over the two days of each week's Plenary sessions.

Tuesday	Wednesday
Government business based on:	Government business:
Questions to the First Minister	Questions to Ministers
Emergency Questions	Non-Government business:
Business Statement	Topical Questions
Ministerial statements	*90 Second Statements*
Approving secondary legislation	*Personal Statements*
Legislative consent motions	*Statements by the Presiding Officer/ Commission*
Government led debates	Standards Committee reports
Financial resolutions	

Tuesday	Wednesday
Legislation – introduction, plus stages 3 and 4	Petitions referred by Petitions Committee Committee inquiry reports Backbench/Committee legislation *Debates initiated by groups of backbenchers* *Debates by political parties* *Short Debates*

Much of the Government's business has been covered effectively in other chapters. Oral Questions and Emergency Questions are detailed in Chapter 13; financial processes in Chapter 12, and legislative processes in Chapter 10. Additionally, from the non-government business, we have looked at non-government legislation in Chapter 11, Topical Questions in Chapter 13, Committee reports in Chapter 9, and we will examine petitions in Chapter 16. The focus of this chapter is on the other business covered in the table, and how you can understand and engage with that. The italicised elements of the table above are the ones explained in this chapter.

Of these different elements, the one that offers the least opportunity for engagement is the 90 Second Statement. This is a relatively new device to allow a Member to make a short statement on a pertinent or topical matter without expecting to tie it to Senedd business or receive any response from the Government. It is simply a way of placing a topical matter on the record and, for some Members, gain some local publicity. The outcomes are very limited and the opportunities for public affairs engagement equally so.

A rarely used mechanism is the ability of Members to make Personal Statements, which are granted by the Llywydd/Presiding Officer following notice in writing. A personal statement must be brief, factual and must not be subject to debate. Examples would usually be when a Member joins the Senedd after a by-election or a change to the regional list representation or, in very unusual cases, where the Member has a disclosure to make. An example of the latter occurred in December 2018 when Darren Millar placed on record some information he had in relation to the late Carl Sargeant.

As neither of these types of statement offer the opportunity for public affairs engagement, in this chapter we will focus on the other italicised elements and how to work on them.

Explaining other Plenary business

Before discussing engagement, it is perhaps useful to be clear on what is the substance of the other elements of Plenary business.

- **Business Statements:** This is led by the Trefnydd (the Government's business manager) who, each week, will formally introduce a statement setting the outline of the following three weeks in the Senedd chamber. Every non-government Member can then rise to request additional business be added. Members usually use this vehicle not just to call for genuine debates but to put matters on the record that they believe should be noted. Some Members are particularly assiduous in using this vehicle, including the Conservative Mark Isherwood, who has been known to call for up to five additional items to be added to the agenda of Senedd business! Other Members have used this device to draw attention to events they are hosting on the Senedd estate. As the Business Statement is not amendable, the thirty minutes or so normally given to this item are more for making a point than achieving anything substantial in terms of process or resolution.
- **Ministerial Statements:** These are issued in writing to Members and then read out by the relevant Minister. It is a matter for the Government which statements are brought forward. Once the statement has been read, the lead opposition spokespeople are invited to respond and usually one or two interested backbenchers from the governing party. The Minister will respond to each speaker in turn, and attempt to answer their questions. No vote is held on Ministerial Statements. The Government can also issue written statements, generally on less contentious matters, which are not the subject of debate in the Senedd and the Government can sometimes attract criticism for issuing a written statement without an opportunity for appropriate questioning.
- **Legislative Consent Motions:** When the UK Parliament wishes to legislate on a subject matter which has already been devolved to Wales, convention requires it to receive the consent of the Senedd before it may pass the legislation in question. Such consent is given by the Senedd through Legislative Consent Motions (LCMs). They are also subject to scrutiny by both the Finance Committee and the Constitutional and Legislative Affairs Committee, but have to be

approved in Plenary session to be binding. A Welsh Government Minister will bring the LCM forward, triggering what is usually a brief debate. LCMs are rarely rejected, the most notable example of which was the Bill to establish police and crime commissioners which was discussed by the Fourth Senedd. As a general rule, external engagement around LCMs by public affairs professionals is generally low, which perhaps reflects that they are under more scrutiny at Westminster than at the Senedd. Having said that, during the 2018-19 period of Brexit arrangements, some Senedd Committees took a much keener interest in the LCMs pertaining to international trade and agriculture.

- **Government led Debates:** The Welsh Government will also table debates in its own time. It does this either to gain views on a proposal when it does not have a clear policy or, more frequently, to set out a policy and point to the success of government actions. Most debates tend to be tabled for an hour and are based on a motion which is open to amendment by Members. A vote is held unless there is unanimity on a motion.

- **Statements by the Presiding Officer/Commission:** The Presiding Officer can make statements on matters within their remit, with the current Presiding Officer, Elin Jones, using this vehicle to update Members on the progress in establishing a Youth Parliament for Wales. As with Ministerial Statements, other Members can ask questions but there is no vote. The Commission, which looks after the Senedd estate and facilities, can also make statements from time to time. Both practices are relatively rare.

- **Debates initiated by individuals or groups of backbenchers:** Backbenchers are also able to table debates for discussion. Sometimes these are done by individual Members on a matter where they are suggesting an initiative that does not require primary legislation. A good example was the debate initiated by the Conservative Suzy Davies on defibrillation and life saving, or her Plaid Cymru counterpart in South Wales West, Dai Lloyd, on protecting Welsh place-names, and Members sometimes group together either on cross-party lines or as backbenchers from the governing party to urge more action on an issue. Good examples of both approaches was the work led by Mike Hedges on a cross-party basis in the Fourth Senedd on establishing a reserved powers model of devolution for Wales; and the initiative taken by a number of Labour backbenchers to get the foundational economy mainstreamed into Welsh Government economic planning, which they achieved.

- **Debates by political parties:** Opposition parties are also able to bring forward motions. They are given the opportunity to do so on the basis of their size in the Senedd, with the bigger parties having more opportunities. Most debates tend to be tabled for an hour, though Plaid Cymru has previously used its time to trigger two shorter debates. Political party debates are based on a motion which is open to amendment by Members and a vote is held unless there is unanimity on a motion. In respect of these votes, the motion is always voted on first, rather than the amendments, allowing an opposition party to at least gauge support for its core proposal without it being amended beyond recognition by the Government.

- **Short Debates:** These are usually held one a week as the final item of business on a Wednesday afternoon. The Llywydd/Presiding Officer holds a ballot to determine the name of the non-government Member who can then propose a topic for a Short Debate, and every backbench Member is guaranteed one Short Debate during each Senedd session. The Member who has succeeded in the ballot must notify the Presiding Officer of the topic not later than five working days before it is to be debated and, during the Short Debate, the Member may speak for up to 15 minutes, and allow short contributions from within their time from other Members. The Welsh Government then has up to 15 minutes to respond, and may also allow interventions within their time. Short Debates are a good vehicle for exploring a policy area in depth and for suggesting new ideas to government. They are often less politically charged and more persuasive than other types of debate, especially since there is no vote at the end. Policy initiatives are occasionally taken on board by the Welsh Government after powerful Short Debates and they also offer the opportunity of engaging the media. In the House of Commons, Short Debates are known as Adjournment Debates.

The timetable for identifying Senedd business is relatively straight forward. An indicative timetable is set out three weeks in advance, which is capable of revision right up until the day a discussion is due to take place. Indeed, if there is a particularly heavy flow of business on a Tuesday, debates can be pulled or statements transferred from oral to written form.

In respect of debates, however, their wording will be published by the end of the previous Thursday before they are due to be debated. The deadline for amendment is then late Friday afternoon. This gives quite a narrow window of opportunity for engagement and influence around amendments, but organisations still work with opposition parties within this timeframe to get them tabled. There is nothing that says you have to wait until a debate motion is published on the Senedd website before working on an amendment. You can begin to work with Members weeks in advance to try and get your concerns and viewpoints shared.

Engagement with other Plenary business

The common factor uniting the different forms of Plenary business described above is that, to varying degrees, they offer the opportunity for external input and are platforms for external engagement and ideas. They are all basically forms of debate.

These ideas can even be as powerful as suggesting a topic. Although Members will have their own ideas for Short Debates, for example, these often arise from interaction with external organisations and the research requirement to produce a 15-minute speech will often mean the Member will be looking for input beyond simply an idea and a title. In terms of the Suzy Davies example cited above, she had particular assistance from heart charities like the British Heart Foundation.

There are also numerous examples of the opposition parties asking for ideas for debates from external organisations, and these can sometimes work well if done constructively. For example, in the Third Senedd the RNIB and other like-minded organisations worked with the Conservatives to stage a debate on wet age related macular degeneration, which was supported by a mass lobby of the Senedd by people with sight loss, including those suffering with this condition. The net effect of this lobby, done in a responsible way, was to impress on the Welsh Government of the need to access these medicines as a matter of urgency. The campaign was a success. Most opposition debates, however, are not so successful and the motions are usually voted down and disregarded. There have also been occasions when they have prompted the Government to take an even harder line against what your organisation is trying to achieve.

The danger of being perceived as being too closely aligned to a particular political party or grouping is very real and every effort must be made to illustrate that you have operated even-handedly and on a cross-party basis. The organisational damage of losing the badge of neutrality can take many years, and potentially a change in personnel, to overcome.

When things spiral out of control from this respect, they can do so pretty spectacularly. During the Fourth Senedd, a multi-organisation campaign to support the passage of the Domestic Violence Bill is a case in point. Nervous that the Bill did not go far enough to meet their aspirations, for months the organisations used every opportunity to put pressure on the Welsh Government to expand the remit of the Bill. It was duly strengthened somewhat but not to the extent they had originally campaigned for. Opposition Members, however, kept on pressuring for stronger legislation still, and threatened not to support its passage in the form it was tabled. At this point, the third sector-led lobby turned on the opposition Members with such fury that several of them condemned the campaign in the Senedd and accused it of being bullying. The legislation passed, but this sort of reaction and labelling was clearly the last thing the campaigners wanted.

Most campaigning, however, is done respectfully and constructively. You need not only confine your interactions to opposition parties either. A government under pressure on an issue may welcome support and information. Praise from a Minister comes with added weight and can be used in your promotional and campaign material as a testament to your effectiveness. It may also bring you closer into the fold of organisations a Minister and officials can work with.

As you can see, there is quite a delicate balance to be undertaken when you are engaging around debates. Further, the consideration of the delicate matter of who to approach is not necessarily just party political. Many organisations use an approach based on the blanket briefing of all Members with the same document. This can be rather a scattergun approach. Many Members will simply not use generic briefings from organisations because they will be nervous of others in the chamber using the same material or might simply consider not enough of an effort has been made to engage them meaningfully.

One useful group of recipients for such a broad based briefing, however, would be the team of research staff in each of the political parties. They might well be able to pass such briefings on in a targeted way to the Members of their party most likely to speak in the debate. In short, they could well do some targeting for you.

More targeted approaches often work better. You could consider approaching a Member that you are particularly close to and offering them an exclusive briefing so that they essentially act as your voice in the debate. This works if you are confident they will clearly raise your concerns – and if they are the right person to elicit a meaningful response rather than being simply brushed aside.

Stratifying your asks so that you approach different people with different points is another way of approaching this challenge. It enables Members to feel valued and well informed, so make sure that you make this level of stratification known to them. It can also work on a geographical basis, and by providing local examples from the constituency or region to a Member who is likely to speak or intervene in a debate can also be very good practice. Yes, stratifying your messages is a lot more time consuming than using a single briefing a multitude of times, but the returns can be worth it.

Which leads on to whether you should spend time, when stratifying your briefings for a debate, with Members implacably opposed to you. Despite showing them goodwill and having the best of intentions to persuade them to change their position to your cause, evidence shows that the likelihood of them changing their minds is negligible. The general rule, therefore, is that the most effective option is to expend your time proportionately on the Members who are on your side, who have an interest in the issue and who are likely to be called to speak.

A final scenario worth considering is where your organisation is the actual subject of the debate. This happens rarely but is not unheard of. In such circumstances you obviously need to treat the debate as both a public affairs priority and an organisational priority and develop a wholesale strategic response. This should see the debate as just one part of a bigger campaign of either promotion or damage limitation (depending on the nature of the motion.) It will also require detailed briefing on a face to face basis, including with officials and advisers to the Minister, and would probably also need a supportive media management operation.

TOP TIP: Choose the right type of debate to engage with. Some opportunities that present themselves may look good at first, for example opposition party motions, but may be counter productive in the longer term if you alienate or harden the opinion of a government you are seeking to influence.

15

Statements of Opinion

In politics, the terminology sometimes varies between institutions, but the essence of a process is the same. In Westminster, what are called Early Day Motions are named Parliamentary Motions in the Scottish Parliament, and Statements of Opinion in the Senedd. The Senedd nomenclature is perhaps more accurate: all of them are statements which, though they are drafted in the style of motions, stand very little chance of actual debate.

Tabling a Statement of Opinion

Only one Member of the Senedd can table an individual Statement of Opinion – on any 'matter affecting Wales' – although other Members, outside the Government, can sign them, regardless of party. It's also worth noting that the subject matter does not have to be within the competence of the Senedd, and in some cases Members table Statements of Opinion outside the remit of the powers of the Senedd as it is one of the few ways of making their opinions formally known on such matters.

Statements of Opinion must be drafted in a certain way. They must not exceed 100 words in total, must begin with the words 'This Assembly/This Senedd' and then must list opinion or required actions based on a series of numbered points. A Statement of Opinion which is not drafted properly or not about a matter affecting Wales, whether or not the matter is devolved, will be ruled out of order and not tabled.

Persuading a Members to table a Statement of Opinion is not challenging. As discussed earlier, they are helpful people who will often be looking for a concrete way to assist you, especially if you are a third sector organisation. If the Member has a long relationship with your organisation it will add to the likelihood of their supporting you in this way. Sometimes, long term, slow burn campaigns can benefit from the strategic use of a Statement of Opinion during their lifespan, so it is not always the right strategy to work for a Statement of Opinion at the outset of any new campaign.

If you do not have an automatic champion to help table a Statement of Opinion, another angle is to research the interests of Members in order to pinpoint one who is likely to work with you in tabling one. Taking a month, by random, from the Fifth Assembly offers a flavour of the type of statements which are tabled. March 2018, for example, saw five new Statements of Opinion laid:

> **Apprenticeships Week**: Joyce Watson (Lab, Mid & West Wales)
> **Apprenticeships Week**: Russell George (Con, Montgomeryshire)
> **Abortions**: Jenny Rathbone (Lab, Cardiff Central)
> **Brexit & working for One Wales**: Mike Hedges (Lab, Swansea East)
> **Earth Hour**: Simon Thomas (PC, Mid & West Wales)

All of these Members were known to have taken a long term interest in the issues they championed through the Statements of Opinion mentioned. Again, the case for a good information flow through monitoring the Senedd is crucial. It cannot be said often enough that context is everything.

You will note from the subject matter of these examples, that the process of producing Statements of Opinion is often influenced by external organisations. Public affairs professionals will ask Members to table statements to reflect days, weeks or months aligned to a specific campaign, or just on a new stand alone campaign. Sometimes Members also table them in relation to local visits they may have done. It is clear that, for the third sector especially, there is real value in engaging with the Statement of Opinion process.

Alternative Statements of Opinion

Sometimes you can get different Members tabling different Statements of Opinion. In the March 2018 example already provided you see two tabled on Apprenticeship Week. These two did not conflict and, in fact, some Members signed both of them.

Nevertheless, in a political environment, it is often the case that political parties often have different standpoints on the same issue, even if they agree with the end objective. Thus, sometimes rival Statements of Opinion can be tabled which different parties find it easier to sign up to. Alternative Statements of Opinion are also tabled when different Members seek to demonstrate that it is they, and not another Member, who is leading on a particular campaign. This is perhaps demonstrated by example.

OPIN-2017-0059 Proposed Super Prison in Port Talbot
Raised By:
Bethan Jenkins AM (PC, South Wales West)
Subscribers:
Rhun ap Iorwerth (PC, Ynys Mon) (12/10/17)
Dai Lloyd (PC, South Wales West) (13/10/17)
Simon Thomas (PC, Mid & West Wales) (18/10/17)
Adam Price (PC, Carmarthen East & Dinefwr) (18/10/17)
Llyr Gruffydd (PC, North Wales) (18/10/17)
This Assembly:
1. Regrets the UK Government's proposal to build a new super prison in Port Talbot.
2. Is disappointed that the Welsh Government has refused to rule out the use by the MOJ of Welsh Government land in Port Talbot for a prison.
3. Notes the proposed site is in an enterprise zone and a flood-risk zone.
4. Disagrees that there is a requirement for more super prisons in Wales.
5. Notes that there is already a surplus of prison places in Wales.
6. Calls for the devolution of criminal justice to the National Assembly so decisions regarding new prisons can reflect Wales's needs

---

Labour Members would find it hard to sign up to this motion, even if they had misgivings about a super prison in Port Talbot, specifically because of the bluntness of the wording of clauses 4 and 5. An alternative Statement of Opinion was therefore for tabled by David Rees, who is the constituency Member covering Port Talbot in the Senedd.

OPIN-2017-0061 Proposed Super Prison in Port Talbot (amendment to OPIN-2017-0059)
Raised By:
David Rees (Lab, Aberavon)
Subscribers:
Mike Hedges (Lab, Swansea East) (20/10/17)

> *This Assembly:*
> *1. Regrets the UK Government's proposal to build a new super prison in Port Talbot.*
> *2. Is disappointed that the Welsh Government has refused to rule out the use by the MOJ of Welsh Government land in Port Talbot for a prison.*
> *3. Notes the proposed site is in an enterprise zone and a flood-risk zone.*
> *4. Notes the lack of evidence that the use of super prisons reduces reoffending rates and calls for the suspension of their development in Wales.*
> *5. Calls for the devolution of criminal justice to the National Assembly so decisions regarding new prisons can reflect Wales's needs.*

Arguably, multiple Statements of Opinion on the same topic weaken the impact of the statement or statements and, from a public affairs perspective, it is always more desirable that a single Statement of Opinion is tabled around which as many Members as possible can coalesce. Ensuring this happens comes down to both wording and the choice of Member or Members to table the Statement of Opinion in the first place.

Additionally, a facility is available where Members can also object in writing to Statements of Opinion, though this is not commonly done.

The value of Statements of Opinion

These devices intend to set out a political opinion on an issue by the person tabling them or the Members signing them, and are essentially tabled in the hope of attracting various forms of attention, be that political attention, stakeholder attention or media attention.

There is no limit to the number of Statements of Opinion that can be tabled. In the first half of the 2016-21 (Fifth) Senedd, 111 statements were tabled, around four per month. This is a radical drop from the first decade of the Senedd, when Statements of Opinion were a much more frequent vehicle for demonstrating a view on an issue.

Statements of Opinion cannot trigger a formal debate. Although they are drafted in the form of motions, they are essentially vehicles to draw attention to issues. Statements of Opinion can, however, be used to bring Members together around an issue and can potentially be used to trigger pressure in terms of staging a more formal debate by other means.

Remember, however, that a Statement of Opinion is a political tool. It is not a campaign in itself, and just getting one tabled changes nothing. It is therefore more important to use a Statement of Opinion strategically as part of an over arching campaign plan. Several major campaigns have successfully utilised the Statement of Opinion process to demonstrate their depth and resonance.

One word of warning on content: if it is too party political, especially in criticism of a government, then a statement will usually struggle to gain cross-party support. A statement which is overtly critical of the Welsh Government will usually fail to get support from the backbenchers of that party. An exception to this rule, however, makes a good case study.

The Disabled Children Matter campaign in 2007 used this device to pull in the signatures of every single Member who was able to sign a statement, tabled by Labour Member Lynne Neagle, calling for her own Welsh Government to follow the UK Government in allocating additional funding to supporting disabled children and their families. The power of this approach was recognised in significant media coverage, including a front page of the *Western Mail*, which supported the campaign for this funding prioritisation. This is an excellent example of where a Statement of Opinion becomes the centre point of a political campaign and the Disabled Children Matter calls were adopted by the Welsh Government, who allocated additional funds to meet their demands.

Building momentum for Statements of Opinion

If a statement is worth tabling, it should be tabled with as much volume as possible. As well as choosing the right issue, you should also try and get the right Member to table it: clearly someone with a strong background or interest in the issue is helpful. Further, if there is a geographical consideration then that will define which Member you choose, whether the constituency or the regional Member.

There is also, however, a more delicate consideration which can only be understood with increased familiarity of the Senedd. This is the extent to which some Members are better choices to approach to act as the initial sponsor of a statement. For example, some have a reputation for energetic campaigning or are known to particularly favour the mechanism of gathering signatures from their colleagues. Without naming names, it is also true that some Members are more popular on a cross-party basis, and therefore are more likely to draw in support from different parts of the Senedd chamber. This may persuade you to try the relevant Subject Committee Chair rather than a lead opposition spokesperson to act as your sponsor. Ultimately, there is a value judgement to be made, and that can only be done with information and context.

Once a statement has been tabled it is then important to build momentum behind it and encourage as many eligible Members as possible to sign. To do this effectively, work with the Member who tabled the statement as they will usually appeal to their colleagues on a cross-party basis to add their names. It is entirely appropriate for you to ask Members directly to add their names too, though courtesy would suggest that you liaise with the Member who tabled the statement to let them know how you intend to build support.

The means that you can utilise to encourage Members to sign would include telephone calls, emails or even direct tweeting to the Member. If it is any form of written communication, then include a link to the tabled statement in order to make it as easy as possible for the Member to add their name and sign up. Obviously, the more Members you have signed up, the easier it usually is to pick off others as no Member will want to be the only eligible Member who did not sign.

Additionally, when a Member has added their name, it is an additional courtesy to email or tweet a thank you for doing so. Using the latter medium also draws further attention to the Statement of Opinion and builds momentum, especially if a link to the Statement of Opinion is again shared.

As with the Disabled Children Matter campaign, the media can be persuaded to take note of a Statement of Opinion if it is about a novel or contemporary matter, or if it has gathered an unprecedented amount of support. This all relates to having a robust and well thought through public affairs campaign plan.

TOP TIP: Don't ever believe that tabling a Statement of Opinion is a campaign in itself. On its own it will achieve absolutely nothing other than ticking a box. You should use Statements of Opinion as part of a clear campaign strategy.

16

Petitions

The petitions process of the Senedd was established in 2007 as a way of connecting the institution more directly with issues of concern raised by the public. From the outset, it was viewed as a way of dealing with and integrating those concerns with the scheduled business of both the Senedd and of Welsh Government, and providing systems for resolution of concerns. Other legislatures in other parts of the UK have now evolved similar structures and approaches, but the Senedd was in the vanguard of this sort of initiative. It has kept its petitions procedure under review in order to maximise and make efficient its impact; while also streamlining the processes to make them user friendly and time efficient.

Why use petitions?

The Senedd stresses the value of petitions in every aspect of its outreach and external relations systems. It works to encourage people and organisations to work together and submit as many petitions as possible.

Skilled public affairs professionals will not just submit a petition every time they want to achieve something but it is, however, one of a variety of tools that can impact on public policy. Done well, it can have real benefits. The changes to the law on organ donation and the introduction of a carrier bag levy, both of which were high profile laws passed by the Senedd, started life as ideas submitted through the petitions process.

Petitions can also add value by bringing Members together for a clear campaign focus, including a mass event to hand over a petition, as described in the end section of Chapter 6 on Working with Members of the Senedd. Additionally, the passage of a petition through different stages also creates opportunities for mass lobbies and popular engagement. It is not just a static process based on submitting a document into the process.

Rules around petitions

The petitions process in the Senedd is governed by clear rules, the most basic one of which says that the issue in the petition must be in the power of the Senedd to, or Welsh Ministers, to change. Petitions cannot ask the Senedd to do anything which it clearly has no power to do (in particular petitions about matters that are not devolved). Further, if the petition is about a service provided in a local authority rather than a Wales-wide matter it may also be ruled inadmissible. Another reason that petitions are ruled inadmissible is when it appears the same as, or is substantially similar to, another petition which is open or was closed less than 12 months earlier. All inadmissible petitions are available on the Senedd website alongside the permissible ones, making tracking this aspect of the Senedd's work particularly easy.

Bearing in mind the rules, the wording of a petition has to be specifically framed around either 'We call on the Senedd to...' or 'We call on the Senedd to urge the Welsh Government to...' The limit on wording (excluding the title) is currently 2,000 characters, but most petitioners tend to confine their petition to a few paragraphs.

For a petition to be valid it must also be signed by 50 people or submitted in the name of a legal organisation such as a charity. A hybrid approach can also be taken, where a petition has come from an organisation but can also be signed by individuals, but you will be in the best position to decide how a petition should be formatted and submitted. If you choose the online approach, remember that, for security reasons, an e-mail address can only be used once when signing a single petition; and multiple people cannot use the same e-mail address.

Submitting a petition can be done in person or online. On submission, you will asked whether you would be prepared to present evidence on the petition to the Senedd, and the strong advice is to agree to do this (for the same reasons as you would respond to consultations in an active way, as outlined in Chapter 8). If something is worth saying, and worth gathering over 50 names in support of, then it is worth saying as loudly as possible.

You can also choose, if you have submitted the petition online via the e-petitions process, to make your petition open to signature by others. Once they are opened online, they can continue to be signed electronically for up to six months (the petitioner specifies the length of the period it is kept open). If an e-petition does not reach the 50 people threshold in that period it is deemed closed, so if you are pursuing an online route to meet your target then make sure you are organising people to sign up online. Online signatures can be added anonymously provided they have been submitted in a valid way.

When you are at the early stage of drafting a petition, especially if you are doing it for the first time or are relatively inexperienced at drafting public facing text, it is perhaps worth consulting the petitions section of the Senedd website. There you can find not only examples of successful petitions, but also the latest rules for submission, laid out in an easy to follow fashion.

The petitions team at the Senedd is also happy to provide advice about the wording of a petition, particularly about whether or not a petition is admissible. However, it's important that the petition is in your own words so that it properly reflects what you would like the petition to achieve.

The Petitions Committee

When a petition has reached 50 signatures or has been submitted by an organisation, it can then be considered by the Petitions Committee of the Senedd. This committee usually meets fortnightly and is generally composed of four or five Members, all of whom have an active interest in external engagement.

The committee cannot itself take any direct action to implement what a petition calls for, or overrule decisions made by the Welsh Government or other public bodies. However, the committee can hold the government and other decision makers to account, seek information from them and give petitioners the opportunity to make their case directly to them as Members of the Senedd. When a petition is received, the actions the committee might take include:

Seek further information from the Welsh Government, other decision makers or organisations that may have a view on, or interest in, the petition – for example, professional bodies, local authorities, health boards, trade unions or community groups.

- Seek further information from the petitioners themselves.
- Invite petitioners, the Welsh Government and others, to attend a meeting of the Petitions Committee to answer questions about the petition and the issues it raises.
- Undertake external visits to gather evidence (though this is rarely used).
- Ask another committee of the Senedd to look at the petition as part of its work programme.

There are two, even more extensive, activities that the Petitions Committee can undertake. One is to conduct a short inquiry into the issue, bringing in some of the elements listed above. The other is to seek time for a debate on the issue at a full Plenary meeting of the Senedd, something the committee will automatically consider for any petition which gathers more than 5,000 signatures, and it need not automatically decide to rule this option in or out while a petition is live. For example, a petition submitted in January 2018 on access to the medicine Orkambi for Cystic Fibrosis sufferers received 5,717 signatures, but the investigation did not conclude for almost two years until the Welsh Government and the manufacturer reached agreement. Throughout this period the Petitions Committee asserted gentle pressure.

In respect of either taking additional evidence from other professional bodies or external organisations, or conducting a full inquiry, there is nothing to stop you contacting the partner organisations in question to talk through with them what you are trying to achieve, and why it is so important. Influencing is, of course, not solely something that is done with politicians.

When the Petitions Committee is satisfied it can do no more with a petition, it formally resolves to close the petition.

All of this should emphasise to you also that a petition should be more than just words. You may well need a strong evidence base to back it up, such as credible evidence and an example of best practice.

Unlike most other Senedd business, petitions under scrutiny by the Petitions Committee can be handed on the next Senedd after an election by means of a report. In February 2019, almost three years into the Fifth Senedd, for example, there were still nine 'live' petitions referred on from the Fourth Senedd that had not been formally closed. This illustrates the length of time that a petition can sometimes sit in the process.

In total, at the start of February 2019, the Petitions Committee had 98 'live' petitions, which demonstrates the extent to which the mechanism is being used. It also illustrates, yet again, the need to make a petition stand out. The following table groups all the active petitions at that particular point in terms of policy area, showing the range of topics that had reached the threshold and qualified for active consideration by the Petitions Committee.

Animal welfare	• CCTV in Slaughterhouses • Slaughter Practices • Support for the Control of Dogs (Wales) Bill • End the Exotic Pet Trade in Wales • Say 'NO' to pheasant shooting on Welsh public land • Ban the USE of LARSEN TRAPS (Multi Corvid Traps) • Control Rapidly Expanding Intensive Poultry Industry In Wales • Ban the sale of puppies by pet shops and all commercial 3rd party dealers in Wales (Lucy's Law) • Introduce a licence to manage land for game bird shooting in an attempt to end raptor persecution.	9
Education	• Ensure schools exercise their statutory powers under regulation 7 of The Education (Pupil Registration) (Wales) Regulations 2010 without interference or bias • Asbestos in Schools • Allow Children in Wales to Have a Family Holiday During Term Time • School Buses for School Children • Keeping Current Guidelines for Religious Assemblies	21

	• Remove the Obligation on Schools to Hold Acts of Religious Worship • Review support for asylum seekers accessing further education • Remove the compulsory aspect of Welsh Baccalaureate • Protecting Class Sizes in Design and Technology Classrooms and Workshops • Ensuring Equality of Curriculum for Welsh Medium Schools e.g. GCSE Psychology • Welsh should not be compulsory for children with dyslexia and special needs • Review and change the guidance for attendance awards in Welsh schools • Fair Deal For Supply Teachers • We need Welsh Government funding for play!! • Reintroduce educational support funding for MEAS and the TES to local authorities • All Schools Should be Welsh Medium and Teach Welsh History • To Amend the School Admissions Code Relating to Summer-Born Children • Presumption in favour of rural schools • Let Welsh Students have the opportunity to choose the best study option for them • Make political education a compulsory element of the new national curriculum • Make Curriculum for Life Lessons Compulsory	
Environment & Energy	• Unconventional Oil and Gas Planning Applications • For Single Use Items: Introduce a Deposit Return System for Drink Containers and Make Fast Food Containers and Utensils Compostable • Give Welsh Fishing Clubs and Salmon and Sea Trout a Chance • Proposed New Fishing Bylaws and failings of NRW • Our natural world is being poisoned by single use plastics...it's time to introduce a tax! • Save the trees and ground in Roath Mill and Roath Brook Gardens before it's too late • Adopt WHO guidelines for air pollution into Welsh law and introduce a new Clean Air Act for Wales • Green Energy for the Wellbeing of Future Generations in Wales • Protect children's lungs from harmful pollution whilst at school	15

	• Ban plastic straws (when drinking milk) in our schools • Ban Single Use Plastic Items in Wales • All New Builds In Wales To Have Solar Panels • Save our Countryside - Revise TAN 1 • Protect the Razor Clams on Llanfairfechan Beach • Create water fountains in the centre of cities and towns to eliminate plastic waste	
Equalities	• To improve access to Education and services in British Sign Language • Close the Gap for deaf pupils in Wales • Lack of Support for Children with Disabilities at Crisis • Reconsider the closure of the Welsh Independent Living Grant and support disabled people to live independently • Recognition of Parental Alienation • Urgent Appeal for a Welsh Veterans Commissioner for the Health & Wellbeing of Wounded, Injured, Sick and Homeless veterans • Male domestic violence victim support services to be independently run & funded • We call for all premises in Wales to be awarded an Access Certificate number similar to the Food Hygiene Certificate • Provide Child Houses in Wales for Victims of Child Sexual Abuse • Make Learning Disability training mandatory for hospital staff • Gender Pay Gap Reporting	11
Health	• Child and Adolescent Eating Disorder Service • Eating Disorder Unit in Wales • To Make Mental Health Services More Accessible • Unacceptable Waiting Times for NHS patients in A & E Wrecsam/Wrexham Maelor Hospital. • Rights to Primary Health Care in Welsh • Better Mental Health Services for Adults • Ensure access to the cystic fibrosis medicine, Orkambi, as a matter of urgency • Causing Nuisance or Disturbance on NHS Premises • Prescription drug dependence and withdrawal - recognition and support	16

	• End the unfairness and discrimination in the financial support for victims of the contaminated blood scandals who were infected in Wales • Specialist prosthetics for child amputees • Implement the NICE guidelines for Borderline Personality Disorder • Pembrokeshire says NO!! To the closure of Withybush A&E! • All men in Wales should have access through the NHS to the best possible diagnostic tests for prostate cancer • Create a National Task Force for Children's Mental Health • Save our Hospital at Prince Philip Llanelli	
Local Government & Community	• Establish Proportional Representation Voting System for Welsh Local Council Elections. • Establish Statutory Public Rights of Access to Land and Water for Recreational and Other Purposes • Port Talbot Community Against the Super Prison • Hi speed broadband to Llangenny village • End Conflict of Interest in Local Authority Constitution • Immediate review of the Neath Port Talbot LDP • More Third party rights in planning appeals • Give young people a voice when commissioning local services in Wales • Fair Funding for Neath Port Talbot County Borough Council and all other Local Authorities	9
Transport	• A Roundabout for the A477/A4075 Junction • Re-open the Cwmcarn Forest Drive at Easter 2018 • Public Petition for the Dinas Powys By-Pass • Put an end to the Cross Border and Sub-contracting Taxi Licensing loophole • Pass Wide and Slow Wales • Roads surrounding Trago Mills/ Cyfartha Retail Park • Allow Free Movement of Taxi Drivers to Carry Out Private Hire Work Anywhere in Wales • Newtown Brimmon Oak Bypass • Improve rail services for Chepstow • Include the alternative 3rd Menai Crossing proposal 'Pont Bendigeidfran' in the formal assessment process • Support the M4 Relief Road Black Route	14

	• No to any Closure of Junction 41 • Remove time restrictions on the layby to the east of Crickhowell • Protect the Gwent Levels and stop the proposed M4 motorway	
Other	• Introducing a Register of Lobbyists in Wales • Small Business Rates Relief Review • Fire Sprinklers are for life, not a fast buck!	3

From this list you will see the prominence of certain types of issue. Unremarkably, education and health concerns seem particularly favoured, but there is also a strong showing from transport and environmental issues. Perhaps unexpectedly, animal welfare also features prominently, commanding some 10% of the total. Of course, you are not confined by any of these topic areas, but it offers a flavour of the balance between local and national concerns, and the type of matters that are raised through the petitions system.

Possible petition outcomes

The petitions process can result in a range of possible outcomes, all of which could be of benefit to your campaign and your organisation. The highest ranking impact would be to bring about a change in Welsh Government policy. This sort of outcome is rare but can happen: the decision to bring in a levy on plastic bags was directly related to a petition considered in 2007-08 by the Petitions Committee.

Most petitions are a good vehicle to raise publicity for, and awareness of, an issue. Organisations supporting a petition will often make the most not just of the media opportunity of submitting the petition, but also offer a periodic commentary as it passes through different stages of consideration by the Petitions Committee. This might well also include the point at which a petition is formally closed.

Another good outcome would be for a petition to be referred, and this could then prompt a Senedd Committee to hold an inquiry on the issue. This was the case with a Kidney Wales petition on organ donation in 2007, which led to a policy review on the Health and Social Services Committee. The Petitions Committee more recently also produced an inquiry report on the issue of type one diabetes in children, triggered by a petition with 2,570 signatures.

Some petitions, as indicated, can lead to a debate in the Senedd, and you do not necessarily have had to hit the 5,000 signatories mark for this to happen. For example, a petition on access to public transport with just 97 signatures led to both a committee inquiry and a subsequent debate in Plenary time. Most strikingly, a petition on Access to Education and Services in British Sign Language, first introduced in the Fourth Senedd, led to a full scale debate in the Senedd in February 2019, some four years after it had originally been introduced. This is a very good example of where patience pays off!

Petitions can also influence the development of new legislation. A very good example of this would be the petition on banning wild animals in circuses, which gathered 6,398 signatures and also triggered a debate on the floor of the Senedd and an undertaking to introduce legislation on the matter.

Finally, petitions can prompt individual Senedd Members to take further action themselves. They might consider asking questions of the Welsh Government or seeking time to debate an issue in the Senedd, or offer a suggestion for the Members Ballot process described in Chapter 11.

All of these outcomes should stress to you that there are a wide variety of ways in which a petition can be dealt with and a range of ways in which it can influence things. Therefore, when submitting a petition it might be beneficial to state precisely in the text what you want the outcome to be. This will then help guide the Petitions Committee in its deliberations on the substance of a petition, as they will be keen to take on board the petitioner's desired outcome as they map out what to do with that petition.

In conclusion, the range and quality of outcomes from a petition does indeed make it an attractive option for external organisations to make their voice heard and to spotlight issues which would struggle to come to the fore otherwise.

TOP TIP: Maximise any petition you submit by collecting signatures before submission and then perhaps leaving it as an active e-petition to gather more names. If you choose this route, then make sure you keep campaigning to gather more signatures and add to the momentum. A half baked petition which doesn't meet the relatively modest criteria for consideration is not really worth the effort in the first place.

17

Cross-Party Groups

An informal and non policy-making part of the functioning of the Senedd are Cross-Party Groups (CPGs). They are not formal Senedd Committees, have no formal role in policy development and should not attempt to replicate the functional areas covered by Senedd Committees. Nor do they have any of the powers of a Senedd Committee. For example, they cannot summon witnesses or Ministers to attend meetings or to provide documentation, and they cannot use the Senedd logo or branding.

Further, CPGs are quite far down the Senedd pecking order. They do not take precedence over formal Senedd business and so will have access to the Senedd's meetings facilities only subject to availability.

In 2013, the Senedd resolved to introduce new rules for the operation of CPGs, following an inquiry by the Standards of Conduct Committee. They came into force on 23 September 2013, requiring existing Senedd CPGs to re-register, and have influenced the way all CPGs have operated since to ensure there is openness and transparency in the way that groups operate.

Organisation and administration of CPGs

CPGs can be established by Members in respect of any subject area relevant to the Senedd, and a group must include Members from a minimum of three political parties represented within the Senedd.

All CPGs much elect a Chair and a Secretary, and the Chair has to be a Member of the Senedd. The Secretary of the CPG, however, may be a Member of the Senedd, one of their support staff, or an individual from outside the Senedd. Very often, the Secretary is an individual from outside the Senedd, however, if this is the case, that person cannot act without the prior approval of the Chair of the CPG, and all notices, correspondence, documentation and other arrangements relating to the activities of the CPG must be issued in the name of the Chair. The Chair of the CPG is always responsible for ensuring that the group complies with the rules on use of Senedd facilities and resources. Indeed, outside organisations and individuals associated with CPGs are specifically not entitled to use the Senedd's resources.

The Chair of any CPG must also call an Annual General Meeting (AGM) of the group every 12 months, at which the group must nominate and vote for office holders. The election of office holders must take place formally at the AGM even if office holders have already been appointed at a recent meeting.

General registered members of the CPGs may also include members from outside the Senedd, but this is at the discretion of the group, and all Senedd Members and all external organisations registered as members of a CPG are then entitled to attend a meeting, along with other invitees. Most CPGs tend to meet once a term, but the group will decide its own frequency of meetings and this may increase if there is relevant legislation or policy passing through the Senedd.

It is generally understood that CPGs can be a particularly effective tool to scrutinise the work of the Welsh Government, especially the implementation of delivery plans, at a national and local level. In order to do this, however, there needs to be both a robust secretariat and an effective Chair in place to drive work forward. Both of these roles are crucial and together can act as the driver of the group, so it is important to get people with the right level of expertise and commitment – without too many personal agendas – in order to fulfil these roles.

As a general rule of thumb, the work of being the secretariat of a CPG is no more than a couple of days a month, though there will be inevitably be busy and quiet periods. Work for the secretariat includes booking the room, creating a list of attendees, liaising with the Chair, writing briefings, inviting speakers, then after the meeting, writing and sharing the minutes. Some external secretariats do less than this, as the burden is carried by an active Chair who leads on the agenda of the group and the focus is very much on what the Chair wants it to be. In such circumstances, the role of the secretariat might be to just turn up and pay for the catering. Some, however, do substantially more, with previous examples of CPGs holding mini conferences for over a hundred people or undertaking outreach work in different parts of Wales.

Range and extent of CPGs

In October 2014, my organisation surveyed a cross section of 15 Senedd Members (about a third of the eligible total) to see how they engaged with CPGs and to determine which they were members of. The figures of membership are as follows:[1]

0	1-3	4-6	7-9	10+
2	2	6	1	3

As of January 2019, there are 68 different CPGs in existence. This compares with a snapshot of 53 back in October 2014. It is perhaps worth breaking the existing CPGs down in terms of subject matter, displayed by the broad topic area they most closely cover:

Broad topic area	Group
Health, Social Care & Sport	1. Asbestos 2. Autism 3. Boxing 4. Cancer 5. Coeliac Disease & Dermatitis Herpetiformis 6. Cricket 7. Deaf Issues 8. Dementia 9. Diabetes 10. Eating Disorders 11. Haemophilia and Contaminated Blood 12. Hospices and Palliative Care 13. Medical Research 14. Mental Health 15. Muscular Dystrophy 16. Neurological Conditions 17. Nursing and Midwifery. 18. Sepsis 19. Skin 20. Smoking and Health 21. Stroke 22. Wales Air Ambulance 23. Vision

---

1   Positif Politics, 2014.

Economy, Transport & Skills	1. Active Travel Act 2. Co-operatives & Mutuals 3. Construction 4. Public and Commercial Services (PCS) Union 5. Small and Medium Sized Enterprises 6. Small Shops 7. Steel 8. STEM 9. Technology and Innovation 10. Tourism 11. Transport 12. Waterways
Local Government, Communities, Housing & Equalities	1. Disability 2. Faith 3. Gypsies and Travellers 4. Housing 5. Human Rights 6. Human Trafficking in Wales 7. Industrial Communities 8. Older People 9. Policing 10. Problem Gambling 11. Violence against Women and Children 12. Women
Environment, Sustainability & Food	1. Beer & Pubs 2. Biodiversity 3. Conservation and Shooting 4. Fuel Poverty and Energy Efficiency 5. Food 6. Rural Affairs 7. Sustainable Energy 8. Woodlands, Forestry and Timber
Education, Young People & Children	1. Children & Young People 2. Further Education (FE) and Future Skills 3. Looked After Children 4. Preventing Child Sexual Abuse 5. Universities
External Affairs & International	1. The Middle East 2. Wales International

Culture & Communications	1. Arts & Health
	2. Welsh Language
Other	1. Armed Forces & Cadets
	2. Funerals and Bereavement
	3. Law
	4. North Wales

This table shows the significant range of issues that can be taken forward. You will notice that not all topics fit easily into the seven Subject Committee's fields of operation. Indeed, you may also disagree with some of the classifications used, especially in relation to some added to the Local Government, Communities, Housing & Equalities, remits which are often broad. That disagreement is, however, not really important. What is important is not only the range of CPGs which exist but also the extent to which a number of them are so broad as to impact on a number of policy areas. Indeed, you can see from this list how some groups are very broad, while others are extremely focused in their work. There is no set rule on how narrow or broad a remit should be.

There is also an element of churn in the number of CPGs as, during every Senedd, new groups are established and other closed. This can happen directly as a consequence of member disenchantment when a CPG is deemed to have lost vision and purpose, or wasn't focussed on a specific goal and therefore the politician makes the decision their time could be better spent elsewhere. A CPG that isn't well supported and seems to be going round in circles, not achieving anything, can harm the reputation of the organisation and individual that supports the group as secretariat. There is no point in calling a CPG meeting for the sake of it, keeping a moribund CPG going, or likewise establishing a CPG without a clear objective.

During the first half of the Fifth Senedd (2016-18), four CPGs were closed down (Circuit of Wales, Cross Border Issues, Fathers and Fatherhood, and Welsh Food and Drink); while both Biodiversity and Arts and Health closed then reopened with new Chairs. Sometimes well established groups, such as those on Healthy Living or Kidney Disease, both of which made a significant impact in the Third Senedd, come to a natural end when key supporters or key organisations move on. There is nothing permanent about any CPG.

Which CPGs should your organisation join?

The first step in answering this question must surely be examining the existing CPGs, which are listed in the Senedd Members to Chair section of the Senedd website. Depending on the remit of your organisation, there will be a variety of groups that might appeal or have relevance.

You will need to go through a process of internal examination not just to relevance, but also in terms of the resources you wish to commit. If your strategy is to simply maintain a favourable profile, the association of your organisation with the CPG, by being a member and attending its meetings is probably sufficient to project the correct message, particularly if resources are scarce. A deeper and more active participation and engagement, if resources allowed, could enhance your organisation's standing and perception amongst elected Members, their staff, and the Senedd's staff. This favourable perception could be further developed by your organisation's membership and involvement with more than one CPG, although the level of engagement within them may need to be varied to avoid becoming overstretched.

Of course, there is always the option to create a new CPG too, providing you can find a Senedd Member to Chair, and Members of two other parties to support the group's establishment. This might be a necessary avenue to deal with a policy area not covered elsewhere, or pertaining to a new piece of legislation or a hoped for piece of legislation. There are obviously clear advantages in setting up a new CPG since you would get a sense of ownership from it and be able to extend the influence and agenda of your organisation. This is particularly true if you end up acting as the secretariat of the new group.

However, establishing a new group could prove to be harder to achieve than you imagine, since Members' time is already stretched between existing CPGs as well as the extensive rigours of Senedd business. Indeed, there are strong examples of where external organisations have been advised not to do so and to instead work within the confines on an existing broad based CPG instead.

Opportunities presented by CPGs

So, why are some CPGs created and not others? We also tested this in the same 2014 research and found a variety of responses from elected

Members which kept emphasising certain aspects of why CPGs are created:

- CPGs are set up for a reason and mainly for publicity or because Members feel not enough is being done on a certain issue.
- Highlight issues of importance to constituents which may not otherwise get appropriate attention.
- Identify areas where there are gaps in policy and meet on a cross-party basis and influence forthcoming legislation and then the implementation.
- To ensure that Members are aware of certain relevant issues.
- A chance to highlight causes
- An opportunity to input into legislation and discuss matters with the Ministers and officials in an unofficial setting, often adhering to Chatham House rules
- An opportunity to raise the profile of a particular area and to discuss on a cross-party basis, free of the whip.

In essence, done well, CPGs look at the development and implementation of policy, are a good opportunity to exert influence on the Welsh Government, and hold it or other service deliverers on its behalf to account.

The opportunities presented by CPGs are often proportional to the effort you are prepared to commit to them. Naturally, being the secretariat offers the greatest level of input but it is also true that with a group which is well established and has a wide range of regular stakeholder input, such as the CPG on cancer, that every participating charity tends to get something out of it. In that example, the CPG has a major benefit of bringing people together and offer a forum for discussion. The focus is as much on joint dialogue within the sector as it is on attracting Senedd Members.

An important facet to bear in mind – which goes back to the point on establishing a new CPG – is the scarcity of time Members have available for CPGs. Most CPG meetings will only attract around three or four elected Members, including the Chair, some of whom may just drop in. The Chair is vital in ensuring other Members turn up, and some target their colleagues with personalised invitations that emphasise relevant subject matter or speakers. Others may send their researchers along, which should also be seen as a positive.

A self evident truth is that CPGs which make themselves relevant tend to have the highest impact. Hot topics come, and hot topics go, often linked to legislation, such as the now defunct Kidney Disease CPG which had its heyday during the passionate debate surrounding the organ donation legislation. Further, the Childhood Sexuality – Sexualisation and Equality CPG attracted a high participation amongst Members when the *Children are Unbeatable* report into smacking children was a big news agenda. Since then, however, as the issue fell off the agenda, the interest and participation of elected Members has tended to wax and wane. This particular CPG did, though, break notable new ground when its report, funded by NSPCC and the Children's Commissioner and undertaken by Cardiff University, was submitted through the CPG itself into the Senedd Subject Committee scrutinising the Domestic Abuse Bill in 2013. Indeed, it is surprising how few CPGs over the years have actually commissioned and launched reports.

A CPG that also scrutinises the work of the Government, be it delivery plans or legislation, and offer input makes itself relevant. Some Chairs consult the forward work programmes of Senedd Committees for matters of relevance, in the hope it will attract attention and impact. Other CPGs have drawn on the delivery plans of the Welsh Government or local health boards to give their deliberations specific focus. This can be especially helpful if officials as well as elected Members are invited to listen to the discussion at CPGs, almost as part of interactive consultation. Some health charities will point to the value they have gained from involving health board chairs or officers in their deliberations too. After all, as is a constant theme in this volume, not everything comes down to the Welsh Government.

There are also examples of CPGs making an impact thanks to the Chair raising the matter as a Short Debate, a device discussed and examined earlier.

External members of CPGs have also banded together during the passage of legislation or the making of policy in the Senedd to write joint briefings, using the CPG approach to emphasise the idea of a coalition of supporters. However, during our 2014 research, one participant from a third sector organisation related to health urged caution at a loose coalition that would not always follow the same line:

'We had a relevant Bill in process and senior civil servants appeared before the CPG, however it backfired slightly as not all members were on message and an aggressive tone was taken, which left the civil servants shell-shocked.'[2]

The value of giving presentations to CPGs is also high. Every CPG will normally include presentation slots on its agenda to give the meeting a focus. These tend to be presentations of no more than ten minutes or so and, delivered well, can significantly enhance the status of your organisation. The golden rule is to ensure your speaker is a renowned leader in their field with a credible understanding of the context within which the CPG is operating, whose expertise is recognised by others in the CPG, and who can respond to challenging questions – whether theoretical or from a service delivery perspective – with ease.

It is indeed valuable to try and capture service user perspective in CPGs. Personal stories bring issues to life, as we explore elsewhere in this guide, but impact is best achieved if the person giving evidence has a good understanding, not just of the topic but also of the nature and culture of the specific CPG. Another respondent stressed this point to our work in 2014, who said that though their CPG was well attended by their stakeholder or service user members, this often meant that discussions were focussed on local issues or a specific family member. Finding a balance is crucial.

Indeed, in respect of the operation of CPGs and inputting into them, finding the balance is the key to a successful interaction. This is as much about balancing your energy and expectations as any other aspect of their operation.

TOP TIP: The effectiveness of cross party groups is often directly related to its ability to generate clear outcomes and actions. CPGs that work best are generally ones that have worked out a way to take their outcomes and actions into the political mainstream.

---

2   Positif Politics, private client research, 2014.

18

Events at the Senedd

The Senedd building is an open public space which contains a variety of rooms that can be booked for external events, and the Senedd estate has been designed to act in a public facing way, with a variety of opportunities and spaces that are available to be booked. There is no charge for space, but you will be expected to use the Senedd caterers and follow the rules.

There are basically three buildings on the Senedd estate which are all close to one another, with the first two being connected by a corridor accessible to Members and staff. The most well known, the Senedd building itself, was opened first in 2005. It houses the Chamber where the Plenary meetings take place, plus committee rooms and a Media Briefing Room. It is the focal point of politics in Wales. The building has been designed in an environmentally friendly way, as is described on the Senedd's website:

> 'It is also a sustainable building, built of traditional Welsh materials such as slate and Welsh oak and other sustainable materials. It also sustainable in the way it is heated; for example, the earth exchange system uses heat from the bottom of the old dock, on which the Senedd stands, before it became the area which is now Cardiff Bay. This is what this building represents. It represents sustainability, it represents democracy but it's more than that too – it is the symbol of the new nation that Wales has become.'[1]

Tŷ Hywel is a redbrick 1980s building in which the Members and the Welsh Government have offices. It contains a small number of rooms

---

1   www.assembly.wales

that can be hired for external events, including some small dining rooms. Also red-brick, the Pierhead building predates anything else around it, and is also part of the Senedd estate. It contains a large room which can host conferences and debates, and some smaller rooms upstairs that can also be hired for different events. You can take a virtual tour of the Senedd estate on the Senedd website in order to become more familiar with the buildings before you actually visit.

Despite this seeming abundance of spaces, it is not always easy to get space on the Senedd estate. Indeed, for some of the most highly desirable spaces (such as the main room in the Pierhead or the Oriel or Neuadd in the Senedd building) you normally have to book months in advance, although you should also be aware that the current rules say all bookings can only be made six months in advance. The Senedd has an events team which can work with you in terms of booking and staging, or you can also engage a company that specialises in Senedd events. The Senedd's event team will normally insist on a site visit usually about six weeks before an event takes place.

Every formal event requires a Member to sponsor it, and also will need an invitation that has to be bilingual and approved by a member of the events team. No event will be permitted if it is deemed offensive or if it raises money for a private or commercial cause, or if it is an overtly party political event. Also, your organisation, or the organisation you represent, cannot hold an Annual General Meeting on the Senedd estate. Also, Members are limited in the number of events they are able to sponsor, so this is another factor which impacts on event booking. Further, the sponsoring Member (or a member of their staff) is required to be at the event; and you should consider that at the event the sponsoring Member usually gives the words of welcome.

Different Senedd estate events can happen at different times of the day when the Senedd is sitting, and if you are planning to stage an exhibition, these are often done over a number of days. Otherwise you are able to hire different spaces for shorter time periods. You will need to make a judgement call over the type of event which you want to stage, compared to the spaces that are available.

The basic outline of building opening hours during Senedd term time is as follows:

Day	Senedd	Tŷ Hywel	Pierhead
Monday	8am – end of business	8am – end of business	9.30am – 4.30pm
Tuesday	8am – end of business	8am – end of business	9.30am – 4.30pm
Wednesday	8am – end of business	8am – end of business	9.30am – 4.30pm
Thursday	8am – end of business	8am – end of business	9.30am – 4.30pm
Friday	8am – 4.30pm	8am – 4.30pm	9.30am – 4.30pm

By agreement, however, you can stage events in the Senedd outside these hours. The Pierhead, for example, is open to the general public during these hours but can also accommodate breakfast meetings or evening receptions by agreement. These are set times for events in the Senedd, but it is possible to pay for extra hours for some evening events such as dinners, but this is done at the Senedd's discretion.

Other impacting factors on your choice of venue might include accessibility. For events in Tŷ Hywel, for example, the downstairs rooms are public but for the dining rooms on level 1 you and other external attendees will need to be escorted at all times, for which the sponsoring Member's office will be responsible. For events happening outside business hours, and for events in the dining rooms of Tŷ Hywel, a list of all external guests and VIPs will need to be given to the sponsoring Member's office.

Finally, for events that are held in the public areas, the invitation has to go to all 60 Members of the Senedd. The exception would be dinner events or ones that are behind the security measures identified above.

Types of event and suggestions for location

You can stage different types of event in the Senedd and different rooms lend themselves to different sorts of event.

Event type	Suggested space	General remarks
Formal dinner	Dining room in Tŷ Hywel	These spaces are close to the kitchens and can accommodate 10-12 people. They are good for intimate, targeted discussions and Members will normally attend for the entire duration, which should probably be about an hour during which you could theme discussions over every course.
Reception or Exhibition / Showcase display	Neuadd / Oriel / Pierhead	These three options are large spaces that work best when they are busy. They contain enough space for a range of stalls and also a staging area which can be used as a focal point for any event.
Lecture	Neuadd / Pierhead/ Conference Rooms C&D	Any of these spaces are big enough to accommodate a formal lecture. The staging available in the Neuadd or the Pierhead is a particular strength for these views.
Factual space or Cross-Party Group	Media Briefing Room / Conference Rooms C&D	The media briefing room is the preferred suggestion as it contains display screens that can be linked up to an IT presentation.
Formal drops in	Any space	Can provide an opportunity for interaction and photographs with attendees.

An informal use of the Senedd estate is the café in the Oriel. You can meet Members for one-to-ones here, perhaps as part of a series of meetings, and some organisations use this space for drop-in sessions with Members. Mass drop-ins usually work best 10am to 2pm on either a Tuesday or a Wednesday. They involve no room booking administration and the only costs would be the price of teas and coffees. These are often excellent vehicles for increasing profile and engaging with Members and their staff on their terms and at their convenience, and the most successful drop-in meetings always have a clear focus and a topical area to discuss. Sometimes the publication of a new report is a good hook.

A checklist for an event

If you're running an event in the Senedd, here is a handy ten-point list of things to bear in mind:

	Event Checklist
1	Choose the right venue – use the advice in the earlier grid.
2	Liaising with Senedd staff on set-up of event – they offer expertise and assistance.
3	Make your event stand out – be creative and eye catching, you will be competing with others for attention and attendance during the same slot.
4	Organise catering – especially if the event falls over lunch-time or after Plenary.
5	Target your audience – don't be afraid to remind Members it is on, including a follow-up to non-respondees on the day of the event. Senedd research staff can also attend as well as Members and can often be really useful contacts.
6	What's in it for them? Think is those terms when you are structuring your invitation.
7	Constituents are the best magnet – if you have constituents coming, tell the Members so that they make an extra special effort to attend.
8	Use a photographer – capture the event for posterity and marketing.
9	Senedd business provides other hooks – can someone plug your event in some way during Plenary before it happens?
10	Media hooks – can you get something in the press before the event happens?

Following up an event

As we will also discuss in Chapter 19, well planned follow-up activity is crucial in maximizing the potential of an event. All too often organisations behave like an event is not part of a sequence of public affairs activity, but a good, high impact, high quality event is not just about the build up, it is about the follow-up – make sure you utilise it to your broader agenda and integrate it properly into your public affairs strategy. It should be a key part of your strategy, but also lead on to other things. While the event is fresh in your mind, make an action list and follow it up.

It is often worth pulling some sort of post-event briefing which you can circulate to key attendees to reiterate your messages. This will also give you the opportunity to thank your attendees, especially the sponsor. You can also provide photographs and a quote for the attendees to use in any local press work. This document can also utilise your contact information or even provide localised data, if such data is available to you.

> **TOP TIP: The key point to your approach throughout staging a successful event should be engaging with Members to actually get them to do things – always be clear how they can help and what they can do to assist you and promote your cause.**

19

Party Conferences

A focal point of the political year are the two party conference seasons. Maintaining a strategic or significant presence at the party conferences is therefore incredibly important for your general public affairs work. For some organisations, especially if public affairs is just a small part of what they do, party conference engagement can be a vital vehicle for engagement. They might also prompt some senior staff members, such as chief executives or UK-wide policy officers, to engage with Welsh public affairs opportunities in a way that they do not do for the rest of the year.

Party conferences occur on a set pattern in Wales but vary slightly between parties as illustrated the table below:

Party	Spring	Autumn
Labour	Full main conference usually from Friday night until Sunday afternoon	No activity
Conservatives	Full main conference covering a Friday and Saturday only	Policy forums in North and South Wales, sometimes offering limited opportunities for external engagement
Plaid Cymru	Two day conference covering a Friday and Saturday only	Main conference, running from Friday through to Sunday (though final day is often internal only)
Lib Dems	Full main conference usually from Friday afternoon until Sunday afternoon	Smaller conference, usually Saturday through to Sunday
UKIP / Brexit Party	No Wales-specific conferences are currently held	

This does not mean that there are no similarities between parties. A general convention exists, though, that most parties vary their conference locations, usually alternating between north/mid Wales and south Wales (athough Labour does tend to go to Llandudno twice as much as any other location). This issue of location is not the only similarity between them. They tend to offer the same sort of engagement opportunities for external organisations. The bulk of this chapter examines the various forms in which that engagement takes place.

So, what do party conferences actually do? Broadly, they have evolved and are used primarily by parties to fulfil a series of actions: to bring parties together for political and social activity; to announce policy; to agree policy; to profile speakers including leaders and, in the run up to elections, candidates in target seats; to engage with the media in a positive way; and also, of use to you, to engage with external organisations in a positive way.

The extent to which these activities are done varies between political parties. For the Conservatives, their Welsh conference is a compact series of speeches interspersed with occasional fringe meetings and very few real debates are held. The focus is much more on UK Cabinet Ministers or front benchers than in other parties. A visit from the UK party leader is the focal point, especially if that person is also Prime Minister, and there is very much a rally feel in operation. In essence, the majority of the conference is geared to presentation, be that to delegates, to media or to the other opinion formers present.

In contrast, the Welsh Liberal Democrats and, to a slightly lesser extent, Plaid Cymru, focus their conference on policy deliberations. This aspect is discussed in more detail in Chapter 20, which deals with the manifesto compilation process.

The ability of a party to engage meaningfully with the media or with external organisations is also a variable factor. Without a doubt, parties in power are usually the most attractive to external forces, and this is clearly the case in terms of attendance numbers. This is not an absolute rule, however. Welsh Liberal Democrat conference sizes started to decline from 2011 onward and did not revive hugely even when Kirsty Williams entered Government as Education Minister in 2016. Further, the closer to a Welsh election, the higher the interest from these groups too. You can perceive the impact of these factors when you have visited a number of party conferences during a cycle.

Another difference between parties in Wales is that of style or tone. A wry observer attending all party conferences once summed it up as follows: 'In Wales, Labour is too powerful to speak to you unless they really have to. The Conservatives are quite welcoming but are suspicious unless they know you. The Liberal Democrats are really pleased you're there and will talk to you for ages, often for longer than you need. And Plaid Cymru are more interested in checking your leaflets are bilingual than for anything they might say.' Only visits to party conferences will illustrate the truth of this satirical overview – but it is meant tongue in cheek. Most external organisations get a great deal out of party conferences, otherwise they would not keep returning.

One of the reasons we keep coming back is that party conferences are usually quite enjoyable. You usually manage to get quite a lot out of them, sometimes proportional to what you put in. Not every organisation will always get a good response, but the general rule is that you usually manage to get something back in terms of engagement and influence. Some of that return will be geared toward the planning and commitment which you show to a party conference and the extent of your contacts there. The good news is that, generally, if you go year on year your web of contacts will increase as you get to know more people, elected politicians, party officials and key policy advocates.

Party conferences can, however, be an expensive business. It is often the case you don't have to just get an observer pass, but also pay for an exhibition stand, a fringe meeting, or dinner tickets before you even start to think about travel, hotel and subsistence expenses. Even a quite basic presence at four party conferences can easily mount up to almost £2,000 once all the core expenses are met. Many organisations therefore consider carefully how they wish to be represented at conferences, and whether they need to be at them all. This means some organisations sometimes opt out of conference seasons outside the election cycles; and other organisations only choose to be represented at the party conference or conferences which might be of most value to them.

An early action should be to reach out and make contact with the person organising each of the party conferences and ensure you're added to their mailing lists. This will allow you to be contacted as soon as the conference dates and venues are set out, and this offers an early input into the opportunities at party conferences. Even if you skip a year or a conference, once you are on the mailing list then you should usually receive ongoing information for future conferences and events. If you are negotiating sponsorship of a dinner or some significant event at a conference, it may be worth approaching the party with a view to negotiating a more reasonable financial package, but generally there is little to be gained from trying to haggle and you can often alienate parties. An exception would be if you are taking a range of opportunities with a single party, such as sponsorship alongside enhanced observer packages and an exhibition stall, where you are then able to exercise a degree of negotiation.

Another aspect to which you should pay proper attention is the security aspects of a conference. This will usually be particularly heightened if a UK Prime Minister is present. Some of us who have done political work for decades well remember the security arrangements surrounding a visit by Tony Blair to Labour's conference in Llandudno, which coincided with the bombing of Serbia by the UK armed forces. You will usually, nevertheless, be required to complete official registration forms for any party conference which you attend. This may require the submission of small passport sized photographs for use in the identification pass you will be issued with.

Options for engagement at party conferences

Once you have established which party conferences you should be represented at, and you have registered to attend, then give some thought to what exactly you want to do there. This will, to a large extent, be influenced by the resources you have at your disposal, but will also be shaped to a very great extent by what you are trying to achieve. Ultimately, being mercenary about it, you may well choose to engage much more heavily in the conferences running up to an election as a vehicle for influencing manifesto development. It may also depend on the extent to which you are working in a distinct policy area. For example, an educational organisation may play a much more active role with the Liberal Democrats during the period that Kirsty Williams holds the education ministry than it ordinarily would. Another big variable is the extent to which you actually have something to say or you just want to be present in order to support networking or tend to your existing political relationships.

Whatever you decide, make sure that as part of your general public affairs planning you communicate with your key contacts – as well as your key targets – letting them know you will be at conference and what activity you are planning to do there. Remember that some politicians, especially Ministers or party leaders, will be remarkably busy during conferences so therefore be realistic over who to engage with and how much time you can expect them to offer. The publication of the conference agenda, usually around a week before the conference opens, will enable you to do this is in a strategic and informed way. The context of the agenda will undoubtedly shape your activities at conference and can potentially lead you to rethink your engagement at a late stage. For example, you may not have planned to go to a conference but find that a key issue to your organisation has been prioritised and timetabled for debate. Of course, if this happens, then engaging before a conference can often be really important as the set piece debates may have already been arranged, and might not be debates in the 'two-sides' sense of the term.

The following table illustrates the main type of conference activities, and some strengths and weaknesses of approaches. As with other aspects of this book, it is subjective and party political conference organisers may well not agree with its content. You may use this book to decide that an exhibition stall is the right choice for you, only to find the organiser tries to persuade you to do a more expensive fringe option instead. Always bear in mind that as well as trying to help you, the conference organiser will also be trying to maximise revenue. They will rarely want you to take the cheaper option when planning any sort of activity at conferences.

Prices are deliberately omitted from this table because they tend to vary between parties but the indication of Low, Medium, High or Very High should tend to indicate the broad bracket you should expect to pay.

Engagement method	Strengths	Weaknesses
General observer Low	• Very low commitment option which allows you to attend and observe (including in the conference hall) but no more than that.	• Limited opportunity for interaction and none for more detailed information sharing.

	• Can work well if you just want to be seen or have a few strategic discussions with a small number of individuals.	• You can get a little lost when other organisations, perhaps competing in the same policy space, are undertaking more direct, prominent and focused engagement.
Special Observer Medium – attendee High – running a session	• Category of engagement particular to Labour which entitles you to attend a day of activities on the Saturday which often include discrete panel events or discussions on policy themes. • Special observers can, for additional sizeable fees, shape and set the agenda for those sessions. They can offer excellent opportunities to float policy directly with Ministers, special advisers and key opinion formers. • There is also usually a Special Observer lounge at Welsh party conferences.	• A more expensive option and one which might not suit every attending organisation. • You may find that the set agenda of Special Observer sessions is totally irrelevant to your organisation and therefore not of interest. • It can also take you out of the conference hall and the exhibition area for extended periods of time.
Dinner places/tables Low - single place Medium – whole table	• Attending a dinner is often the most relaxed and enjoyable part of a conference. If you attend solo then you can sometimes get a lot out of it, depending where you end up being sat and what your expectations are.	• Going as a solo attendee gives you little control over who you sit with, and this can end up as a bit of a lottery with variable results.

	• Taking a full table at a dinner gives you control over guests and if your targets are just a small number of politicians this can work well in terms of proving a forum for targeted engagement. • Sometimes tables work well if they are developed and managed thematically (health or education) or focused around a structured discussion, but this can be difficult when your table is just part of a bigger event. • If you take a full table, you usually get a thank you from the host (often the party leader).	• Conversely, the cost of a full dinner table can often be prohibitive. • Also filling a table of ten may end up being a real challenge if elected Members are in short supply or people end up dropping out. • The quality of dinner speakers can often vary considerably between political parties too
Sponsored dinners or drinks receptions High to Very High	• This approach is often costly but can get you noticed and can be a big boost to profile. • You will get a chance to make a speech to everyone attending the dinner and to meet a lot of new people, including some very senior ones. • It will also come with a chance to network with politicians of your choice and is usually the most expensive part of any conference, though usually some observer passes are thrown in.	• The cost will usually deter most organisations from pursuing this route. • Speeches also need good content if they are to be engaging: do it badly, or go seriously over time, and you are certain to be remembered by conference goers for years to come – and for the wrong reasons.

	• This option can be very time efficient: attending just for three or four hours really gets you noticed and, if planned properly, can tick all the boxes of your public affairs strategy.	
Exhibition spaces Medium	• Offers the most consistent form of engagement at any party conference. • Gives you an anchor space to reach out and connect with as many people as possible, often with photograph opportunities with key politicians and candidates. • Party leaders and spokesperson usually tour the exhibition hall at least once. • This option works well if you have good, eye catching material and messages, especially if you offer some sort of interactive element to get people to engage with you. • Exhibition stands usually come with observer passes, so this can help reduce the overall cost of attendance.	• Location, location, location is everything: every long-term stall holder will have good and bad stories about different conferences, and the location will usually feature in both. • Be prepared for your stall to be ignored if it is in the wrong place, often just a matter of luck. • The staffing commitment is usually quite strong too, with most organisations usually sending more than one person to staff a stall. • Factor in the cost of not just the stall but also any literature or materials you have to give away.

| Fringe meetings | • Fringes tend to be held in the same buildings as the main parts of conference, so they are much more mainstream and less 'fringe' than in their UK counterparts. The fringe guide is also officially published as part of the conference business, setting out the themes for debate and the hosting organisations.
• Hosting a fringe does give you the chance to set out a stall very clearly and, for an hour, to get a great deal of focus.
• Fringes work best when you have put the work into them to get the right politicians on panels, or to involve experts, or to present reports or data which are key catching and impactful.
• You can also boost attendance by using flyers or targeting potential audience attendees via email or social media.
• Timing is also an issue – middle of the day fringes usually attract a bigger audience than the ones at the start or the end of the day (and are sometimes priced differently for that reason). | • Can be particularly expensive, especially if the fringe meeting is catered (you will be expected to do this if it falls over lunchtime).
• The level of competition can also be fierce, especially if more than one is being held on the same topic area.
• You are also reliant on the quality not only of the speakers but also the quality of the speakers from the floor of the meeting. As fringes will generally be open to all delegates, many people will turn up just for the lunch or also may ask very uninformed questions or make very left field contributions from the floor. |
| High | | |

Sponsored debates High	• A feature of Plaid Cymru conferences where, for a fee, organisations can offer a topic for a debate of an hour and host a panel discussion on centre stage. This option only works if you either want to raise your profile or have something significant to contribute in policy terms. • It offers an excellent opportunity for engagement with key party spokespeople and general profile raising either for your brand or an issue which you wish to promote.	• Is usually too expensive an option for most organisations. It should also be avoided if you have policies and standpoints that are controversial to that political party, which will not be attracted to a heated debate either. • The quality of the event will depend not just on the speakers you provide, but the politicians available for the panel, and also the questions that might come from the floor (as with fringe meetings).

Follow-up actions

Engagement through conferences doesn't have to end when the conference finishes. When you get back, use online communications to thank the politicians who have engaged with you, especially if you have photographs. A good Twitter feed will demonstrate the public value of your conference engagement.

On a deeper level, you may have a number of action points to undertake in relation to supplying some of the people you have met with more information, or writing to them inviting them to visit your work or meet with you on a formal basis. The best public affairs professionals tend to capitalise on informal networking and turn it into something more meaningful and substantial for future working.

An effective follow-up cannot be stressed enough. It could be the 'make or break' that helps ensure that the considerable financial investment in attending a conference is rewarded with tangible progress with a campaign priority. Moreover, a successful campaign outcome that was enhanced by focused activities at a conference can be evidenced if conference-related spending is challenged within your organisation.

Another useful exercise to undertake at the end of each conference is to prepare a list of outcomes or outputs you have achieved, which might be broader than just follow-up actions. It might be worth writing this in such a way that it captures all the conferences over a given period, such as the intense spring conference season, in order to try and establish an overview of what you achieved. This can serve as a useful record for internal purposes and lead to you refining your presence or activities at future conferences.

> **TOP TIP:** In the run up to an election some of the cannier public affairs people use party conferences to make contact with the candidates most likely to get elected for the first time. This short cut to getting to know a politician can be helpful to working together in the future.

20

Manifesto Compilation

Once every five years, a new Senedd is elected and the parties that contest them do so on the basis of the manifestos they have constructed. While every party approaches this task in slightly different ways, the one thing that unites them all is their readiness to listen to outside influences and to engage meaningfully with civic society.

Of all the periods in the life of a public affairs professional, the year running up to a Senedd election can be both the busiest and the most rewarding. It is, of course, a challenging period, but get it right and you will reap the rewards for the following five years by seeing your priorities and ideas mainstreamed into the work of the party of government.

Politically savvy public affairs professionals pay a great deal of attention to the political backdrop in the few years running up to an election. There are usually a lot of political runes that can be interpreted to set the direction of travel for potential formal and informal coalitions from some way out from an election.

The manifesto compilation process

On assuming the office of First Minister for the third and final time in May 2016, former Labour leader Carwyn Jones AM promised the Welsh Parliament that his government had "No monopoly on good ideas". This was intended to reassure the other political parties, especially Plaid Cymru, that the Welsh Government was open to ideas in terms of how it governed, and of the policy and financial priorities of his administration. Whether this happened remains a matter of political conjecture.

For a lobbyist, however, it is has long been known that the political parties of Wales openly acknowledge they do not have that monopoly on good ideas. The 2017 and 2019 General Elections aside – when political parties compiled manifestos in record time without the trappings of external engagement, or just dusted down parts they had used two years earlier – most election periods are accompanied by the development of political manifestos that involve a great deal of external stakeholder input.

The process of manifesto compilation for external organisations tends to begin from about two years out from the date of the election. Some organisations leave it a lot closer to the day to begin which, although it can work, does leave a lot more to chance, especially if you are trying to seed big ideas – such as changing the rules on organ donation or abolishing the physical chastisement of children – then setting out the aims of the policy over a longer period has been shown to be necessary. Both of these big ideas were eventually legislated upon in the Senedd following the one in which they were first raised by organised campaigns, and raised within the Senedd itself. In essence, the first few years of work was about building momentum to make sure that parties committed in their manifestos to make such a change.

Just as the way that different external organisations will approach the manifesto compilation process in different ways, so too will the political parties. A general rule is that all of them will seek to engage externally in some way, though this will vary between parties. Labour, for example, will draw from its own internal policy forums and will take a weighted approach to evidence gathering, leaning particularly heavily on trade unions and the co-operative movement for evidence and input. These are integral components both of Welsh Labour and also of its policy development process.

In the Chapter 19 we discussed the role of party conferences in determining policy. Both Plaid Cymru and the Welsh Liberal Democrats set great store in the way policy motions passed by party members after conference debates will generally work their way into the manifestos they present. The same is also true, to a lesser extent, of Welsh Labour, which also respects conference resolutions, though the amount of policy created at its conference is far less than in the two other parties. The Conservatives are somewhat different since they focus their conferences virtually entirely on presentation as opposed to policy making. Being conscious of these differences in approach helps you to be better informed and better positioned for seeking to influence policy development and manifesto development as a whole.

Another key way in which parties approach policy development is the structures they develop to capture ideas and input. Welsh Labour has a full-time policy officer, and Plaid Cymru has a similar role. These are not currently mirrored in either the Conservatives or the Liberal Democrats (their policy development staff disappeared with the crash in their popularity and funding after their Westminster coalition with the Conservatives). Each party will also appoint a manifesto co-ordinator, usually an elected politician and usually either a rising star or a trusted team player at the heart of that political party. These officers or appointees will have the job of pulling an outline manifesto together, feeding back to their national executive committees, and steering a policy platform forward until it is published as a manifesto.

At a basic level, therefore, you must be sure of context in order to achieve maximum effect and this includes knowing how the manifestos of parties will be developed, who will undertake that, how they will go about it, and how they might be influenced. In short, a manifesto compilation process is best shaped by remembering the lessons from the first three chapters of this book.

Influencing the manifesto process

Since manifestos are influenced by external input and develop mechanisms to capture external perspectives, then it is perhaps not just a question of how to input and influence, but how to input and influence successfully. Here are ten suggestions of key factors that you might consider to help you frame your input effectively.

- **Informed:** You can learn a lot from what has gone before. Not only do parties tend to approach manifesto building in broadly the same way as they did at the previous election, but you can also see what they said on that occasion. The first point in developing your manifesto asks is to look at what the parties pledged the time before, and also what their spokespeople had said on that issue since then. Also, if you were not the person leading the manifesto input last time but you are now, try and talk to the person who did it last time. Information on the past equals context, and context once again can equal success.

- **Evidenced:** Don't lose sight of the fact that politicians and parties are good people wanting to make a difference. Just coming forward with an idea, no matter how eye catching, is not enough on its own. In 2007 Plaid Cymru's pledge to introduce free laptops for school children gained a lot of media interest. What was less clear was the potential benefit of such a move, which was not particularly well explained even though international studies on children and laptops were available. When Plaid Cymru entered the coalition, they compromised on the policy and agreed instead to a pilot scheme being rolled out in 2010-11. This was subsequently discontinued when the pilot showed that the £660,000 spent on the pilot had not delivered the promised improvements. This is a classic example of a policy lacking an evidence base which, even though it was briefly enacted, has subsequently disappeared without trace. Make sure you have a strong evidence base for any ideas that you are proposing. This can also be international evidence or examples from within other parts of the UK.

- **Costed:** Money matters. One of the first things party manifesto builders will think when they examine your suggestions, is how much will they cost? This can often be particularly challenging, but every party will want to enter the election with manifesto pledges that are costed and therefore more robust because the same party will want to set out in financial terms how much its policies will cost to implement. You may find it difficult to cost a potential policy, but the political parties will have to so, so you should help them and do this work yourselves to the best of your ability. On the same topic, a low cost but high return policy will often be seen as particularly attractive.

- **Contextualised:** No policy is produced in a vacuum. Whatever you are suggesting needs to be examined in terms of what the existing government policy and approach is. Maybe your ask isn't a new one at all, it is simply the implementation in a certain way which is new. This can often be the case where you are looking for local health boards or local authorities to do things differently (as discussed in more detail in Chapter 21).

- **Clear:** Structure your asks in a single document based on pledges accompanied by a description of benefit, cost and a description of potential outcomes. You might also want to put in the potential costs and outcomes of not doing something you suggest. The important point is to be extremely clear what you are asking for and how it might be implemented. Some organisations do this by means of producing manifestos of their own, others by releasing policy papers, and others simply by working to one or two pledges. There is no right or wrong way to do this providing that there is clarity in the approach taken.

- **Stratified:** A lot is made of stratification in this book, and this is also true of stratifying messages during manifesto compilation. That may sound counter intuitive to other suggestions, but it need not necessarily be. If you look at the content of party political manifestos you will find that there are significant amounts of overlap. I once took part in a political quiz where excerpts from different manifestos were read out and the teams had to try and identify the parties offering such policies. It was virtually impossible to do, since the content was so similar. Clearly some organisations had indeed managed to sell their ideas across the whole political spectrum, but such an approach is not always the best. Remember why manifestos are pulled together – they are supposed to be distinct offerings by political parties to the electorate. Think in those terms and you may choose to seed some ideas more actively with some parties more than others. After all, if you can provide them with a Unique Selling Point, it might be much more attractive than a more generic sell in.

- **Tonal:** Politics has its own language, but different political parties speak in their own dialects. How you express an idea can have a real impact on how different parties respond to it. Try relating anything you are trying to sell into a political party's policy processes to their overarching philosophies or the direction in which they are travelling. Strongly worded pledges that are politically aligned are a gamble: they can win you favour with some parties, while simultaneously alienating others.

- **Targeted:** Think back to the way in which different parties develop and build policies in different ways and apply the lessons of Chapter 3. Treat each party as a target for your public affairs asks and identify the people who are the gatekeepers to the manifestos being assembled. It is often worth beginning discussions at an early stage with these gatekeepers before your final asks are solidified and published.

- **Thematic:** Before presenting your final asks, also discuss with the gatekeepers the types of themes that are likely to emerge in their manifestos. You will see from reading previous examples that parties tend to group policies into themes. It will be helpful to them if you are able to tweak and shape your asks depending on the themes they are seeking to develop and elucidate.

- **Weighted:** Not every party stands an equal chance of forming the next government. In Wales, Labour has been part of every administration for 20 years, the Liberal Democrats have been part of two, Plaid Cymru has served in one, and the Conservatives have never been in power. Without, for a moment, suggesting this will never change, from a historical perspective there would obviously be more value in talking to Labour than any other party. You might therefore consider weighting your asks so they are more palatable to the party likely to be in power beyond the election, or spend more time targeting such parties in the hope of making it into the manifestos of those parties most likely to form a government. After all, in a coalition scenario, things that appear in multiple manifestos stand the most chance of making it into the programme of government. This suggestion may be controversial or be outside your organisation's *modus operandi*. Charities, for example, often have to work in a way that treats all parties equally and cannot distinguish between them.

Collaboration to achieve impact

Every other organisation in Welsh public life will probably be seeking to do exactly the same as you during an election period: to exert their influence. This can often create a remarkably crowded and noisy field, and obviously, not every policy initiative which you and others propose will be adopted and taken forward. In most cases, parties will just be looking for enough material to create a coherent and thematic manifesto rather than a more detailed programme. There are, of course, exceptions to this rule. This commentator remarked that the 2007 Welsh Liberal Democrat manifesto was so verbose and detailed it would have been un-implementable in a single Senedd, let alone if the Liberal Democrats had entered any sort of coalition.

Do not lose sight of the point made earlier about different parties saying the same things in their manifestos and being virtually undistinguishable. By extension, the same could also apply to you in the crowded market place in which you are trying to sell your ideas. In this space, building alliances on thematic grounds often helps cut through. In the run up to the 2016 Senedd election, around ten different organisations in the housing sector combined for a joint manifesto, the central points of which were matters on which they could all agree, such as the need for a Housing Minister at Cabinet level. This brought together, for the first time, organisations that weren't natural allies, such as Shelter and the Residential Landlords Association, in making the case for their common action points.

Further, even if manifesto asks aren't aligned between different organisations, that does not stop you working together to demonstrate common approaches. Often politicians welcome the symbolism of this, as well as it being a time effective way for them to engage with you. A good example of this approach can be seen at election periods in the health lobby. This section of the lobbying community is probably larger and louder than any other single grouping, They recognise their strength is not just volume, but diversity and a co-operative ethos. In the run up to most elections they tend to group together at party conferences and stage drop-in events where the manifesto gatekeepers, candidates and other interested parties can try and visit as many health organisations as possible in organised campaign fairs or 'speed dating' sessions.

Direct internal input into party policy making

It is the nature of the beast that many people involved in public affairs tend to also be party politically active, often at a national level. Most codes of practice for public affairs professionals are clear that you should keep separate your roles with a company or organisation and your role within a political party. It would thus be seriously inappropriate for a lobbyist to be head of policy for a political party. However, other forms of overlap may be permissible. For example, if you are a party activist then there is probably nothing wrong in working with others to get your party to adopt a policy motion at conference if that is something you believe in as an individual. However, be sure to check what your employer feels about your party political activity when it impacts on anything related to your employment.

TOP TIP: Develop a clear, straight forward and well researched set of policy objectives and use them continuously to make your case, perhaps over a longer period of time.

21

Working at a Local or Regional Level

The Welsh Government directly delivers very few services. Indeed, the only major areas where it interacts with individuals or businesses in terms of the actual delivery of policy are few and far between. One is farm subsidy payments, where it is the body which directly works with farmers in their distribution. Another is the process of grant aid to businesses.

In most cases, however, the Welsh Government engages other bodies to deliver the services that it pays for. The level of flexibility given to those providers may vary considerably or may not, depending on the type and nature of the legal direction issued by the Welsh Government when it allocates the responsibility or funding for a method of delivery. There will also, of course, be examples where a delivery body innovates completely for itself within its legal powers to deliver services, which they are also able to do.

The most notable and extensive deliverer of services in Wales is local government. Since 1 April 1996, Wales has been divided into 22 single-tier principal areas for local government purposes. The elected councils of these areas are responsible for the provision of all local government services, including education, social work, environmental protection, and most highways. Councils have to provide certain statutory services by law, and these are set out in legislation and cover services like social care, environmental health inspection and planning. They can also provide other services such as leisure and art centres at their discretion. This is the distinction sometimes referred to as between statutory and non-statutory services.

An exhaustive list of local government services is too long, but this summary covers the main areas of their operation:[1]

---

1   https://www.wlga.wales/local-government-in-wales

- **Education;** for example providing schools, transport to get children to school and providing opportunities for adult learning.
- **Housing;** such as finding accommodation for people in need and maintaining social housing.
- **Social Services;** for example caring for and protecting children, older people and disabled people.
- **Highways and Transport;** including maintaining roads and managing traffic flow.
- **Waste Management;** including collecting rubbish and recycling.
- **Leisure and Cultural Services;** for example providing libraries, leisure services and arts venues.
- **Consumer Protection;** such as enforcing trading standards and licencing taxis.
- **Environmental Health and Services;** for example making sure that the food provided in pubs, restaurants and take-aways is safe to eat, and controlling pollution locally.
- **Planning;** including managing local development and making sure buildings are safe.
- **Economic Development;** for example attracting new businesses and encouraging tourism.
- **Emergency Planning;** for things like floods or terrorist attacks.

The second notable deliverers of local services are the Health Boards of NHS Wales. On 1 October 2009, the 22 Local Health Boards (LHBs) and 7 of the NHS Trusts in Wales were replaced by a new structure made up of 7 new Health Boards. Their remit is the funding and delivery of three types of health services on a local level:

- **Primary care services**; such as GPs, community pharmacies, dentists and optometrists.
- **Hospital services**; for both inpatients and outpatients.
- **Community services**; including those provided through community health centres and mental health services.

For the purposes of this book, we will focus on engaging with local government rather than local health boards, but the processes of doing both are actually quite similar and based on the same principles. Indeed, the similarities between them are especially acute since they are both dealing with the need to provide increasingly complex and expensive services with local sensitivity and in response to local demand, while at the same time ensuring legislative and other instructions are obeyed and delivered upon. Since over 90% of all Welsh Government spending is currently delivered through either local government or the health service, it is no real surprise that there is an enormous importance attached to their operation and functioning.

Despite this importance, both in resource and delivery terms, working at a local level through either local authorities or health boards can be challenging. There may also be significant variations of opportunity and culture between one organisation and its neighbouring authority. The trade-off, in terms of developing locally focused and locally accountable services, is of course that this element of variability can and should exist. Public affairs practitioners often need to accept that variability, and work within it to try and ensure that the best practice achieved by one body in a specific matter is replicated by another. Considering the number of authorities involved, none of this is easy.

Indeed, the pattern of local service delivery is one of the most contentious areas of Welsh public policy. It is often subject to change or threat of change, such as the numerous attempts to change local government structures and reduce the number of local authorities during the first two decades of devolution. In respect of health boards, there have already been two wholesale reorganisations since 1999.

Even with the relatively calm period over recent years, with wholesale local government structural reform off the table (other than potential voluntary mergers), and no plans to restructure health, it is still a fruitless pursuit to focus on structures. We are, at the same time, living through a series of other innovations such as City Regions and Public Service Boards which are making significant alterations to the landscape of service delivery. It is best therefore not to get too bogged down in the inter-changeability of the present, so this chapter will address themes and patterns alongside the more immutable parts of the local and regional delivery systems.

Representing local government

With over 1,000 local councillors spread across 22 authorities, the way in which the diffuse opinions and experiences of local government is communicated is critical. The key body in this respect is the Welsh

Local Government Association (WLGA). The WLGA promotes the important role of local government to both Welsh Government and the Senedd, and seeks to enhance and protect councils' reputation and secure positive change to legislation. It is, in effect, a representational and lobbying body, and arguably the most effective example of such in Wales.

The WLGA is a member-led organization through its main decision-making bodies are the Council – comprising 79 members proportionately representing the populations they serve – and the Executive Board, comprised of the 22 council leaders. Although Labour currently forms the largest group within the WLGA and holds the post of leader and deputy leaders, the WLGA operates on the basis of consensus across all the political groups running the 22 authorities: Labour, Independents, Conservative and Plaid Cymru. Therefore, balance is achieved in the executive overall, and leaders and other WLGA Council members act as spokespeople for the WLGA covering a range of local government services or portfolios. These portfolio areas cover every aspect of local government services, though the spokespeople on finance, education and social services are generally the key portfolios.

The WLGA also possesses its own team of expert staff, headed by a chief executive, who act as the *de facto* civil service to the different local authorities in terms of their work. The WLGA's staff include policy leads to support the lead spokespeople and also deal with policy development. The WLGA also facilitates networks of practitioners amongst the officials operating in local government, such as the Association of the Directors of Social Services (ADSS).

For a public affairs practitioner, there is value in establishing links with the lead WLGA spokesperson, and also their deputies/alternates, plus any officials working in the WLGA on your policy areas, in the same way that you should engage with lead officials or the lead opposition people on a subject area in the Senedd. A full list of the executive board members is available on the WLGA website.

Another important element in the representation of local government is the operation of the Local Government Partnership Scheme (LGPS). Embodied into law since 2006, this provision was previously entrusted to the Local Government Partnership Council that had existed since 1999 and is part of the partnership working approach that will be considered in more detail in Chapter 22. The LGPS places a legal obligation on the Welsh Government to mutually beneficial ends:

'The Welsh Government and local government in Wales are committed to working together in partnership, within an atmosphere of mutual trust and respect, recognising the value and legitimacy of the roles both have to play in the governance of Wales.'[2]

The importance and legal basis of the LGPS means it is hardwired into the operation of both the Welsh Government and the WLGA, which takes on the local government representative role in respect of the scheme.

Beneath the WLGA, and in each local authority, there will also be three types of contact that could also be worth a public affairs practitioner identifying and engaging with – the Cabinet lead, the appropriate service manager or director, and the Chair of the relevant scrutiny committee. In effect, local government structures in each local authority mirror the structures of the Welsh Government and Senedd but at a smaller level. If your area of interest is social services, for example, there will be at least one designated lead in the Cabinet of each local authority who has a statutory remit in this area and is responsible for delivery. I say at least one because, in respect of Social Services as the taken example, there may be different Cabinet leads for adult services and children's services. There may also be more than one lead, therefore, amongst officials. Every council will also have its own distinct structure for policy scrutiny, and each committee will also have a Chair.

Public affairs practitioners who are serious about engaging with local government should take time to produce a stakeholder map for local authorities, logging names and contact details and parties (where appropriate) for each of these different types of post-holders. Although time consuming, you should do this for every local authority where you are operating. The information will all be publicly available on the relevant local authority websites, it just takes time to work through it.

Establishing good relationships with relevant councillors and officers at local authority level can also lead to relationships beyond the boundaries of a single local authority. As pinpointed above, there are sectoral networks in existence bringing together officers on a topic basis (social services, IT, housing etc) and these often mean that

---

2   Local Government Partnership Scheme, point 2.1

a useful connection with one or two specialist leads can result in a sharing of information or an idea through a wider network within local government. In essence, these networks are as penetrative as Wales-wide ones established at a national/governmental level, the difference being that they are driven forward from a service delivery rather than a policy development angle.

It is important to recognise the potential of good and deep relationships with local authorities and, through them, the many locally based community and voluntary organisations in Wales who are funded by or deliver services on local government's behalf. This network can also be extended to a range of local businesses that have a significant level of engagement with local government in, for example, planning, environmental health, health and safety and trading standards. In order to nurture useful relationships with these three locally-based sectors – community, voluntary and commercial organisations – the primary focus for public affairs activities would be with the local government officers and the key elected members themselves.

Other opportunities for engagement at a local level

Public Service Boards (PSBs) are a relatively new innovation at local government level, formally created through the passage of the Well-being of Future Generations (Wales) Act. The intention of PSBs is to improve joint-working across all public services in each local authority area in Wales. Some counties, such as Conwy and Denbighshire, have used the powers in the Act to merge their PSBs into a single unit.

Each PSB must undertake a well-being assessment and publish an annual local well-being plan, which is a statutory obligation under the Act. This plan must then reflect the seven statutory well-being goals that apply throughout the public sector in Wales:

* A prosperous Wales
* A resilient Wales
* A healthier Wales
* A more equal Wales
* A Wales of cohesive communities
* A Wales of vibrant culture and thriving Welsh language

- A globally responsible Wales

If your work affects these well-being goals in any way, then it is probably worth giving some thought to how you can engage with these PSBs in their delivery of the relevant statutory responsibilities as they affect you. PSBs tend to meet quarterly, have websites and also have secretariats with whom you can engage.

The core membership of every PSB is defined to comprise, identically, the relevant local authority or local authorities, the local health board covering that area, the relevant fire and rescue authority and also there are representatives of Natural Resources Wales. In addition, Welsh Ministers (when relevant), chief constables, the relevant police and crime commissioner, relevant probation services and at least one body representing voluntary organisations are invited to participate.

The voluntary representative will be drawn from the local organisation of voluntary organisations, which operates under the ambit of the Wales Council for Voluntary Action (WCVA). Again, this can be a helpful area of engagement, especially if your work is particularly focused in one or two counties. If you are a locally focused third sector organisation, then engaging through these can provide a plethora of support as well as significant resource and networking opportunities.

Collaborative working on a regional level

As the second decade of devolution comes to a close, one area that has seen considerable growth is collaboration. This happens not just between different public service bodies through statutory creations like PSBs, but also between different local authorities and other bodies. Indeed, the central thrust of Welsh Government policy, which has a great deal of cross-party support, is that if they are not to be compelled to merge to discharge their functions then they should at least co-operate together in the delivery of public services.

The most notable of these innovations has been the creation of four regional education consortia, which have been in place since 2012 and act on behalf of their constituent local authorities to deliver aspects of school improvement in each region. As well as assessment and peer support activities, these four consortia also oversee and manage education grant allocations to schools on behalf of the authorities in their region, and work to business plans jointly agreed by the local authorities. The consortia are accountable to the local authorities in their region, are governed by a joint committee of elected members and are subject to local authority scrutiny in the same way as any other local authority service.

The direction of travel for Welsh Government is clearly to increase the powers and role of the Regional Educational Consortia, with legislation promised to increase the regional footprint. However, the discussion on their future has also thrown up some areas of concern, not least this from the Public Accounts Committee of the Senedd:

'Evidence from the establishment of the regional education consortia clearly points to the need to establish a clear mandate and direction from the outset when establishing regional structures. Furthermore, consideration needs to be given to how the impact of regionalisation is measured and communicated, which is evidenced by the lack of clarity over what regional consortia have delivered and the negative response this generated.'[3]

Nevertheless, the regional approach remains the thrust and focus of public policy at present. It is also exemplified in the existence of the four Regional Skills Partnerships – as opposed to the three Regional Educational Consortia – which are in place to drive investment in skills by developing responses based upon local and regional need.[4] The RSPs produce Regional Employment and Skills Plans to analyse and influence the provision of skills based on regional economic need, and to support growth and key infrastructure projects in each region. The plans are refreshed every three years and provide recommendations to Welsh Government to influence the prioritisation and deployment of skills funding including apprenticeship and further education allocations.

The Regional Employment and Skills Plans build on and support priorities identified by Enterprise Zones, cross-border collaborations, and also City Deals/City Regions. This is where it gets even more complicated, as four potential City Deals/Regional Deals exist in

---

3   Public Accounts Committee - Response to the White Paper on 'Reforming Local Government: Resilient and Renewed' (10 April 2017)
4   https://businesswales.gov.wales/skillsgateway/skills-development/regional-skills-partnerships sets out the map as it stands and more detail around the operation of the Regional Skills Partnerships.

Wales, all at different stages of maturity, and with variable output and success. They are also massively different in size: the Cardiff City Region constitutes ten authorities, the Mid Wales Growth Deal just two.

The overlaid map of Regional Educational Consortia, Regional Skills Partnerships, police and fire authorities, growth deals, and local health boards is widely considered to be a mess, with the only commonality being they are all built from the building blocks of 22 local authorities. Taken from this perspective, there seems to be an increasing amount of sense from this appeal by the Public Accounts Committee in its same report on Regional Education Consortia:

'The Committee believes that going forward the aim should be for as much co-terminosity as possible between regional structures. This is the simplest approach for the public to understand and to administer.'[5]

Nevertheless, despite the complexity, the seeming illogicality and the lack of co-terminosity when it comes to regional arrangements and regional working, it does seem that this is the future direction of public service policy in Wales. In short, the message is collaborate within local authority units, and collaborate within different regional arrangements. Public affairs professionals would do well to heed those messages as clear opportunities for influence and engagement.

> **TOP TIP: Spend time mapping out local government and building up a picture of how your policy area is delivered locally and who by. Many public affairs professionals underestimate or deprioritise the work of local government, and thereby miss out on engaging with opportunities it brings, especially in respect of service delivery.**

---

5   Public Accounts Committee - Response to the White Paper on 'Reforming Local Government: Resilient and Renewed' (10 April 2017)

22

Partnership Working

An important part of the culture of politics in Cardiff Bay is the notion of partnership working. One of the greatest strengths, and greatest successes, of public policy making in a devolved Wales has been the emphasis on co-production and partnership. It is displayed particularly heavily in the health and social care sector, and is a reciprocal relationship of equals between provider, recipient and other stakeholders.

This ethos has permeated every part of the working of Welsh Government. Indeed, there has been a huge and longstanding emphasis on this approach, as constant as the presence of Jane Hutt, its arch proponent, in government. "It's about how do 'we'," was one her regular phrases during the first decade of devolution. It is embedded as a central policy principle of pieces of legislation like the Social Services and Well-Being Act 2014, and in the operation of voluntary networks like Co-Production Wales.

Partnership working has been hard wired into devolution since the beginning. Way back in 1999, three partnership councils were created to try and embed this approach into the very heart of the devolution project. In the First Senedd, the Partnership Councils for Local Government, business and the voluntary sector played, arguably, as prominent a role in the general functioning of the politics as did the general Subject Committees of the Senedd. Over time they may have faded in prominence, but the modern incarnations of them still exist, providing a bridge between partners in policy development.

Local government working is discussed in Chapter 21, but it is, perhaps, worth briefly considering the nature of interactions between policy makers in the other two fields.

Voluntary sector

The Third Sector Partnership Council (TSPC) continues to be an embedded part of the work of both the sector and the Welsh Government. Facilitated by the Welsh Council for Voluntary Action (WCVA), it is always chaired by the Welsh Government Cabinet member who has lead responsibility for the voluntary sector. It meets at least twice a year and brings Welsh Government together with 25 representatives of different types of voluntary organisations including: education; animal welfare; sport; international development, and others.

A core function of the Third Sector Partnership Council is to ensure the Third Sector Scheme is operating effectively, which is the working document underpinning the relationships, and embodying the principles of the partnership relationship.

From a public affairs perspective, becoming one of the sectoral representations on the TSPC can provide a good networking and learning experience. It can also enable the sharing of interested aspects of information, since the council tends to work in a thematic and networked way.[1] It is probably true to say that this body has not made a great deal of external impact, though its supporters will say its real focus is intended to be internal within the sector, and a mark of its success is that it shows how confrontation can be avoided. However, as with any large body of this nature, views on its overall effectiveness will vary due to personal experience and expectations.

Economy

A Business Partnership Council was established in 1999 which, it is fair to say, didn't make as much headway as the other two bodies. It was revived as the Economic Renewal Council in 2010 after a period of some stagnation. At the time of the rebrand, then First Minister Carwyn Jones said:

'The Council for Economic Renewal indicates a fresh start. It will enable both the employer and employee voices to be heard at the heart of the Welsh Assembly Government, and help inform our

---

1   https://www.wcva.org.uk/what-we-do/influencing/third-sector-partnership-council

policies. We learnt valuable lessons from the economic summits. In particular, we are keen to capture the action-orientated nature of the early summit meetings. We want the Council for Economic Renewal to provide us with a high level of strategic debate to help guide policy.'[2]

The same body has now undergone a further rebrand to become the Council for Economic Development (CED) and meets on a quarterly basis. The First Minister used to chair every meeting, but Mark Drakeford has indicated he wishes other Ministers to share this role, and he will only periodically chair it himself. You can either look at that as great leadership and delegation or something less positive.

As with the TSPC, whether the Council for Economic Development is considered functional depends on the different expectations there seem to be of it. At best, it can be seen as an useful forum to get the social partners together to debate and update on issues affecting the economy. Further, a lack of common appreciation and understanding of the notion of social partnerships may also be a limiting factor in terms of its potential effectiveness.

Sectoral networks

Partnership working in Wales has also developed naturally between organisations operating in common areas, without the encouragement of government. For example, Wales Environment Link has developed to act as an umbrella body for a significant number of organisations in its sector.

In another space, the Wales Industry Group of the Association of the British Pharmaceutical Industry (ABPI) was set up soon after devolution, and brings together those members of the ABPI who want to have a Wales enhanced presence. To participate, ABPI members pay an additional fee, but it is a distinctive network that has brought together a number of interested companies in the pharmaceutical world who wish to better engage with the political process. From a public affairs perspective, this co-ordination and co-operation undoubtedly

2   *Western Mail*, 16 November 2010

provides more impact for the pharmaceutical industry generally than any one company could achieve on its own.

More broadly, in healthcare, networks of friends and colleagues have emerged that find a balance between operating alone and distinctively on the one hand, while also co-operating with others in the same space. Small networks like the therapists have a long culture of doing this (speech therapists, physiotherapists and occupational therapists) and meet regularly, sometimes submitting joint evidence to consultations. Even in the space where organisations might be seen as competitors, either for the same funding or for attention, such as cancer, there is genuine joint working and partnership approaches are common. Perhaps they are brought even closer together by the functioning of Cross-Party Groups, such as the one that exists on cancer.

Sometimes networks spring up when the occasion arises. The Social Services Bill, which dominated a lot of time in the Fourth Senedd, was perceived as being so complicated and so concerning to interested organisations in the sector, that over a dozen of them jointly clubbed together to co-ordinate their lobbying, amass their briefings and co-ordinate their amendments.

Others come together at times of crisis or challenge, such as the coalition led by Cymorth Cymru to defend the Supporting People Fund during the budget round of 2016, which was assessed in the earlier chapter on the Senedd budget process. Financial concerns were also the motivation of the Disabled Children Matter Wales campaign during the work it did to increase funding and profile for disabled children and their families back in 2006.

Whatever the motivation for such partnership approaches, they are genuinely welcomed by the Welsh Government. A Health Advocacy Day, organised by Positif Politics, then in its infancy back in 2007, which provided a platform for over 60 health organisations with stalls, attracted over 40 Members of the Senedd and a number of candidates for the upcoming Senedd election too. It was welcomed by the then Presiding Officer, Dafydd Elis-Thomas AM, as 'historic' in its reach and impact.[3]

---

3   Chartered Society of Physiotherapists account of the Health Advocacy Day, 28 March 2007

Joint campaigning

As this book will hopefully have illustrated, in a number of ways and in a number of places, there is a genuine advantage in partnership approaches and joint working which can result in real and tangible benefits. A good example of this was the approach taken by the Kidney Wales Foundation in building a coalition of those making a case for increased levels of organ donation. Their creative joint-working in a coalition which included not just the obvious suspects of the British Heart Foundation and the British Lung Foundation, also included the British Medical Association, giving it additional gravitas and reach.

Partnership working does have its drawbacks, however, and may not be the correct option for your organisation. The necessary requirements of joint-campaigning with partners, whose hierarchy of decision-making may result in longer sign-off times, may be off putting for smaller, agile organisations, so a degree of patience and professional discipline is essential if the partnership is to enjoy and success.

Despite these undoubted pitfalls, partnership working has genuine and extensive advantages since in most cases your voice will always be magnified. If you are a small, possibly cash strapped, organisation then it could be a particularly good use of resources.

When partnership working happens, particularly on a larger scale, there is often a tactical decision to be made around who leads or fronts it. This will depend on how the campaign is resources and who is able to bring what skills to the table. For example, on organ donation, it was Kidney Wales that had the time and money to shape the campaign, and they fronted it. In respect of the Disabled Children Matter Wales, it was a combination of one of the smaller charities that had time to commit, plus Labour backbencher Lynne Neagle, a passionate advocate for children's rights.

Indeed, involving a politician as a public face of a campaign can often be a positive advantage. They will usually be much more receptive to taking on such a role on behalf of an umbrella rather than an individual organisation, since it will not mean prioritising the needs and demands of one charity over a myriad of others. However, when choosing a Member to work with, bear in mind also that some of those who are the most campaign orientated – such as Mark Isherwood, Bethan Sayed or Hefin David – also tend to be very in demand and get pulled in lots of different campaign directions. Sometimes, working with a single politician who is not subject to the same pressures and competing demands works better.

Indeed, one of the biggest worries about partnership working can lie with who your partners are. Negative behaviours, such as behaving in a more confrontational or unreasonable manner, can be heightened by partnership working as organisations fall into an echo chamber of egging each other on and losing track of external appearance in doing so. This is more than a hypothetical situation. Every partnership run campaign I have worked on has had the potential to head in that direction, as one partner can operate in a confrontational or unhelpful way. I've seen it happen in campaigns I haven't been near too. For example, in 2014 the 'Don't Kill the Bill' alliance around the domestic violence legislation mentioned earlier was a classic case in point. The passion of the campaign turned into the perception of aggression because of the behaviours of a small number of those involved, and Members of the Senedd openly condemned the tactics deployed. Unfortunately, every organisation in the coalition became tarred with the same brush because of the antics of a few of the less measured members of the alliance.

Of course, one way of avoiding or seeking to limit rogue and damaging behaviours, is to take control or leadership in a partnership yourself and ensure a clear tone and style are both established. Indeed, an important part of the construction of partnerships is to practically assess what you can get out of them, and 'what's in it' for you or your organisation. If you haven't been able to get profile or traction on your own, maybe a partnership approach is exactly what you need.

Media and partnership working

It may be much more possible to gain media attention for your campaign work by taking a partnership approach, especially if you are a smaller organisation with a low or non-existent profile. More collaboration generally means more attention, especially if there is, within the partnership team, someone who has a strong or appropriate media voice or is someone with strong media connections who can help get the partnership noticed, and note that they need not necessarily be the same person delivering on both of these attributes.

In Wales, despite the prevalence of partnership working, it is still a newsworthy story if a number of organisations come together to campaign on a single issue. Ten logos on a press release has way more impact than just one.

Clever, well publicised campaigns are also magnified if a wide range of media resources are utilised. Without crossing into the territory of bombarding the media and civic society, you can work with your coalition partners to generate a myriad of noise. This can include lead features in the *Western Mail* but also be supported by particular local media activity utilising case studies. As discussed elsewhere, the use of constituents usually does tend to pique a politician's interest.

Organising partnership events

Thought should also be given as to whether any events you are planning might be improved in reach and impact by making them partnership endeavours. There is the usual trade off in terms of control and branding in doing this, but there are obvious benefits to it too, and your chances of success are heightened if the partners can impress policy makers by presenting a united front.

However, the same tensions if not all partners behave in a similar way can also particularly manifest itself at events and this can cause huge tensions and lead to accusations of hierarchies and hijacking. This scenario can sometimes come to pass because a resource-rich partner wants to stand out or show off. In the run up to the Senedd elections in 2016, a number of health charities clubbed together to form a health marketplace to connect with candidates from all parties at their individual party conferences. Interest was so high that there was a degree of over subscription. To enable as many organisations as possible to actually participate, everyone was asked to bring stalls and material of certain sizes. All but one did, and that one brought an over-sized presence. They obviously didn't care about the impact, despite being told it was inappropriate, because they did exactly the same on another ocassion.

The bottom line for partnership events is the same as for partnership working: you are only as good as your collective whole and you are limited by the lack of partnership commitment by your most difficult member of the partnership. It is therefore always worth considering dissolving a partnership approach, or the right person having strong words with a partnership member who is not operating in an agreed way.

TOP TIP: Be as clear and strategic about what you want out of a partnership as you are about any other public affairs activity, especially if you are contributing significant money or time to one.

23

Working with the Media

An important element of a high-profile public affairs strategy is working with the media, which tends to have a degree of geographical focus. About 1/20 of the UK population live in Wales (c5% of the UK total) and, according to the Office of National Statistics (ONS), the population of Wales is 3.1 million and expected to grow.[1] As of 2019, the largest urban areas are Cardiff (361,500), Swansea (244,500) and Newport (149,100), with significant other bases of population in both north east Wales (Flintshire and Wrexham) and south east Wales (Newport and its hinterland valleys to the north). It is no surprise, therefore, that where local media exists, it generally tends to be focused around these four urban centres.

Since the creation of the Senedd in 1999, as has been demonstrated throughout this book, there has been increased policy divergence in Wales from the rest of the UK. With powers over education, health and parts of the economy, Wales is now pursuing different policies and having different results in these areas. Yet, perversely, there is common consensus that the ability of the media to report on these Welsh developments over this time has actually declined.

Indeed, in October 2013, Ofcom's Advisory Committee for Wales warned that the risk posed by a lack of plurality were 'of pressing importance' and that it was essential that public service broadcasters and the print media 'provide news and current affairs services covering the whole of the Wales which can hold democratic government in Wales to account'. Nothing has really changed in the years since then. Writing in 2018, Senedd politician Bethan Sayed noted:

'A free press and media has long been the mark of a free society. Without frank and independent journalism the people may not be fully informed of what is done in their name and governments, and others with power, will not be held to account for their actions. The decline of commercial news journalism in Wales should therefore concern us all. As in other parts of the world, the circulations of Welsh newspapers have dropped sharply in recent years while online circulation has grown. However, this growth in digital readership has not improved newspaper profitability. Instead, we have seen job losses, mergers and newspaper closures.'[2]

The vexed subject of media capacity in Wales is not a matter in this guide, and others have already provided an excellent overview on the way a distinctive Welsh media has developed in the past.[3] Moreover, the mapping of the current state of the media in Wales is done annually by the Media Summits of the Institute of Welsh Affairs. Unfortunately however, as each year passes, a bleaker and bleaker is painted of the robustness and total capacity of news reporting in Wales. Indeed, in her committee report, Bethan Sayed's Culture Committee made a series of hard-hitting recommendations to help reverse the trend, including publicly funded journalism.

Perhaps the important element for the public affairs professional to realise is that capacity is a constraint in Wales. Thus, although bilingualism might make it appear there are actually a wide range of outlets, in reality there are far fewer available than in Scotland. It is therefore absolutely critical that when shaping your public affairs engagement you are very focused and targeted in your use of media. You should gear activity in a very precise way to offer much leverage as possible, including Welsh language media, which is dealt with in this chapter, but is also touched upon in Chapter 25.

Television in Wales

Ofcom reported in 2015 that TV was the main source of news for Welsh citizens: 'nearly six in ten (58%) adults aged 16+ said that the TV was their main source of UK and world news. Websites or apps were used by two in ten adults as a source of news, more than any other nation and the UK as a whole. Use of radio and newspapers for UK and world news was used by a similar proportion of adults in Wales (9% and 8% respectively).'

Television remains the most powerful communication medium for news in Wales, with BBC Wales and ITV Wales' early evening, 30-minute, news bulletins attract a greater share in Wales when compared to the UK average for the same weekday slot. *Wales Today*, BBC One's early evening news bulletin, for example, had an average 30.7% share of TV viewing in Wales between 6.30pm and 7.00pm in 2015, higher than the average audience for BBC One's regional news broadcasts in England for the same time period (29.6%).

ITV Wales' evening bulletin, *News at Six*, attracts a lower share than BBC One's *Wales Today*, although, at 20.1%, it was also higher than the UK average (18.5%) for the regional news bulletins across England. The feel of ITV Wales' flagship news programme also differs to the BBC Wales offering, and is often softer, more conversational, with more health related and more family related stories.

The Welsh language channel S4C also has a news service provided by the BBC. *Newyddion 9*, broadcast at 9pm, often gathers stories separately and in addition to the main BBC Wales output. It can therefore also be beneficial to target journalists who are specifically working on the *Newyddion 9* programme.

As a general rule, a story generated through public affairs will only have real traction if you are also prepared to provide someone who can do a clip for television outlets. TV news is a visual medium and relies heavily on short items that are pre-prepared and edited. For Welsh language content on *Newyddion 9*, normally only a Welsh speaker is acceptable for interview, apart from exceptional circumstances. It's also worth noting that it is not necessary to provide the same person for both Welsh and English language TV, but it is often more convenient if you do.

Another tip is that unless your story is strong enough to demand attention on all channels, then you may find that news outlets are looking to be distinctive and so may only be interested if there is a degree of exclusivity on the story. This is particularly true in relation to the rivalry between BBC and ITV. You can get around this sometimes by offering a case study to one outlet (a service user perhaps) and an organisational person does the clip for the other outlet.

Radio in Wales

BBC Wales operates two national radio stations, BBC Radio Wales in English and BBC Radio Cymru in Welsh. For public affairs professionals, the opportunities presented by radio are both numerous and extensive, especially to feed into the news programmes in the morning and the evening. In general, BBC radio stations prefer live items for these flagship programmes and are used to people coming into one of their studios to be recorded and broadcast as live. If people are not available for studio, then live recordings can be made, but the readiness of broadcasters to undertake this is often dependent on the number of other people booked on the same programme who are also intending to do the same thing. Also, you may only have a few hours notice of a radio interview, especially if it is during the day.

A third national service is provided by Real Radio Wales. There are also a number of commercial and community radio stations throughout the country which broadcast in both Welsh and English. The following list is not definitive but does provide an overview of the scale and variation between them.

Rank	Radio station	Location	Weekly reach (Dec 2014)
1	Heart Wales	Cardiff (Bay)	497,000
2	BBC Radio Wales	Cardiff (Llandaff)	427,000
3	Capital South Wales	Cardiff (Bay)	207,000
4	Nation Radio	Cardiff (Bay)	176,000
5	Capital North West and Wales	Wrexham	174,000
6	The Wave	Gowerton	138,000
7	Heart North Wales	Wrexham	107,000
8	Radio Cymru	Cardiff (Llandaff)	106,000
9	Smooth North Wales	Cardiff (Bay)	74,000
10	Swansea Sound	Gowerton	69,000
11	Smooth South Wales	Cardiff (Bay)	59,000
12	Smooth North Wales	Cardiff (Bay)	74,000
13	Radio Pembrokeshire	Narbeth	45,000
14	Bridge FM	Bridgend	43,000
15	Nation Hits	Neath	42,000
16	Radio Carmarthenshire	Narbeth	39,000
17	Radio Ceredigion	Narbeth	18,000

As a general rule of thumb, there tends to be less news content on non-BBC channels. Naturally, if your public affairs activity is geographically focused then it will have a particular resonance to the local news radio channels and they may look for an 'as live' interview. Some outlets, such as Nation or Heart, are also often ready to do clipped interviews by Whatsapp or Facetime for broadcast on their news bulletins.

Also of note are the BBC's feature style programmes dealing with broad themes like the economy, politics and public services or equalities. Some of these radio programmes may also be open to a direct pitch for an idea for a feature on their programme.

Newspapers and news magazines

Unlike Scotland and Northern Ireland, the Welsh national press is limited. The only English-language Wales-based daily national newspaper is the *Western Mail*, produced by Trinity Mirror, now called Reach UK: its Sunday counterpart is *Wales on Sunday*. The *Western Mail* also includes set sections on different days related to the economy, health and education.

One study in the 1990s found that the most widely read newspaper in Wales was *The Sun*, although by 2019 its sales has been overtaken by the *Daily Mail*. Despite the popularity of London-based newspapers in Wales, most UK newspapers do not produce regional editions for the Welsh audience, although until 2003 *The Mirror* was branded as the *Welsh Mirror*.

The most popular local newspapers are the Cardiff-based *South Wales Echo*, the Swansea-based *South Wales Evening Post*, and the Newport-based *South Wales Argus*. In north Wales the market is dominated by the Welsh edition of the Liverpool-based *Daily Post*, while the *Evening Leader* is the main evening newspaper for north east Wales.

Additionally, there are four editions of *Around Town* magazine covering Bridgend, Cardiff, Swansea and Rhondda Cynon Taff. Across all four titles they have the biggest print run in south Wales.

In the Welsh language, the weekly magazine *Golwg (Sight)*, established in 1988, covers current events and features and claims a monthly circulation of 12,000, the largest circulation of any magazine in Wales. Recently, *Golwg360* was launched as a website offering a rolling Welsh and international news service in Welsh, which attracts over 100,000 visits per month. *Y Cymro* (*The Welshman*), first published in 1932, was the longest running Welsh language weekly newspaper, which ceased publishing in 2017 before re-emerging in 2018, under new ownership, as a monthly publication. The monthly Welsh language magazine *Barn* is also usually a good source of politically focused writing, while *Planet*, a bi-monthly magazine covering the arts, literature and politics in Wales and the wider world, is produced in Aberystwyth. Each edition features poems and short stories alongside cultural reviews and political analysis.

Generally, however, print readership is declining rapidly. Data compiled by the print industry body ABC in 2018 confirmed the *Daily Post* remains Wales's most popular newspaper, but its readership had slipped 11%, selling an average of 19,842 copies per edition in 2017. During the same period, the *South Wales Evening Post* shifted 18,029 copies (-14%), the *Western Mail*'s average circulation was 13,419 (-12%), while the *South Wales Echo* had an average circulation of 13,394 (-10%).[4]

It is important to note, however, that media outlets are increasingly turning to online publication in preference to print production in order to maximise reach, engagement and advertising revenue. This is especially the case with the *Western Mail*, which has for some years prioritised its online version over its print version in order to capture new readers and react to the way in which people are now receiving and absorbing news. It is important to remember when engaging with print media that their online versions probably have even greater reach and traction.

The best source of online traffic data for news websites is the *Press Gazette* website, which reports on ABC figures.[5] The following table compares 2017 and 2015 news stories, to provide some historical context to the figures:

Website	Daily unique users (June 2017)	% year-on-year change	Daily unique users (average, second half of 2014)	% change 2014 to June 2017 figures
Wales Online	429,656	9.5	178,382	141
Daily Post	130,604	60.4	42,343	208

Website	Daily unique users (June 2017)	% year-on-year change	Daily unique users (average, second half of 2014)	% change 2014 to June 2017 figures
South Wales Argus *	47,119	2.2		
South Wales Evening Post**			48,943	

*No figures are available for the *South Wales Argus'* website for 2014.

**Following the Local World group's acquisition by Trinity Mirror, *South Wales Evening Post* content is carried on the Wales Online site.

Generating effective public affairs media content

All of this context is intended to help you successfully navigate the media in Wales. In terms of a public affairs intervention, the interview or the press feature is not the end product. That is the focus for public relations, but for public affairs it is somewhat different. The role of the media in public affairs is to give a platform and to give voice to a campaign or a moment of activity, which is then supposed to impact on the policy maker to get them to take your intervention and perspective on board.

Not all campaigns need media attention. Some are particularly sensitive and are focused on quiet persuasion or negotiation. In such circumstances, a media story can actually be quite counter-productive. It can push the decision maker into a more hardline stance where they are less willing to compromise especially if, because of the media attention, they find it harder to reach a compromise. Indeed, in some circumstances when you are negotiating to achieve specific ends in public affairs, it may be part of the deal done with the decision maker that absolutely no media publicity is sought and that way no party looks weak or wrong in public.

From an opposite perspective, you may have a campaign or an objective that requires no media activity at all, so don't feel under pressure to always launch a media element to fulfil your ends. In some cases, a public affairs strategy does not necessarily need any sort of media activity at all.

In a good proportion of cases, however, the assessment of your public affairs strategy will generally point you toward some sort of media activity. Often this can be driven forward by a combination of public affairs, policy and media specialists within an organisation, though in smaller organisations it also may be one person fulfilling all three roles. An important rule of thumb, however, is that if your organisation does have a media capacity then you, as a public affairs professional, should work with them in crafting your media strategy. Expertise and delivery are best deployed when you are utilising all resources possible. Further, even if you have some previous media expertise, then it can be construed as rude and unhelpful to not work with colleagues. After all, many in-house media professionals also have some public affairs experience, but that does not make it right for them to plan and launch policy and political campaigns without engaging with the public affairs team.

News releases

Most media activity around public affairs will be centred around news releases, specifically created to draw attention to your campaign or public affairs objectives. No matter how skilfully you put your release together, however, you are subject to competition. Just like events at the Senedd, a big part of your impact will be who else is trying to capture the spotlight on the same day. To minimise the potential for clashes you should, from a public affairs perspective, try to horizon scan as much as possible in order to time your news releases to clash with as few other stories as possible: it will always clash with something. Mondays are always a good day if you have a particularly hard hitting story to start the week, although Fridays or during Senedd recess periods are usually good times to get attention because there is less competition around, even though the political pick up may not be as strong during these periods.

This balance will also be influenced by the central hook of your public affairs activity. It could be a report launch, or it could be a mass lobby of the Senedd, or it could simply be an announcement of some kind. In respect of all these options, it will probably be more effective to stage your media activity to coincide with the hook and that will of course probably be most effective when the Senedd is actually in session. Thus Tuesdays and Wednesdays can be particularly competitive days for media attached to public affairs activities.

Just like when you are pitching an event or an idea, it's important to think like the person you are intending to engage with when putting a news release together. To make something newsworthy, it has to be hard hitting and noticeable. You can achieve this, for example, by framing statistics or quotes in a particularly noticeable way. There may also be a temptation to be critical of a government or of a service provider such a local health board or local authority. Be careful, however, as criticism, especially when hard hitting, often increases news value but it might simultaneously decrease your ability to actually achieve your public affairs ends. It's not just about the column inches you succeed in generating, it's about the influencing of the Minister and the Government.

There is also a particular use of news releases after events. Often your event will include some form of indication that a politician is in support – they might be signing something or holding a copy of a report or engaging with someone – and a photo of this is then is helpful to share with them as soon as possible. Often supplying a few statistics (localised to the politician's constituency if possible) or maybe a quote can then enable the politician in question to generate their own localised press release, which can play a significant role in cascading your campaign outward into different parts of Wales, maximising its impact at a number of levels. This can also be achieved be sending a standard 'local' release to the politician for adaptation and use in their area.

Another key use of news releases is to use them as points of commentary linked to a piece of legislation or the twists and turns of the budget process as described earlier. This need not just be limited to the point at which the legislation or the budget is passed, it can take the form of news releases as commentary throughout a process, and the news release need not be especially detailed if it is part of an ongoing commentary on the process. Indeed, brevity is sometimes more effective, with just a comment succinctly illustrating your view based on a narrative that has already been developed and rolled out.

The Welsh Local Government Association is a particular master of using the media during a budget round to create and develop a narrative of under-funding. In most years, this has created a climate where the Welsh Government comes under particular pressure to make financial concessions. Perhaps the most infamous news release the WLGA ever put out was in the first decade of devolution, where they complained their financial uplift was only 5% when that for NHS Wales was a few percentage points higher.

Basically, and it cannot be stressed enough, is that providing press activity which is not deemed to be counter-productive adds a valuable extra dimension to other public affairs activities you undertake. This applies as wholly to events on the Senedd estate, as it does to interventions in the passage of legislation, as it does to the submission of notable evidence to a Senedd Committee, as it does to the lodging of a petition with the Senedd, where a photo on the steps with Petition Committee members is often seen as a compulsory action.

Some final advice on media activity

As mentioned previously in relation to TV coverage, you may need to consider an element of exclusivity in your media engagement. The guarantee of an exclusive can often make a channel take a public affairs story more seriously. The case for exclusivity may indeed get stronger if, for example, you are dealing with a particularly complicated issue or detailed report.

Similarly, building up a relationship with a single journalist and supplying information should definitely help your case. BBC Wales, ITV Wales and *WalesOnline/Western Mail* each have a designated health correspondent, for example, and so building up a close media relationship with those people can pay dividends for any organisation lobbying in health.

Deepening relationships with journalists will also present additional opportunities. An economic development organisation, for example, must prioritise the building of a good relationship with the business editor of the *Western Mail* as can result in regular opportunities to comment on economic issues or budget announcements. It is not unduly difficult to increase your profile and the profile of your organisation by being ready to offer expert opinion on the stories and initiatives of others, and not just confine yourself to initiatives you have spearheaded yourself. Don't worry unduly about being a journalist's go-to for comments on key issues, a so-called 'rent-a-quote'. As long as what you're contributing is appropriate and engaging it will your organisation's profile in a positive manner, and remember, there are plenty of other public affairs professionals who'd love to replace you in that slot.

Perhaps the peak of public affairs practitioner media activity is a regular monthly column in the *Western Mail* or another of the major newspapers in Wales, perhaps in the form of a regular health or education column. To achieve this status, you need to have built up not only a strong reputation with journalists, but also a reputation for actually saying something and saying it well. It is a privilege reserved for the very few.

TOP TIP: Factor in media activity to every significant piece of public affairs activity you do, but remove that element if it is deemed counter-productive to any stage of a campaign or to the overall public affairs objectives as a whole.

24

Online Communications

The increasing use of social media is now an integral part of political life. This is not just because politicians use social media extensively, but also because 'thought leaders', campaigners and constituents (not necessarily in that order) use it extensively too. It is a worldwide communications phenomenon which has revolutionised political engagement. Some may argue the changes are not necessarily always for the better, but the scale of the online revolution cannot be argued against or resisted.

So, what is social media?

> 'Social media is the term commonly given to Internet and mobile-based channels and tools that allow users to interact with each other and share opinions and content. As the name implies, social media involves the building of communities or networks and encouraging participation and engagement.'[1]

The potency of social media lends itself particularly well to public affairs campaigning because its interactive nature enables two-way or multi-user engagement, simultaneously and immediately. It also enables small organisations with effective social media skills to communicate directly, and influence, much larger organisations and key policy makers.

This is important to bear in mind in terms of how you approach the different mediums. Another consideration is the amount of resources you are able to commit to your social media presence. Developing a presence can mean you need to make it an active presence, requiring

---

1   Chartered Institute of Public Relations, 2013

regular updating, input and engagement in order to keep it vibrant and relevant. This capacity angle is one you need to examine within your organisation as part of your overall social media planning.

Something else you might want to consider is developing a social media policy for your organisation which anyone within it can access. This might set out clearly the platforms to use, the tone that is appropriate, and ideas for content. It might address the capacity problem but at the same time you will need to be assured that the people in your organisation likely to use social media on the organisation's behalf adhere to the agreed social media policy.

Tone and content

Making statements or sharing information will not just help you engage with your target audience (as per any public affairs strategy) but will also open you up to engagement with others too. Some of these others might approach social media in a different way from you. What starts as a relatively straight forward statement might soon escalate into a bigger discussion, involving people you do not know and who may not agree with you.

There is always a degree of strategising around the tone you use. Naturally, you will probably want your post to generate some sort of interaction, so trying to say something meaningful is probably beneficial. There are more ultra bland postings on social media than there are provocative, meaningful or provocative ones.

Remember that social media lends itself to conversation. Try and prompt one or engage with other conversations. Avoid one-sided conversations where you end up just talking to yourself, and also respond quickly and constructively to new ideas, questions or criticism. As in any debate or discussion, there is therefore a need for you to be prepared to enter into a debate and explain or defend your position. You must also be prepared to support your views and statements with evidence. Language and tone are critically important. Try and avoid inflammatory language, unless you want to make a point really stand out and make people think. It is also true that different people approach social media mediums in different ways and for different ends.

An important rule of thumb is, if you find a debate has become too heated you don't have to stay within it, even if your original social media post started it. You can also play a role in calming things down or returning people to the original posting or statement, and if individuals get extreme or persistent you can always block them on social media. The 'mute' function on some social media platforms can also come in very useful.

Also, it is true that nobody is always right. Sometimes you may make an error in dealing with someone on social media or have communicated the wrong data. In such circumstances a short correction and apology can remedy the situation.

In general, social media works best when it is used positively. Short messages thanking people for interactions and support can often work particularly well, especially if utilising photographs to make your point and express your thanks.

Returning to the matter of content, you can also use social media platforms as a good way of sign posting to your own activities. This could be appearances before committees, launches of campaigns or advertisements, or public statements on a contentious issue of the day. If you are releasing a report, always share it on social media too, with a link to an online version and, very importantly, in the loud space of social media you may need to do this several times and in several ways to be noticed and heard.

Content sharing is especially true of any media activity you have undertaken, either through mainstream media or blog pieces. You can translate media impact into social media impact by using the same material in different ways. You can also use the same approach with media material with which you disagree. Things have moved on a lot since your only recourse to a challenge press story was a letter in the following day's newspaper.

Social media is not an alternative to traditional print and broadcast media, so effort and thought must be given to integrate the two fully with your public affairs and communications strategies. Even if you run these aspects independently, they will not remain independent in the eyes of your multi-level audiences. It is important to recognise that in the platforms and messages you choose to embrace.

Also consider your bilingual policy when you engage on social media. The reasons for this will become apparent in Chapter 25.

Finally, whatever platforms you are using, think of them as ways of explaining and extending your brand. Keep to organisational colours and brand guidelines. In this modern digital age, social media is one of the strongest methods you have to get your brand across.

Different types of Social Media

Figures for 2019 show that the following ten forms of social media are the most popular in the UK:[2]

Platform	Description	UK Users	World Users	Comment
Facebook	Social sharing networking site	35,130,000	2,417,000,000	Highest traffic occurs between 1-3pm, however more engagement can be found between 7-8pm
YouTube	The top website used for video uploading and viewing	23,000,000	1,900,000,000	1 billion hours of Youtube are watched daily
WhatsApp	Platform that allows users to send text messages as well as voice and video calls		1,500,000,000	55 billion messages are sent each day on the platform
Instagram	Photo and video sharing social networking	14,000,000	1,000,000,000	95 million posts are shared each day on Instagram

2.   social-media.co.uk

Platform	Description	UK Users	World Users	Comment
Twitter	Micro-blogging platform	13,000,000	883,000,000	Year-on-Year the total ad engagement rate was up to 91%
Snapchat	Send images and videos with a short life span over an app	16,200,000	600,000,000	528,000 Snaps are shared every minute
LinkedIn	B2B platform for networking professionally	20,000,000	590,000,000	More than 50% of all social traffic to B2B sites and blogs comes from LinkedIn
Tumblr	Popular microblogging platform used to broadcast messages	9,000,000	550,000,000	45% of Tumblr's audience is people under the age of 35
Reddit	Entertainment, social news and social networking website	6,600,000	330,000,000	The average time a Reddit user spends on the site is 16 minutes
Pinterest	A popular photo sharing website	10,300,000	266,000,000	50% of users have made a purchase after seeing a Promoted Pin on their feed

A health warning on this table: it is very much a time limited table and preferences for usage can change. Social media platforms evolve and regress rapidly. The Friends Reunited platform of the early part of the 21st century is now a dim and distant memory. New platforms will evolve, but the principles of social media engagement will remain relatively constant.

Twitter

Twitter is the preferred method of online communication for elected Members of the Senedd and, every single one is now present on the platform. The list is contained in the following table:

Senedd Member	Twitter Handle		Senedd Member	Twitter Handle
Adam Price	@Adamprice		Julie James	@JulieJamesAM
Alun Davies	@AlunDaviesAM		Julie Morgan	@JulieMorganLAB
Andrew RT Davies	@AndrewRTDavies		Ken Skates	@KenSkates4AM
Angela Burns	@AngelaBurnsAM		Kirsty Williams	@Kirsty_Williams
Ann Jones	@ann_jonesam		Leanne Wood	@LeanneWood
Bethan Sayed	@bethanjenkins		Lee Water	@Amanwy
Caroline Jones	@CarolineJonesAM		Lesley Griffiths	@lesley4wrexham
Carwyn Jones	@AMCarwyn		Llyr Gruffydd	@LlyrGruffydd
Dafydd Elis-Thomas	@ElisThomasD		Lynne Neagle	@lynne_neagle
Darren Millar	@DarrenMillarAM		Mandy Jones	@MandyJonesAM
David Melding	@DavidMeldingAM		Mark Drakeford	@MarkDrakeford
David Rees	@DavidReesAM		Mark Isherwood	@MarkIsherwoodAM
David Rowlands	@DavidRowlandsUK		Mark Reckless	@MarkReckless
Dawn Bowden	@Dawn_Bowden		Michelle Brown	@MishBrownAM
Dai Lloyd	@DaiLloydSwansea		Mick Antoniw	@MickAntoniw1
Delyth Jewell	@delythjewell		Mike Hedges	@MikeHedgesAM
Elin Jones	@ElinCeredigion		Mohammad Asghar	@MohammadAsghar
Eluned Morgan	@Eluned_Morgan		Neil Hamilton	@NeilUKIP
Gareth Bennett	@GarethBennettAM		Neil McEvoy	@neiljmcevoy
Hannah Blythyn	@hannahblythyn		Nick Ramsay	@NickRamsayAM
Hefin David	@hef4caerphilly		Paul Davies	@PaulDaviesPembs
Helen Mary Jones	@HelenmaryCymru		Rebecca Evans	@RebeccaEvansAM
Huw Irranca-Davies	@IrrancaDaviesMP		Rhianon Passmore	@rhi4islwyn
Jack Sargeant	@JackSargeantAM		Rhun ap Iorwerth	@RhunapIorwerth
Jane Hutt	@JaneHutt		Russell George	@russ_george
Janet Finch-Saunders	@JFinchSaunders		Sian Gwenllian	@siangwenfelin
Jane Bryant	@JBryantWales		Suzy Davies	@suzydaviesam

Senedd Member	Twitter Handle		Senedd Member	Twitter Handle
Jenny Rathbone	@JennyRathbone		Joyce Watson	@JoyceWatsonam
Jeremy Miles	@Jeremy_Miles		Vaughan Gething	@vaughangething
John Griffiths	@J_GriffithsAM		Vikki Howells	@VikkiHowells

Members are not averse to being contacted via Twitter, and just because they might not reply to you directly, it does not mean your communication has not been noted. It is also highly likely that the politician will usually retweet something positive about them personally, or certainly acknowledge it.

Twitter feeds are also exceptionally public. Most Members have many thousands of followers, even if they choose to follow a more limited number of people. Members will also expect proper political engagement through Twitter. There is no distinction between personal and public as you might find in relation to the use of Facebook. The same rule generally applies to politicians at every level, and Twitter can often be a very good means of raising issues at local government level.

You can also use Twitter in a very specific way to highlight specific asks of elected politicians. For example, if there is a Statement of Opinion you want someone to sign, ask them to do so via Twitter. Similarly, you can use Twitter to tag politicians and remind them to come to events or meetings of Cross-Party Groups. Macmillan Cancer Care was one of the first organisations to build such persuasive targeting into its outreach work with politicians, and since then many other organisations have followed.

A really good application of Twitter can be live tweeting an event and encouraging others to do so. The use of a catchy #hashtag will undoubtedly help you do this effectively. Hashtags enable you and others to 'brand' a series of tweets about something specific. You can also use them in the context of creating and sustaining longer term campaigns. An extremely effective international example was the #MeToo movement, which operated on an international basis. Part of its success was undoubtedly the succinct nature of the hashtag, so that must always be a consideration.

The reach of Twitter is also demonstrated by its viral nature. Things can be spread very easily and quickly, both good and bad, which means this particular medium is a double-edged sword. Both campaigners and politicians have been caught out by a badly thought out tweet.

Remember, social media disasters do not respect normal nine-to-five working hours too.

It is also worth noting that, in many cases, staff look after an elected Member's total communications, including their Twitter account.

Facebook

The power and ever increasing reach of Facebook seems undiminished and ever growing. There are two broad ways in which it can be used from a public affairs sense. The first is to spread messages to opinion formers. Like Twitter, it has the power to engage and prompt debate and the same potency for immediate action and reaction. There are, nevertheless, limits to this since Facebook tends to be confined to designated Friends or Followers to leave comments. The distinction is important. In many cases, elected politicians have split their Facebook presence into a wide, public facing campaign page for their political work and a private page for their personal contacts and comments. It is important to respect this distinction if the politician has chosen to do so. Indeed, some politicians specifically avoid politics on their own personal pages.

The other application of Facebook is through targeted messaging. You will have seen an increase of this form of messaging in recent years and, though occasionally controversial in its application, it is a growing way of connecting with a wider audience for campaigns or fundraising. It has been mainstreamed now into many forms of political communication, especially during election periods. Facebook is the biggest media platform in Wales, with over 2,000,000 daily users. This quantum can then be divided into different types of user based on factors such as age, gender or geographic location. This allows campaigners to buy targeted advertising space for messages. Those who interact with the ads – by sharing, commenting, or clicking links – can then be further engaged with to encourage more interaction with your organisation.

Other platforms

There are other social media platforms which can be used for political activity but are less familiar as mediums for such communication. However, their lesser use may actually make them more attractive options as your campaigns might reach different audiences. A good example is the business-focused Linkedin, which contains significant potential to connect with potential business supporters of a campaign, or to allow postings on issues of relevance to business.

Visual methods of campaigning are often underestimated. Scope in Wales had been campaigning for years about access to polling stations, pointing to this as a major issue by collecting anecdotal data from people unable to get into a polling station and exercise their democratic right to vote. Scope broke through with the campaign when they started using photographs of how inaccessible these places actually were, and this resulted in legislation to ensure accessibility. This is a good example of how some forms of social media, such as Instagram or Snapchat, could potentially be integrated into campaign work.

One quirky and noticeable technique online is the use of Thunderclaps. These are pre-planned and synchronised social media blasts to create a buzz around a product launch or event. They utilise the Thunderclap app and are particularly effective when done on Facebook and Twitter.

Another potential use of images is the development and transmission of memes, which lend themselves to a variety of social media platforms including Instagram, Twitter and Facebook. This light, visually based approach can really help with cut through and is often a lot more impactful than just words. It can lend itself particularly to familiarising a campaign slogan or promoting a hard- hitting statistic or quote.

Based on its reach and potency, YouTube may well figure more heavily in public affairs work in the future, though at the moment its potential is applied in a very limited way.

Politician-led engagement

The interactive nature of social media means engagement is sometimes led by the politician or the administration as well as the campaigner. This means that you should be prepared to respond as well as to initiate. Some politicians use social media in a very impactful way in order to gather supporters, but can also occasionally use it to test opinion or probe issues.

Senedd Committees, Welsh Government and local authorities will also sometimes use social media, both to sign post their own consultation exercises or meetings as well as to conduct online outreach. This is a relatively modern phenomenon. One of the downsides of some of the partnership working models in Wales (as covered in Chapter 22) is that it can sometimes result in closed models of partnership working based on organisational engagement rather than public engagement. If the first decade of devolution was characterised by managed engagement, the second decade has been about using social media and other methods to involve more people in the conversation.

Martin Donnelly's speech on the integrity of civil servants also adds a valuable addition to the analysis, when he places engagement by officials in the broader analysis. He asks pointedly:

'How do officials convince a sceptical wider world that Whitehall really is good for them, or at least better than any plausible alternative model?'

He then draws conclusions that the changing nature of the world means the official can no longer stay cocooned away from wider political processes.

'There is also a much greater level of transparency and media engagement now with civil service processes and decisions. This means civil servants need to be more assertive in helping citizens to assess information about complex issues. It is also increasingly clear that much trust-related dialogue takes place on social media. Digital literacy is becoming a core skill for policy officials. Agreeing how officials can engage directly in the digital world while respecting both political boundaries and their own private space is a key challenge for us all.'[3]

It seems likely that over the next decade this form of outreach and engagement by administrations rather than just by politicians and campaigners is set to continue.

---

3   Martin Donnelly, The Positive Neutrality of Civil Servants, October 2014, UK Government website

Key things to remember about social media

The tips for using social media can be expressed in 10 simple rules which you could follow:

- **Capacity:** Remember to match your social media presence with the amount of capacity you have available to feed into social media.
- **Freshness:** You need to find a balance between commenting and sharing continuously while not allowing your presence to become stale by not sharing regular content.
- **Learning and sharing:** Develop a tone which sets out your case in an authentic, informing and engaging way. You will never make everyone on the internet agree with you, so don't bother trying. Rather, take an approach in which you are contributing to common learning and sharing, and be prepared to learn from others too.
- **Multi-platform:** Don't confine your presence to a single platform. If something is worth saying or worth sharing, it is worth saying and sharing prominently and loudly. You can utilise Thunderclaps or platforms which co-ordinate posts such as Hootsuite or Tweetdeck.
- **Authority:** Your brand may come with implicit authority on certain issues. This is both a strength and a weakness. It means that your postings will gather more gravitas if you speak with implicit authority, but you can also damage that same brand with an unwise post.
- **Visual:** Remember the power of an image is often much more potent than the strength of a sentence, statistic or quote without a strong image to accompany it.
- **Clarity:** As is a constant refrain throughout this volume, message clarity is really important. The succinct nature of many forms of social media demand absolute clarity and may require you to be careful with every single word that you use.
- **Repetition:** Don't be afraid of using your message or your memes on multiple platforms and at multiple times. Nobody is continuously on all forms of social media so don't expect people to have engaged if you say something only once.
- **Media-savvy:** Don't forget that the media follows social media too. They will spot positives and negatives. Sometimes a well crafted tweet in a conversation can lead directly to media opportunities from watching journalists.

- **Integration:** A social media presence works best for campaigning organisations when it is properly integrated into your broader public affairs and communications strategies.

In summary, social media is a very useful campaigning tool when used sensitively and intelligently. It is also not a static tool. No social media plan should be set in stone, not just because plans need flexibility to succeed but also because platforms are evolving. It is also the case that you should evaluate your social media presence periodically. Analytical tools developed by the platforms can be really helpful. Facebook and Twitter are especially good at providing data on impact and reach, and their analysis and applications are free (at least at the time of writing!). You can use this data periodically to evaluate your social media effectiveness.

> **TOP TIP: Use news hooks for regular comment. Even if you don't have something to publish, then just providing a comment can get you noticed and sometimes lead to a presence on the mainstream news coverage.**

25

Operating Bilingually

Wales is a bilingual nation and the parity of both English and Welsh is enshrined in the operation of both the Welsh Government and the Senedd. The most successful public affairs professionals do not see the Welsh language as a burden or a barrier, but work with Welsh as a positive and enriching factor in their public affairs work.

Although very, very few people speak only Welsh, with nearly all being bilingual with English, the point about the Welsh language is that a large number of Welsh speakers are more comfortable expressing themselves in Welsh than in English, and it is perceived as a basic right to be able to communicate in the language of one's choice.

A speaker's choice of language can also vary according to the subject domain (which is known in linguistics as code-switching). There has been a serious attempt over the decades to avoid or minimise code-switching within the operation of public affairs practice. Indeed, the number of Welsh speakers elected to the Senedd has also gradually increased over time, with many Members learning once they have been elected.

According to the 2001 census the number of Welsh speakers in Wales increased for the first time in 100 years, with 20.5% of a population of over 2.9 million claiming fluency in Welsh.[1] In addition, as the same source indicates, 28% of the population of Wales claimed to understand Welsh. It also shows that although there was an uplift in Wales as a whole, it was increasing particularly quickly in Cardiff, climbing from 6.6% in 1991 to 10.9% in 2001. Cardiff is, of course, the epicentre of Welsh public affairs practice.

---

1   Dr John Davies (14 February 2003). "Census shows Welsh language rise Friday, 14 February 2003 extracted 12-04-07". BBC News. Archived from the original on 5 January 2009. Retrieved 17 October 2009.

The 2011 Census showed a similar set of results, with 19% (562,000) of usual residents in Wales aged three and over reporting that they could speak Welsh. The estimate of Welsh speakers is a decrease of two percentage points on the 2001 estimate of 21% (576,000), although in 2001, the estimate of people who 'Can speak Welsh' did not include those who listed speaking Welsh as one of their skills in the 'Other combination of skills' category. However, amongst Welsh speakers 30% (169,000) of this group were aged between three and 15 years old, showing a significant demographic change.[2] The number of younger people able to speak Welsh continues to grow and grow.

The Office for National Statistics breaks down all of this data by local authority, educational and skill level, and other factors like gender. Interestingly, it also has data on projections and trajectory for the number of Welsh speakers aged three and over, from 2011 to 2050.[3] This data set estimates that, based on current growth rates, Welsh language speakers will rise from 562,000 in 2011 to 666,000 in 2050.

Building on this increasing demographic, at a political level the current Welsh Government has pledged to hit one million Welsh speakers by the same 2050 date.[4] To boost by this number will of course need serious concerted action – not least from amongst the public affairs community itself – but it is notable that there is little political dissent from this target, only discussion on how it might best be met. In the launching of its policy to reach this target, the responsible Ministers in the Welsh Government at the time noted:

'we need to reach a position where the Welsh language is an integral element of all aspects of everyday life. If we want to achieve this, the whole nation has to be part of the journey – fluent Welsh speakers, Welsh speakers who are reluctant to use the language, new speakers who have learned the language, and also those who do not consider themselves to be Welsh speakers.

---

2   Data from the Office of National Statistics (ONS) on 2011 Census data for Wales.
3   Welsh Government statistics collated from the ONS, https://statswales.gov.wales/Catalogue/Welsh-Language
4   A drive to almost double the number of Welsh speakers to one million by 2050 has been unveiled by then First Minister, Carwyn Jones, at the National Eisteddfod on 1st August 2016.

Everyone has a part to play, and we want everyone to contribute to realising our ambition.'[5]

By every indicator, both demographic and political, the importance and size of the Welsh language cohort in Wales is likely to increase. No public affairs practitioner can afford, for emotional or practical reasons, not to be part of this general direction of travel.

Why is using the Welsh language important in your public affairs activity?

Demographic change, especially in Cardiff, linked to increasing public affairs practice and an increasing number of Welsh speaking Members of the Senedd mean that proficiency and fluency in Welsh is increasing year on year in Welsh public affairs. From a strategic public affairs perspective, it is therefore a really positive step to try and use the Welsh language in your public affairs activity.

From a cold, strategic perspective you might also consider that working bilingually potentially increases your exposure and can open the door to a wider audience than English-only content may provide. There may only be a small number of people who cannot speak English, but there are a large number of Welsh speakers who are much more engaged through Welsh medium communication channels in terms of receiving news, opinion and debate. In terms of the media, for example, BBC Radio Cymru and S4C's *Newyddion 9* are well established and significant outlets that take political/public affairs journalism seriously, often cover stories that do not appear elsewhere and can break news that others can then pick up. Indeed, according to October 2018 data, Radio Cymru is gaining listeners while it's English language counterpart Radio Wales is shedding them.[6]

Allied to this, remember also that since stories are sometimes specifically run through the Welsh language media, using Welsh can also provide an opportunity to target a specific audience. It could well be the case that your message has a specific or targeted resonance with

---

5   "Cymraeg 2050: A million Welsh speakers", Welsh Government, 2017
6   https://www.bbc.co.uk/news/uk-wales-45967244 BBC coverage of listener figures, October 2018

a Welsh language audience and therefore it becomes a central element to use the language in such communication.

There can also be direct financial benefit for charities to adopt a bilingual approach. Recent research into marketing and fundraising by charities in Wales was conducted by the Welsh Language Commissioner following many requests by charities for evidence to show that bilingual marketing can increase a charity's success with their appeals and campaigns. It was specifically weighted so that the results are representative of the population of Wales, with the responses of Welsh speakers capped at 19% of the overall 700+ interviews conducted. The research showed that people in general were more likely to give to locally focused charities, and that Welsh language use was a strong denotation of localism. Further, interviewees were asked if they thought that charities operating in Wales should market bilingually and 70% stated that they agreed or strongly agreed with this statement, with that percentage only falling back to 67% when Welsh speakers were excluded from the data. It is also worth noting that this research showed that only 2% of the respondents noted that bilingual marketing would have a negative effect on how much they would give.[7]

Above these tactical reasons to respect and use Welsh, however, there are also natural and respectful reasons for using the Welsh language. The simplest – and the most powerful – is that using the Welsh language as a matter of course is the clearest and most basic step to demonstrate an understanding of, and respect for, the Welsh context you're working within. It is a mark of good practice and a boost to equality. This can be especially important if your organisation has a pan-UK remit, and you are seeking to demonstrate or enhance your Welsh reach. Even some basic steps will indicate that you respect the language and recognise its value and significance.

What are the legal requirements for different organisations?

There are also legal reasons to use the Welsh language. The Welsh and English languages have official and equal status in public life in

---

7   The Benefits of Bilingual Marketing by Charities in Wales, Welsh Language Commissioner, 2014.

Wales. The Welsh Government is in the process of introducing new Welsh language 'standards' to improve the services Welsh speakers can expect to receive from organisations. The aim is to also increase the use of such services.

The Welsh Language (Wales) Measure 2011 places duties on organisations relating to the use of Welsh in the workplace and with the public.[8] It also created the role of the Welsh Language Commissioner to oversee the application of the way the measure would operate and specifically set out the following key remits for the role:

- Promote and encourage the Welsh language.
- Investigate if someone isn't allowed to speak Welsh.
- Powers to set standards on organisations.
- Regulate organisations, and ensure they comply with the standards.
- Establish the Welsh Language Tribunal if there is any dispute about the commissioner's decisions in relation to the standards.

Looking at this list of five, you should definitely abide by the law and seek to incorporate the first two bullet points within your organisation. For all the reasons outlined above, strategic and cultural, there should be a natural place for Welsh language provision in your organisation; and you should never, for serious moral and legal reasons, seek to prevent someone speaking Welsh in the workplace.

What are Welsh Language Standards and to whom do they apply?

Welsh language duties or standards are legally enforceable requirements for basics of service which apply in Wales and are applied specifically to designated organisations. Public sector organisations in Wales have to provide a Welsh language service, which may be through Welsh language standards or schemes, depending on the particular organisation. (Welsh Language Schemes are dealt with later). The Welsh Language Commissioner's own website sets out the over-riding aim of the standards as follows:

---

8   http://www.legislation.gov.uk/mwa/2011/1/contents/enacted The Welsh Language Measure 2011

'The aim of the language duties is to ensure that organisations in Wales should not treat Welsh less favourably than English. According to the Welsh language standards, organisations should also promote the Welsh language, ensuring that Welsh has an active role in the organisation's internal administration, and that the language is accessible to the public.'[9]

The Commissioner also sets out the purpose of Welsh Language Standards, which is to ensure clarity to both organisations in relation to the Welsh language and to Welsh speakers on what services they can expect to receive in Welsh, which should therefore provide greater consistency in Welsh language services and improve quality to users.

Every public services organisation that must comply with Welsh language standards will have received language duties at different periods, from 2015- 2019. According to the Welsh language standards, organisations should also promote the Welsh language, ensuring that Welsh has an active role in the organisation's internal administration, and that the language is accessible to the public.

You can identify the standards that apply to each public service organisation by visiting their website or consulting with the website of the Welsh Language Commissioner.

Even if you are not affected by the standards as a designated organisation, they are still important to you as a consumer of public services. You may therefore want to play an active role in ensuring compliance by raising any concerns on the application of those agreed standards with the public service body in question.

Welsh Language Schemes

A significant number of smaller public sector organisations, for example housing associations, town and community councils and UK government departments, implement Welsh Language Schemes. Welsh Language Schemes derive from the Welsh Language Act 1993 and predate Welsh Language Standards. Similar to Welsh Language Standards, they place language duties on organisations.

---

9   Website of the Welsh Language Commissioner, sub-section on Standards http://www.comisiynyddygymraeg.cymru/English/Organisations/Pages/What-are-standards.aspx

When preparing their language scheme, an organisation must carry out a public consultation on their scheme and must also adhere to the Welsh Language Commissioner's statutory guidance, which is freely available. The organisation and the Welsh Language Commissioner will also discuss the language duties, before coming to an agreement on the final language scheme.

Importantly for you maybe, businesses and charities can introduce Welsh Language Schemes on a voluntary basis following the Welsh Language Commission guidance. This provides an opportunity for many organisations to embrace the spirit and practice of working through the medium of Welsh in a proactive manner that sends a clear signal but also introduces consistency and clear internal guidelines for all staff to follow.

Welsh language considerations for events/ campaigns/ social media activity:

So now that the legal basis of bilingualism has been laid out, alongside a hopefully persuasive case as to why such an approach should be adopted, let's consider what a bilingual provision of services might actually look like for a public affairs professional.

Bilingual printed materials are now pretty standard. It is rare to find a monolingual copy of a report in modern Wales. Indeed, shorter printed briefings or campaign leaflets will usually also be printed in both languages too. Increasingly, organisations are also producing their short briefings to Senedd Members ahead of debates in a bilingual format too. Indeed, some Senedd Committees are now also actively encouraging this approach and asking for submissions to committee inquiries to be produced in a bilingual format too. At minimum, these are sort of things you should be looking to make sure are available in both languages.

Another area where bilingualism is now standard is the event invitation. Indeed, the Senedd Commission stipulates that all events on the Senedd estate must now include both Welsh and English text in order to be fully accessible. At events, it is now becoming more commonplace to see bilingual slides for presentations, although they tend to work best if the presentation is actually quite short or not particularly text heavy. Many organisations, especially those organising conferences, will also give consideration to providing simultaneous translation for events. If done on the Senedd estate, this service can be provided for free. It is also worth noting that in the case of best practice, though not necessarily in the cases of most practice, any material/pop up displays used at the event should be bilingual too.

Most organisations will also conduct their media relations in a bilingual manner. It is generally seen as best practice to issue press releases bilingually, not least to maximise the amount of exposure an announcement is likely to get, but a good piece of advice is also to bear in mind that media outlets such as TV and radio may also require a spokesperson to do a clip or an interview, and it is also worth considering this aspect. If you have Welsh speaking staff who are comfortable with the media or have been media trained, they will undoubtedly add to the potential impact of any press release which you are attempting to get noticed.

External general communications are also increasingly being delivered bilingually, which is seen as standard now for public bodies, as is tweeting and posting to Facebook in both languages. As with all aspects of bilingualism, however, here will need to be a balance here between resource and rapidity of commenting.

Some final advice on bilingualism

The worst use of the Welsh language is when it is done badly. We have all seen the horrific examples of using Google Translate to produce literal but inaccurate translations. The key rule is to factor bilingualism into your core campaign work, and allow enough time for material to be translated, so don't leave it until the last minute. If something is worth doing then it's worth doing properly, so make sure that the Welsh language provision you have is accurate or it may well go down in infamy as part of a viral meme. To help you get it right, the Welsh Language Commissioner provides a free proofreading service – note that it is free proofreading and not free translation.

It is also worth thinking through your entire branding, from image through to strapline, to make sure it is coherent and resonant through the medium of Welsh. Remember too that direct translation doesn't always work, and that distinct messages in English and Welsh can sometimes be more effective. It's often better to consider both languages from the outset in a campaign and developing your messaging and materials accordingly. Indeed, translating to Welsh as an add-on at the end could mean that the message gets lost in translation.

TOP TIP: Embrace the opportunities of the growing numbers of people learning Welsh, and become an active and visible partner of the Welsh Government in seeking to achieve one million Welsh speakers by 2050. The public affairs community has a key leadership role in making this happen, and unless you seize the opportunity with sincerity and prioritisation, you will get left behind when others do so.

26

Any Other Business

Hopefully this guide has demonstrated the truism that it set out to prove: successful public affairs is about talking to the right person, or an influencer on the right person, in the right way, about the right things, at the right time. It has been written, hopefully and with hope, in an accessible way which should enable the near novice to better understand the world of public affairs in Wales but should also have guidance of value for even the most experienced public affairs expert.

The nature of public affairs is that it is never static. We live in interesting times and sometimes it becomes almost bewildering for even a seasoned public affairs practitioner to remain on top of their game. Looking at the overall pattern of politics these days, change seems inevitable. Regrettably, the disregarding of some conventional wisdoms seems inevitable too.

A couple of years ago I would have thought that there was nothing in the next decade to suggest that the Senedd would change much other than its name. Now I am 50-50 as to whether the Welsh Government will change from Labour for the first time ever. The last time I felt that sense of total alteration was back in 2007, but I have hopefully written this book in such a way that even if the colour of the government changes, the fundamental truths of effective public affairs will not. There should be plenty of advice and guidance here that would support interaction with any type of Welsh Government or any type of Senedd. For example, the arrival of a once seven-strong group of UKIP members in 2016 changed nothing in terms of the architecture of political structures. A change of government will not alter the fundamentals of 'doing' politics either. The Fifth Senedd would have been dominated by Brexit, with or without a UKIP presence.

As we enter a third decade of devolution, I might almost be drawn to suggest that it might focus on Brexit as an excuse for what cannot be done. If that happens there will almost be a sad pattern to much of Welsh Government and Senedd politics. The first decade was obsessed with a lack of powers. When those powers came, the second decade was obsessed with a lack of money. Could a third decade be obsessed about the negative impact of the lack of EU membership, or would a new debate be sparked on Wales' constitutional position and the possibilities of an alternative future.

Those varying scenarios will unfold over the coming years but, I have to comment that far too often the Senedd and Welsh Government have focused on limitations and neglected opportunities. It is an easy trap to fall into, but with the advent of useable Income Tax powers post-2021, coupled with a strong base for legislative activity, there is a good argument that more can be done in a Wales which seizes the opportunities available to it, rather than become trapped in a victim mentality which reverts to focusing on what cannot be done. Institutional maturity is about more than just a renaming exercise. It is about taking full responsibility for the governance of the nation.

To do so effectively, a culture of optimism and enablement needs to be imbedded. Public affairs professionals need to play a key role in doing this. We should not shy away from our professional status and our varied skills and enthusiasms. Collectively and individually we have played a key role in shaping policy and politics in Wales to get it to the point where it is now. We can certainly keep contributing more to shape improvement over the decade and decades to come.

Public affairs professionals do make a difference, and McGeachy and Ballard offer a typically upbeat assessment on the value of our profession:

> 'Your organisation should, therefore, approach its public affairs strategy with some optimism that the issues you are raising will be considered on their merit, and with renewed confidence from reading this guide that it has developed and strengthened its existing skills and capacity to deliver a highly successful, cost effective public affairs strategy to achieve its policy aims and objectives.'[1]

---

1   McGeachy & Ballard, *The Public Affairs Guide to Scotland*, op. cit., p.191.

In concluding their book, they also reaffirmed the need for a successful public affairs strategy to be rooted in the knowledge that politicians are there to help and are genuine, effective people. They do not need your expertise, they need your input, guidance and direction. An hour long meeting may leave them – maybe briefly – seriously better informed about your issues, but without clear asks and without the sense that you are in a dialogue rather than a one-sided or one-off conversation, then you are likely to fail to make the impact you want or need.

To make sure that happens, you need to have a clear set of objectives. The politician will not deliver those objectives for you. In fact, this book will not deliver them for you either, and neither will copying what someone else is doing. The road to your success is your own and you can only map it by bringing focus and deploying public affairs skills and techniques. Hopefully this book will have assisted you with the latter at the very least; though it has maybe enabled you to be clearer in deciding your objectives too.

Above all don't be gloomy or overwhelmed. With relatively new legislative powers and the significant boost of fiscal powers, we are in a third decade where there is much to play for and much to influence. The opportunities to do things differently, more ambitiously and more creatively in Wales are greater than ever. It is up to us as public affairs professionals to rise to that challenge and play as full and energetic a role as possible. In some small or large way, I hope this book will have helped you to do so.

TOP TIP: The constant change in the public affairs landscape in Wales is an opportunity to do things differently, to experiment, to succeed and to fail. If you want for permanence and overt stability you may be waiting a long time, and will have missed the opportunities to really achieve results by trying things differently.

Index

A

Additional Learning Needs and Education Tribunal (Wales) Bill 82, 92-4
Andrews, Leighton viii, 36, 47
Antoniw, Mick 101, 219
Asghar, Mohammad 30, 101, 219
Association of Directors of Social Services 67

B

Backbenchers 50, 54-6, 58, 72-3, 93, 100, 127-30, 139
Barrett, Lorraine 48
BBC Wales 38, 117, 205, 212
Bennett, Gareth 102, 219
Bevan Foundation xv, 117
Black, Peter 101-2
Blythyn, Hannah 36, 219
Bowden, Dawn 219
Brexit 33, 42, 54, 62, 75, 102, 129, 136, 235-6
British Heart Foundation 19, 131, 199
British Lung Foundation 199
British Medical Association 19, 67, 199
Bryn Melyn Group 49
Budget xv, 4-6, 16, 23, 31, 33, 55, 58, 71, 74, 103-16, 198, 211-2
Budget (s), Supplementary 113
Bullying 52, 62, 132
Burns, Angela 49, 219
Business Committee 6, 71-3, 89, 91, 126

C

Cabinet Ministers xiv, 119, 168
Cabinet (Welsh Government) x, xiv, 10, 25, 29-30, 36-8, 87, 93, 110, 122, 184, 190, 196
Carrier Bag Levy 14, 16, 18, 78, 141, 149

Chapman, Christine 55
Children, Young People and Education Committee 63, 72, 89
Civil service 8, 27, 38-43, 189, 223
Climate Change, Environment and Rural Affairs Committee 63, 72
Committee of Scrutiny of the First Minister 73
Communities First 55, 113
Constitutional and Legislative Affairs Committee 64, 71, 73, 90, 93, 95, 128
Consultations xvi, 15, 19, 24-5, 33, 38, 60-70, 74-5, 79-80, 86, 88, 90, 99-100, 123, 143, 159, 198, 223, 232
Counsel General 29, 94, 119
Cross-Party Groups 49, 75, 152, 160, 198, 220
Culture, Welsh Language and Communications Committee 64, 72
Cuthbert, Jeff 87
Cymdeithas yr Iaith 66

D

David, Hefin viii, 48-9, 199, 219
Davies, Alun vii, 55, 87, 219
Davies, Andrew RT 219
Davies, Paul viii, 28, 101, 219
Davies, Ron xv, xvii
Decision Reports 25, 38
Deputy Ministers 27, 119
Disabled Children Matter Wales 139-40, 198-9
Donnelly, Martin 39, 223
Drakeford, Mark 10, 28, 35-6, 42, 106, 113, 115, 117, 119, 121, 197, 219

E

Economy, Infrastructure and Skills Committee 64, 72

Electoral Commission xvi
Electoral system 1,3, 99
Elevator Pitch 17
Elis Thomas, Lord Dafydd vii, 28, 30, 55, 198
Equality, Local Government and Communities Committee 74, 72-3
Evans, Rebecca 49, 219
Explanatory Memorandums 88-9, 92, 98
External Affairs and Additional Legislation Committee 64, 72, 75

F
Facebook 217, 220-2, 225, 233
Finance Committee 5, 64, 66, 71, 73, 90, 110-11, 128
First Minister xiv, 3-6, 10, 28-9, 31-3, 35-6, 41-2, 44, 73, 79-81, 109, 113, 119, 121-2, 124, 126, 178, 196-7, 227
Fostering Network 49
Friends Reunited 218
Fringe meetings 168, 175, 176

G
German, Lord Mike 29
Government of Wales Act 1998 ix, xv
Government of Wales Act 2006 1
Government of Wales Act 2014 xvi, 1, 4, 115
Government of Wales Act 2017 7, 115

H
Hart, Edwina 68-9, 121
Health, Social Care and Sport Committee 64, 72, 154
Hedges, Mike 55, 102, 129, 136-7, 219
HM The Queen (Monarch) 28-9, 79, 94
Hootsuite 224
Huckle QC, Theodore 29

I
Instagram 217, 222
Isherwood, Mark 101, 128, 199, 219
ITV Wales 205, 212

J
James, Julie 36, 219
Jones, Ann vii, 219
Jones, Caroline 3, 219
Jones, Carwyn xv, 28, 31, 33-5, 44, 79, 178, 196, 219, 227
Jones, Helen Mary 48-9, 121, 219

K
Kidney Wales Foundation 19, 78, 149, 199

L
Law, Peter 29
Legislation, Primary 95-6, 129
    Secondary 38, 62, 71, 90, 95
Legislative ballots 100-2
Legislative Competence Orders xiv
Legislative process Stage One 65, 86-7, 89-91, 100-1
    Stage Two 86, 89, 91-4
    Stage Three 86, 92-4
    Stage Four 86, 94, 101
Legislative programme 4-5, 81, 84, 102
Liberal Democrats 2-3, 31, 35, 108, 168-70, 179-80, 183-4
LinkedIn 218, 222
Lloyd, Dr Dai 3, 101, 129, 137, 219
Llywydd/Presiding Officer 27-8, 71, 89, 91-4, 99-100, 120, 124, 126-7, 130
Local authorities/local government 5, 10-1, 15-6, 27, 49, 57, 64, 78, 103, 105, 107, 112, 115, 148, 155, 181, 186-91, 194-5, 220, 223
Local Health Boards 11, 27, 61, 68, 159, 181, 187, 194

M
Macmillan Cancer Care 47, 220
Melding, David 48, 50, 219
Members' Research Service 76, 81
MeToo movement 220
Michael, Alun 4
Milburn, Alan 33-4
Millar, Darren viii, 50, 101-2, 127, 219
Morgan, Eluned viii, 4, 219

Morgan, Julie 36, 50, 55, 87-8, 219
Morgan, Rhodri x, 42

N
National Infrastructure Commission 36
Neagle, Lynne 55, 139, 199, 219
NHS Confederation 67
NHS Wales 68, 187, 212

O
Ofcom 203-4
Office of National Statistics (ONS) 203,
    227
Ombudsman (Wales) Bill 64, 100
One Wales agreement 28, 34
Oral Questions 56, 119-21, 123-4, 127
Organ donation, law change 19, 63, 78,
    141, 149, 159, 179, 199
Owens, Cathy 43

P
Papers to Note 24
Parkinson's UK 47
Permanent Secretary of the Welsh
    Government 39
Petitions Committee 6, 14, 64, 71, 73,
    127, 143-5, 149, 150
Pinterest 218
Plaid Cymru 2-3, 28, 30, 32, 34, 50,
    54, 57, 73, 108-9, 112, 121, 129-30,
    167-8, 176, 178-81, 183, 189
Plenary session of the Senedd 6, 22, 25,
    69, 76, 79, 90, 92-3, 109-10, 119,
    126-7, 129, 131, 144, 150, 161, 165
Programme of government 4, 32-5, 61,
    183
Public Accounts Committee 40, 71, 73,
    193-4
Public Affairs Cymru xviii
Public Health Wales 61, 85

R
Ramsay, Nick vii, 57, 219
Randerson, Baroness Jenny xviii
Reckless, Mark 219
Regional committees xiv

Reserved matters to Westminster 8
Review of Lobbying in Wales xviii
Rowlands, David 102, 219
Royal College of Nursing 67

S
Sargeant, Carl vi, viii, 87, 127
Sargeant, Jack viii, 219
Sayed, Bethan (formerly Jenkins) vii, 3,
    48, 101, 137, 199, 203-4, 219
Scope Wales 222
Scottish National Party (SNP) 15
Senedd: First 29, 55, 195
    Second 3, 29, 55
    Third 30, 55, 73, 121, 131, 156
    Fourth 15, 30, 55, 76, 85, 100-2,
        108, 110, 129, 132, 145, 150,
        198
    Fifth 30, 49-50, 55, 73, 75, 81, 85,
        100, 101, 110, 138, 145, 156,
        235
Senedd Commission 98-9, 119, 232
Senedd TV 25
Sepsis Trust 16
Shared Prosperity Fund 64
Short Debates 127, 130-1
Skates, Ken vii, 36, 101, 219
Snapchat 218, 222
Social media 52, 175, 214-8, 221-2,
    225, 232
Special Advisers (SpAds) 27, 35, 41-3,
    125, 172
Stakeholder map 12-3, 18, 190
Standards Committee xvii, 64, 71, 73,
    126
Statements of Opinion 23, 135-40
Supporting People 5, 16, 113, 198

T
This Is Not a Suitcase campaign 49
Thunderclap 222, 224
Trade Union (Wales) Act 2017 82, 85
Tumblr 218
Tweetdeck 224
Twitter 176, 218-21, 225

U

United Kingdom Independence Party
(UKIP) 2-3, 167, 235

V

Voices from Care Cymru 49

W

Wales Environment Link 49, 67, 197
Warner, Chris 93
Watson, Joyce 50, 136, 220
Welsh Assembly Government xiv, xv,
43, 196
Welsh Conservatives xvi, 1-3, 30, 50,
57, 131, 167-9, 179-80, 183
Welsh Government ix-x, xv-xvi, xviii,
4-5, 7, 10, 14-6, 18-20, 25, 27, 29,
31-4, 36-44, 47, 54-5, 57, 60-3, 65,
67-9, 73, 76, 79-81, 85-90, 93, 95,
98, 101-19, 125-5, 129-32, 137-9,
141-4, 146, 149-50, 153, 158-9, 161,
178, 186, 188-90, 192-3, 195-6, 198,
211, 223, 226-8, 230, 234-6

Welsh Labour Party xv, 2-4, 15, 28-32,
34-5, 45, 50, 54-5, 73, 102, 108-9,
119, 130, 137, 139, 167-70, 172,
178-80, 183, 189, 199, 235
Welsh Language Commissioner 229-33
Welsh Language Schemes 230-2
Welsh Language Standards 230-1
Welsh Local Government Association
(WLGA) 16, 78, 112, 186, 211, 189,
212, 190
Western Mail (inc. WalesOnline) 43,
212, 139, 197, 201, 207-8, 212-3
WhatsApp 207, 217
Whip (s) 30, 54-5, 71-2, 98, 158
Wild Horses, legislation on 15
Williams, Kirsty 31, 34-5, 101-2, 168,
170, 219
Wood, Leanne 28, 50, 219
Written Questions 22, 50, 119, 123

Y

YouTube 217, 222

welsh academic press

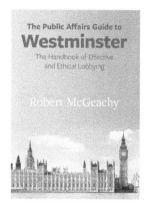

The Public Affairs Guide to
Westminster

Robert McGeachy

'Lobbying is an essential part of effecting necessary change and this is a must read for any aspirational organisation seeking to change the law for the public good.'
Brendan O'Hara MP

'an essential tool for anyone who wishes to lobby the UK Parliament in a cogent and successful way. This comprehensive book covers it all. Robert McGeachy has drawn on his long Parliamentary experience to produce a fascinating book full of insight and explains, in an easy to understand way, how to develop a public affairs strategy, how to monitor Parliament and gather political intelligence and how to influence key policymakers.'
Michael J Clancy OBE

978-1-86057-134-3   330pp   £23.00   PB

The Public Affairs Guide to
Scotland

Robert McGeachy & Mark Ballard

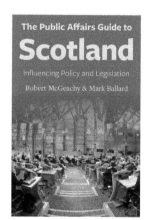

'I've worked in Scottish public affairs for many years but this book is still a great resource for clear guidance, ideas and planning. We keep one in our office and refer to it often. Colleagues new to the field of public affairs describe it as invaluable.'
Kim Hartley, Head, Royal Col. of Speech & Language Therapists Scotland

'Whether you need to engage with the legislative procedures of the Scottish Parliament and its policy development or hope to inform the development of a Bill, this book provides in depth help.'
Satwat Rehman, Director, One Parent Families Scotland

'Both authors have used their tremendous experience to really good effect. I really can't praise their efforts highly enough.'
Bill Scott, Policy Director, Inclusion Scotland

'...contains all a person needs to know to engage with the Parliament, the Government, local authorities and civic society in an effective and efficient way.'
Michael P Clancy OBE

'Mark Ballard and Robert McGeachy, through the pages of this important book, are ... doing democracy a service.'
Michael Russell, MSP for Argyll & Bute

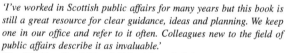

978-1-86057-126-8   224pp   £19.99   PB

welsh academic press

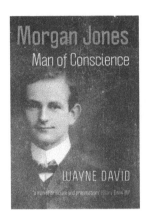

MORGAN JONES
Man of Conscience

Wayne David

'Wayne David deserves great credit for bringing Morgan Jones to life in this well-researched and very readable book.'
Nick Thomas-Symonds MP

'Wayne David writes of one of his predecessors as Labour MP for Caerphilly with the understanding of the political insider and the contextual knowledge of the historian.'
Professor Dai Smith

'Jones was a man of principle and pragmatism.'
Hilary Benn MP, from his Foreword

Imprisoned in Wormwood Scrubs for his pacifist beliefs during the First World War, Morgan Jones made history by becoming the first conscientious objector to be elected an MP when he won the Caerphilly by-election for Labour in 1921.

978-1-86057-141-1   128pp   £16.99   PB

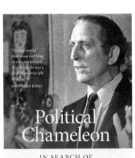

POLITICAL CHAMELEON
In Search of George Thomas

Martin Shipton

'Compelling'   **Kevin McGuire**
'A brilliant book'   **Guto Harri**
'By far the most brutal political biography I have ever read.'
Daran Hill

'I picked up this book expecting it to be a hatchet job, but it is a very fair book and a very well researched book. The problem with George Thomas is that one can write a book that is very fair and very well researched yet he still comes out of it very badly.'
Vaughan Roderick, BBC Radio Wales

Drawing on previously unpublished material from Thomas' vast personal and political archive in the National Library of Wales, and interviews with many who knew him during his career, award-winning journalist Martin Shipton reveals the real George Thomas, the complex character behind the carefully crafted facade of the devout Christian, and discovers a number of surprising and shocking personae – including the sexual predator – of this ultimate *Political Chameleon*.

978-1-86057-137-4   304pp   £16.99   PB

welsh academic press

ABERFAN
Government and Disaster
(Second Edition)

Iain McLean & Martin Johnes

'The full truth about Aberfan'
The Guardian

'The research is outstanding...the investigation is substantial, balanced and authoritative...this is certainly the definitive book on the subject...Meticulous.'
John R. Davis, Journal of Contemporary British History

'Excellent...thorough and sympathetic.'
Headway 2000 (Aberfan Community Newspaper)

'Intelligent and moving'
Planet

Aberfan - Government & Disaster is widely recognised as the definitive study of the disaster and, following meticulous research of previously unavailable public records - kept confidential by the UK Government's 30-year rule - the authors explain how and why the disaster happened and why nobody was held responsible.

978-1-86057-1336   224pp (+16pp photo section)   £19.99   PB

GARETH JONES
Eyewitness to the Holodomor

Ray Gamache

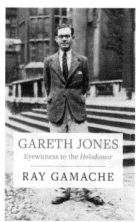

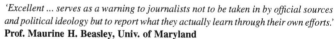

'Excellent ... serves as a warning to journalists not to be taken in by official sources and political ideology but to report what they actually learn through their own efforts.'
Prof. Maurine H. Beasley, Univ. of Maryland

'...meticulously researched book [that] returns Gareth Jones to his rightful status, as one of the most outstanding journalists of his generation'
Nigel Linsan Colley, www.garethjones.org

'Extraordinary ... Jones' articles ... caused a sensation ... Because [his] notebooks record immediate impressions and describe events as they were happening, they have an unusual freshness ... Jones' reputation has revived thanks to the Ukrainian government's broader efforts to tell the history of the famine.'
Anne Applebaum, The New York Review

Gareth Jones (1905-1934), the young Welsh investigative journalist, is revered in Ukraine as a national hero and is now rightly recognised as the first reporter to reveal the horror of the Holodomor, the Soviet Government-induced famine of the early 1930s, which killed millions of Ukrainians.

978-1-86057-122-0   256pp   £19.99   PB

Lightning Source UK Ltd.
Milton Keynes UK
UKHW021213081219
354991UK00012B/383/P